BY BILL BOYARSKY

LOS ANGELES

CITY OF DREAMS

BY BILL BOYARSKY

LOS ANGELES

CITY OF DREAMS

URBAN
TAPESTRY
SERIES
TOWERY
PUBLISHING INC.

ART DIRECTION BY BRIAN GROPPE

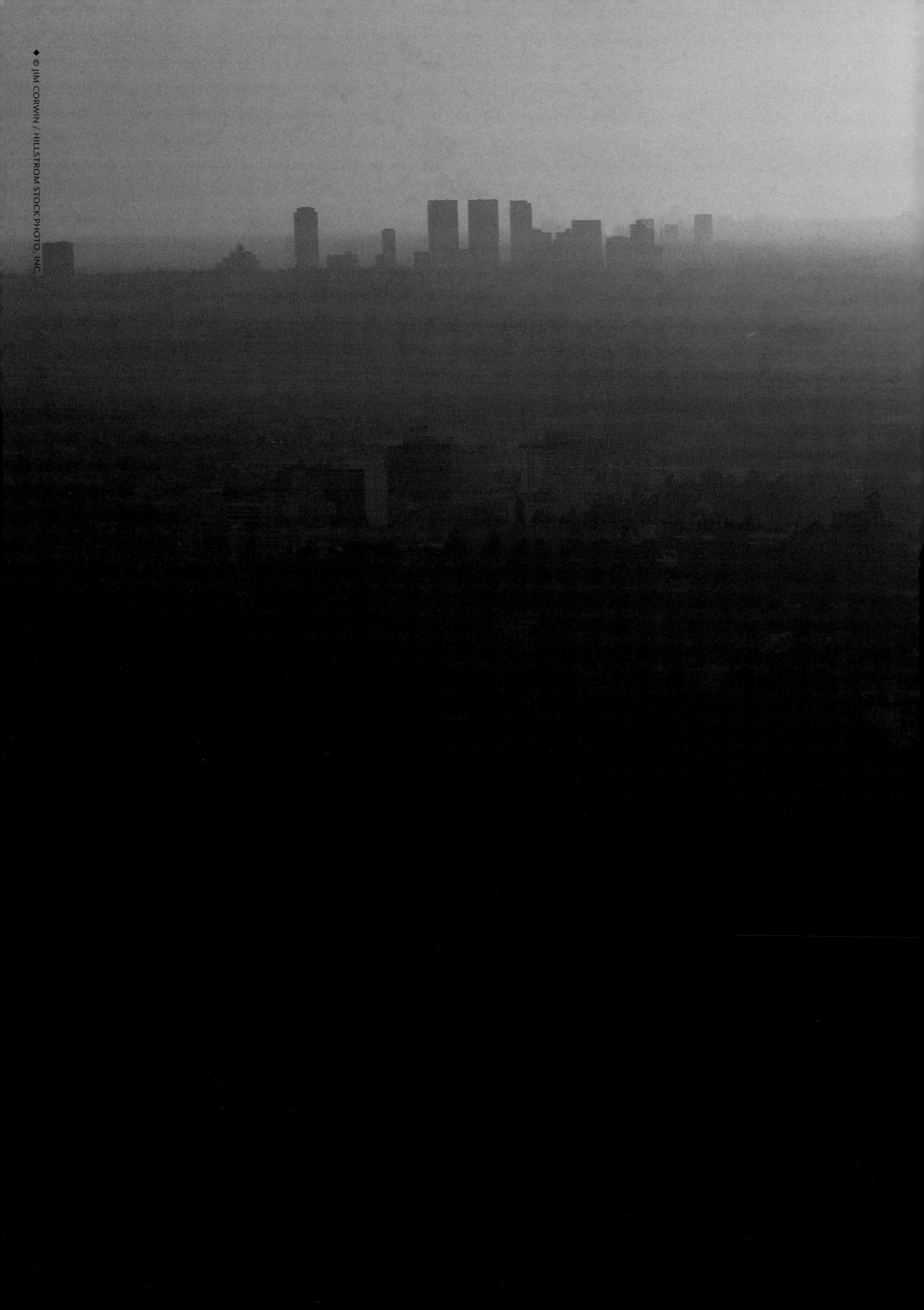
◆ © JIM CORWIN / HILLSTROM STOCK PHOTO, INC.

C O N T E N T S

Library of Congress Cataloging-in-Publication Data is available on page 525.

or nine years as a columnist for the *Los Angeles Times* and for almost 20 years before that as a reporter, I prowled the huge city of Los Angeles. I also ranged far beyond the official boundaries of L.A. into the vast environs that are best described by a wonderfully expansive phrase coined by early-day boosters—the Southland. ⚜ I immersed myself in a way of life that first put me off, but, in the end, seduced me, as it has done with so many others. Now, my prowling days are over. I've been promoted to city editor, and my job is to direct others in the task that had long occupied me. What a perfect occasion, I thought, to show them *my* L.A.—the Southland—and to share with others my thoughts about a place that so often defies definition or description. ⚜ It's easier to

describe the Southland a piece at a time. A few years ago, I was speaking to a class at the University of California at Berkeley, trying to explain the politics of L.A. As I jumped from one politician to another, and skipped from town to town, Tom Goldstein, who was then dean of the Graduate School of Journalism, shook his head. "You make it sound like you're covering a bunch of small towns," he said. "It's one of the biggest cities in the world." That may be, but to understand the Southland, the visitor must look at it as a collection of communities—some small, simple, and unpretentious; others exceedingly famous, wealthy, and ostentatious.

The scope of metropolitan Los Angeles staggers the imagination. I stand on a hill in the countryside some 75 miles to the east of the city and look down on a valley that will soon become a reservoir. It will hold water from faraway Northern California and the Rocky Mountains, the lifeblood that made possible the development of the semiarid Southland.

A landmark equally important to the Southland lies 100 miles west of the hillside. It is the Los Angeles harbor, dredged from tidelands by early-20th-century visionaries who, in doing so, created a port that became an economic engine for the entire area. This place, which encompasses San Pedro and Wilmington, is an L.A. unknown to outsiders, more reminiscent of the Northeast than California, with tight enclaves of Serbs, Croatians, and Latinos. Catholicism is at the center of this strongly religious neighborhood, as evidenced by the parishioners at Mary Star of the Sea Church—its name fitting for the generations of sailors, fishermen, and longshoremen who have made their living from the sea and pray with their families in the church on Sundays.

Few streets in the world have been as immortalized as Sunset Boulevard (ABOVE, PAGES 12 AND 13). In film, on television, and, most recently, on Broadway, Sunset evokes an image of Los Angeles that embodies its past and future glories. Its name derives from the serene nightly spectacle that is among the city's most wondrous natural beauties.

I visit East L.A. and I think of the Japanese garden at Theodore Roosevelt High School that I once wrote about, where the student body, like the neighborhood, is almost entirely Latino. The garden fell into disarray when Japanese students and their families were interned at the outbreak of World War II, and was ultimately destroyed. But recently, Latino students learned about the old garden while they were studying the history of their neighborhood, and they set about rebuilding it.

I could have started my tour of Los Angeles in East L.A., the harbor, or at 100 other equally memorable spots. Instead, I chose Sunset Boulevard.

The boulevard, immortalized in show business hype, in movies, on television shows, and on the musical stage, presents every face of sprawling Los Angeles. Driving along Sunset, from one end to another, it's easy to see the power and promise of the Southland, as well as its problems and challenges. L.A. has had a reputation, since the days of the Spanish conquistadors, as a place where dreams come true. At least some dreams. ➤

Sunset
17300 W

The best way to experience Sunset Boulevard is to drive to the point where Sunset meets the beach, across from which is a big parking lot, perfect in its symbolism for the Southland's long marriage to the motor vehicle. At the edge of the parking lot is a small cliff with a stairway that leads down to the beach. Nearby, surfers in wet suits ride the breakers toward the shore. This is Palisades Beach—the L.A. of travel posters and movies—just one stop along a 70-mile stretch of magnificent beach, most of it accessible to the public. This long ribbon of sand gives unity to a region with no real center. ⚜ The boulevard rises sharply from the beach, traveling along the lower reaches of the Santa Monica Mountains, which run through the heart of the city. The mountains are a seasonal reminder of the Southland's precarious relationship with fire and rain, the forces that can quickly turn this land of eternally sunny skies into a dangerous place. In the late summer and fall, hot Santa Ana winds blow in from the desert, bringing with them clear skies. Sometimes, the winds also bring fires that sweep across the mountains, leaping from one hillside to the next, and roaring down the canyons with dangerous power and speed. Always just under the surface, there is a tension to living in L.A. that comes from knowing that fire, flood, earthquake, or urban riot—as happened in 1965 and 1992—can strike with devastating quickness.

A few years ago, during a particularly disastrous fire season, I found the beach parking lot at Sunset Boulevard filled with fire trucks and firefighters catching a quick rest. I hiked north along the Pacific Coast Highway, watching the smoldering hillside on the land side of the road, until I met some other journalists with a utility vehicle. I hitched a ride up into the mountains, past small smoldering fires that looked harmless—until they exploded

into big ones. We saw that a substantial fire was coming down the hill in our direction. We weren't in trouble—yet—but trouble was not far away, so we turned around and headed back toward the beach.

Cruising along Sunset, few of the city's visitors would notice the ever present fire danger, so bemused are they by the amount of wealth displayed along the boulevard as it climbs up from the beach past a community of expensive homes known as Pacific Palisades. I first visited the Palisades before I moved to Los Angeles. Based in Sacramento, I was a political writer for the Associated Press, covering a campaign for governor. One candidate I was assigned to was an actor who lived in the Palisades, and one morning I hooked up with the traveling campaign party at his house. Ronald Reagan's home was large and comfortable, but modest compared to the ostentation of most Hollywood stars. He wasn't pretentious, and no doubt that was one of the reasons he was so popular.

What's striking about these upscale neighborhoods is the confluence of rich celebrities with the obscure rich. It's nothing unusual to have a famous star living in the mansion up the street, just as it's commonplace to find yourself sitting next to one at a restaurant or a deli. The presence of celebrities, however, can bring the unwanted glare of publicity to such retreats, mocking the millions residents pay for what they thought would be a safe haven.

That's what happened on Rockingham Drive in Brentwood in the summer of 1994 when one of the neighbors, O.J. Simpson, was arrested for the murders of his ex-wife, Nicole, and Ronald Goldman, a waiter in a Brentwood restaurant. Simpson was handcuffed in his front yard in a scene duly recorded by the media horde. He was released but later, when the cops tried to pick him up again, he fled in the famous low-speed chase, shown on national television, that ended at his Brentwood home. Viewers got to know the grounds, the house, and the neighbors as they watched the trial. Brentwood has never been the same, not even after Simpson moved away. Still, the comforting presence of another famous Brentwood resident—the mayor of Los Angeles, Richard Riordan, tended by police bodyguards—provides evidence that things are returning to what, at least for Los Angeles, is normal. ⋙

It's somehow fitting in L.A. that the city can turn its negatives into achingly beautiful imagery. Events like the disastrous Malibu fires in the early 1990s became Technicolor snapshots beamed out to the rest of the world.

Union Station is the last of the great railroad stations built in the United States (RIGHT). Open since 1939, the terminal boasts a harmonious blend of Spanish mission-style architecture with elements of streamline moderne. Naturally, the site has become a perennial movie set, most notably in the 1991 film *Bugsy* and the 1950 classic *Union Station*.

Remarkable not only for its collection of roughly 2.5 million books and historical photographs, the Central Library downtown is also renowned for its stunning beaux arts architectural detail (OPPOSITE). Completed in 1926, the structure incorporates numerous Egyptian motifs, including its gilded pyramidal tower and the sphinxes that wait outside the 5th Street entrance—all of which get a big thumbs-up from actor Arnold Schwarzenegger.

CITY OF DREAMS

he O.J. Simpson case introduced the nation—and a substantial number of Angelenos—to downtown, the often overlooked part of the city, where Simpson was tried in the Criminal Courts Building. Many Southlanders—probably a majority—never venture downtown, preferring the familiarity of their own particular suburban community. The daily freak show of the Simpson trial may have strengthened suburban Angelenos' resolve to stay away, but at a personal loss. Downtown Los Angeles is one of the most vibrant parts of the city. In fact, just up the street from the Criminal Courts Building is the Music Center of Los Angeles County, consisting of three theaters on a seven-acre site overlooking downtown. Fund-raising is under way for a fourth venue, the Walt Disney Concert Hall. A few blocks away is the newly restored Central

Library. By the standards of a city where it's commonplace to tear down a 50-year-old building and put up something new, the library, built in 1926, is historic. It was designed by architect Bertram B. Goodhue, who, like the designers of the old movie palaces, drew his inspiration from many styles and cultures—Hellenistic, Islamic, Mediterranean, and Egyptian. When fire swept through the interior in April and September of 1986, some demanded that the library be bulldozed. But this time, L.A. said no. Instead, the city rebuilt the structure and added a handsome new wing that rises four stories above an interior courtyard.

That's where my wife and I often head after dinner in the garden of the Café Pinot (which sits adjacent to the library) for readings sponsored by the Library Foundation and hosted by Gregory Peck, the actor. Afterwards, everyone has coffee and dessert under the great glass ceiling of the new wing. Among the other actors we've seen in the library's elegant little auditorium are Kathy Bates, Roddy McDowell, Ted Danson and Mary Steenburgen, Morgan Freeman, and Angelica Houston. The events are relaxed and casual, audience and actors bound together by their devotion to the public library. This is a side of L.A. that never makes the news.

© DAVID PEEVERS / HILLSTROM STOCK PHOTO, INC.

Surrounding the library are the high-rises of a downtown, once the commercial and political heart of the entire Southland, that has today ceded power to the economic giant of Orange County and to other population centers once dismissed as the hinterlands.

The history of this change can be seen in the buildings. A few blocks south of the library is L.A.'s own Broadway, which early-20th-century merchants hoped would become as big as New York's version. For a while, it looked as if their dream would be realized. Interurban trains—the Red Cars—were crowded every day with people, coming downtown to shop, work, and do business. Tens of thousands of people lived nearby. Broadway was lined with movie theaters, some of them grand palaces with marble floors and great crystal chandeliers, which even today are classics of the genre.

Downtown's fortunes changed, however, with the arrival of the automobile. For it was the car that gave the Southland its mobility and led to the development of the sprawling subdivisions that came to define the Southern California way of life, centered far away from any urban core.

But powerful economic and political forces kept downtown alive. The 73-story Library Tower, situated across from the actual library, is flanked by a fanciful imitation of Rome's Spanish Steps, leading past restaurants and coffeehouses. On blocks nearby, seven other buildings reach beyond 50 stories, with much of their space devoted to law firms and companies serving the Pacific Rim trade that contributes heavily to the Southland's economy.

Downtown's restaurants range from the Biltmore Hotel's elegant Bernard's to an old-fashioned diner called the Pantry, which sits on the fringe of downtown and is owned by Mayor Riordan. No, he's not a short-order cook. A multimillionaire venture capitalist, Riordan bought the restaurant, one of his favorite places, when it was in danger of closing several years ago. But despite downtown's long list of amenities, it's no Manhattan, nor will it ever be. ⮞

Taking full advantage of modern conveniences and technological innovations, today's Los Angeles workforce has redefined the meaning of the word "office." Highly mobile and nontraditional in their approach, L.A.'s businesspeople are emblematic of a city that's relentlessly moving forward.

City of Dreams

On July 1, 1993, Richard Riordan—a lawyer, entrepreneur, and self-made millionaire—succeeded five-term mayor Tom Bradley, and was reelected to office in 1997. Along with a 15-member city council, Riordan makes his professional home in the art deco confines of City Hall, featured prominently in the *Superman* and *Dragnet* television series (OPPOSITE).

CULTURE *y*
CULTURA:
How the U.S.– Mexican War
Shaped the West
May 2 - Sept. 7

AUTRY MUSEUM OF WESTERN

owntown—home to the Museum of Contemporary Art (MOCA), housed in a handsome brick structure among the high-rises—is also a gateway to the Los Angeles art scene. Like the Southland itself, the art produced and collected here is so eclectic, widespread, and diverse that its essence is difficult to capture. On a recent Sunday, I could have driven to the Ronald Reagan Presidential Library and Museum, north of L.A., and viewed an exhibition of Grandma Moses' paintings. Or I could have hit Wilshire Boulevard, another of the broad avenues extending from the beach to the central city, and visited the Dan Bernier Gallery near Los Angeles' Museum Row. That day, the gallery was showing an unusual sculptural installation, which resembled a shack sitting on huge springs that vibrate and create an audio track.

Artists flourish everywhere—in studios on Venice Beach, in Santa Monica, East L.A., South Central, Laguna Beach, and in the many art schools. I once interviewed artist Robbie Conal, a political satirist of devastating wit, in the perfectly landscaped garden of his home. Conal lives in Mar Vista, a middle-class suburb a few miles from the ocean, where his neighbors are lawyers, accountants, teachers, and businesspeople. A world away from Mar Vista, 20 miles to the east of Conal's pleasant home, is a vibrant artist colony, centered in loft apartments and studios in old warehouses on the fringes of a squalid and dangerous Skid Row. Low rent for ample space first drew the artists here. With them came restaurants, coffeehouses, and galleries. At the Warehouse Gallery on East Fourth Place, for example, emerging Los Angeles artists exhibit paintings, sculpture, and mixed media assemblages.

I've also admired the work of Latino muralists on the sides of stores, in courtyards of housing developments, and other public places. The wall mural, in fact, is a true Los Angeles art form. So is what you see in the Peterson Automotive Museum on the Miracle Mile of Wilshire Boulevard. The Peterson celebrates the vehicles—beautiful and ugly—that made the Southland what it is today.

Exactly how many galleries exist in the Los Angeles area is unclear. A few years ago, the guidebook *Artscene* reported that there were 74 galleries and museums in West Hollywood and Beverly Hills; 67 on the Westside of Los Angeles, including Santa Monica and Venice; 19 in Pasadena and the eastern reaches of the county; 18 in downtown Los Angeles; 17 in Hollywood; and 15 in the San Fernando Valley and Glendale. And that's not counting Orange County, which is loaded with galleries of its own, such as those in Laguna Beach and other coastal communities. ⇒

The mural-sized, artful creations of native Angelenos burst forth from banners and building walls throughout L.A., a reflection of the area's diverse ethnicity.

Also putting their mark on the city today are Father Gregory Boyle (OPPOSITE) and painter R. Kenton Nelson. Boyle's Homeboy Industries brings gang-related youth a vital message of responsible living and moral values. Nelson's rich images, reminiscent of WPA-era works, hang in many of the city's celebrity homes.

Shopping is another Los Angeles art form. Its most famous manifestation is in Beverly Hills, especially the Golden Triangle, an enclave of most-expensive shops that extends north from Wilshire Boulevard. The Los Angeles Visitors and Convention Bureau suggests shoppers first fill up on a breakfast of eggs Benedict or sun-dried-cranberry French toast at the Beverly Hills Hotel and Bungalows. That sounds good to me. The hotel opened in 1912. In its early years, famous drinkers like W.C. Fields and John Barrymore hung out there. Old age afflicted the place for a time. A dozen years or so ago, I brought my family there from Sacramento for a brief stay while I was on a book publicity tour. Excited by the prospect of a few days in a world-class grand hotel, we were surprised by the tackiness and faded decor of our rooms, an experience that became part of our family lore. Recently, a $100 million remodeling project restored the hotel to its former glory, and it remains a favorite gathering spot for Hollywood's elite.

Rodeo Drive is not far away. The street has been around a long time, but it didn't become what it is today until retailer Fred Hayman decided he wanted to make it one of the world's famous shopping boulevards. He succeeded, and Rodeo Drive is today occupied by designer stores, like Tommy Hilfiger, Ralph Lauren, Gucci, Giorgio Armani, Versace, and Chanel. Elegant silver and glass gifts are sold at David Orgell, where at Christmas, Arnold Schwarzenegger can be spotted examining the crystal in a wall cabinet, while Priscilla Presley talks to a salesperson amid the Versace china, Waterford crystal, Chopard watches, and Mont Blanc pens. Nearby are Saks Fifth Avenue, Neiman Marcus (with its smart basement restaurant, the Mariposa), and Barneys New York (with its excellent deli, Barney Greengrass).

While Rodeo Drive is the Southland's most famous shopping place, it's just part of the story in this shoppers' paradise, where appearance and image are everything. Fifty miles south of Beverly Hills, the well-to-do in Orange County have their own Rodeo Drive. Since it is part of a suburban mall, however, it doesn't have quite the same cachet. South Coast Plaza, which is just off the southbound San Diego Freeway, has a full complement of designer shops, including several, like Calvin Klein, that are not in Beverly Hills.

The huge complex also features moderately priced goods at large retailers like Macy's, Robinsons-May, and Sears, as well as hundreds of smaller shops—some unique and some common to every mall in America. Above all, South Coast Plaza operates with a suburban sensibility suited to people who boast that they wouldn't live in places like L.A. or Beverly Hills.

Don't think Southland shopping is all high end. I'm reminded of that fact whenever I stop at Ontario Mills some 40 miles east of Los Angeles. This complex, surrounded by undeveloped flatlands, serves a fast-growing population extending from Palm Springs and its satellite communities up into the hills and valleys of Riverside and San Bernardino counties. The area is called the Inland Empire, where subdivisions cover what was once fertile farmland.

I pulled into this remote shopping outpost one blazing day, walked through the 102-degree heat to a row of one-story warehouse-like buildings, their facades bearing the names of famous stores, designer labels, and well-known brands of housewares and leather goods. On this particular day, the Brooks Brothers outlet was offering some good bargains, although its selection of summer suits had been picked bare. I bought a shirt and poked around in some of the other stores, edging my way through a determined crowd of shoppers on the same mission. It was thirsty work, a far cry from Fred Hayman's on Rodeo Drive, where the stress of shopping can be relieved at the store's handsome oak bar.

© ROBERT LANDAU

Affectionately known as the Pink Palace, the ultraswank Beverly Hills Hotel (opposite)—the ultimate in "trendee"—has played host to Hollywood aristocrats, including Frank Sinatra, Elizabeth Taylor, and Marilyn Monroe, not to mention actual royalty, from the Duke and Duchess of Windsor to the Crown Prince of Monaco.

If there's a European center of Los Angeles, it has to be somewhere along Rodeo Drive, where you'll encounter the fashion flair of Paris, the architecture of Berlin, and, of course, the banks of Zurich.

n Los Angeles, it's the freeways that connect the many far-flung shopping centers and hold the Southland together as a region. These crowded, high-speed thoroughfares may be ridiculed and condemned—I know Angelenos who avoid them unless absolutely necessary—but they are as vital to the region's prosperity as is water. Although water made possible the cultivation of arid soil, even the most fertile land is useless if the produce can't be brought to market. Thus, as architectural historian Reyner Banham wrote, "Transportation (became) the next great shaper of Los Angeles after land and water. From the laying of the first railway down to the port at Wilmington . . . transport has been an obsession that grew into a way of life." First, there were the interurban railroads, reaching in five directions from where the city was founded in 1781 by colonists from Mexico. The harbor, Santa Monica and its beaches, Orange County, the Inland Empire, and the San Fernando Valley—all were linked to the center of L.A. by rail. The railroad builders worked with real estate developers, creating residential subdivisions and commercial centers along the lines. The pattern of L.A. sprawl was established long before the first freeway, the Pasadena, opened just before World War II. Today's freeways, in general, follow the routes of the old railroads.

But Angelenos never did love the trains the way they love their cars. To immigrants from New York and Chicago, public transportation was part of the crowded urban scene they were trying to put behind them. The idea of one person alone in a car, with complete control over route and destination, the freedom to go where you want without having to worry about train or bus schedules—this is the vision of freedom and mobility that has drawn so many people to California. It also is an expression of the desire for privacy that is a major characteristic of the area's suburban way of life. The backyard with a swimming pool and a barbecue still represents the dream of large numbers of Southern Californians.

When the freeways are not crowded—at certain times during midday or on the weekends—they are a marvel of convenient transportation. They also offer easy access to a world of different cultures that exist within the metropolitan area.

Take, for example, a recent Saturday night when I took the Santa Monica Freeway east, past the high-rises of downtown and through low-lying hills into the San Gabriel Valley. My destination was Monterey Park, a city where most of the residents are Asian-Americans. I've chronicled that area's historic development, watching its sometimes tense but always peaceful evolution from an Anglo city, to one where Latinos shared power with whites, to its current domination by Asians. I've marveled that it has occurred in a state where, less than a century ago, Asians were not allowed to own land.

At Monterey Park's Ocean Star Seafood, a restaurant stretching over a space more than half the size of a football field, I join huge numbers of Chinese families enjoying the excellent cuisine, and afterwards, stop at a large supermarket stocked with Asian goods and pick up imported tea and bananas to take home. Within 35 minutes, I am in urban Westwood again. Among other things, the freeway allows me to play foreign tourist in my own town.

On one spring day, I decided to test the mobility this freeway system provides. I took the San Diego Freeway over the Santa Monica Mountains to the San Fernando Valley, a vast, flat area surrounded by mountain ranges. This was ranch land until water was brought over the mountains, permitting the development of one of America's first residential subdivisions. Halfway across the valley, I switched freeways and headed east toward the San Gabriel Mountains. It was midday, and my speed never dropped below 65 miles an hour.

As the mountains neared, I switched to a third freeway along the very edge of the mountain range, and later left it for a snaky mountain road called Angeles Crest Highway. I climbed above Pasadena to the road's highest elevation, Dawson Saddle, 7,986 feet above sea level—an easy drive but a world away from the San Fernando Valley's suburban sprawl. Then I headed back down the mountains, traveled two more freeways, and was back at the paper. From crowded city streets to mountain isolation and back again—and all between breakfast and lunch.

There are some who like to romanticize the freeways, which have been featured in songs and novels. To me, they're strictly utilitarian. When a section of the Santa Monica Freeway was destroyed by the 1993 earthquake, my editor wanted me to write a poetic tribute to the road. I thought he had spent more time listening to songs about the ill-fated freeway than traveling it.

For me, it's always easy to see the negative effects of road construction on the surrounding community. In many places, freeway builders hacked a straight line through long-stable neighborhoods, causing irreparable harm. Dig deep into the history of the Santa Monica Freeway, for example, and you learn a lot about how such public works projects can isolate communities and further racial segregation. ➤➤

Intricate enough to boggle the minds of autobahn engineers, the L.A. freeway system is a functional—if occasionally baffling and often infuriating—automotive raceway. Unfortunately, it is not immune to natural disasters in this earthquake-prone area.

As reflected in a poignant Union Station mural, the early railroads brought booming industry, hopeful immigrants, and optimistic dreamers into this land of fertile orange groves and ranchos (OPPOSITE). Along the same pathways forged by the rails, the freeways continue to define the city's prosperity.

n so many aspects of life in Los Angeles, the surface is deceptive, lending itself to gags about a materialistic and shallow people with no sense of self or history. The trick is to dig below the surface, to play the urban archaeologist. It took me a while to like the place. Part of it was because of my own roots in the San Francisco Bay area, where L.A. is held in great contempt. It's also a tough place to understand. Other cities are easier to characterize. Chicago is loud, crude, and up front. Philadelphia is compact and rich with history, as is Boston. Washington is the major leagues of politics. L.A. is more difficult to define, but it is well worth the trouble. At first, I explored the city as if I were a foreign correspondent covering a strange land. The turning point was when I found myself thrust into covering a raging school integration crisis, just as my daughters were in public school. Suddenly, I was not covering abstractions, but events that directly affected my family's life.

We settled into the routine of L.A., where Disneyland became a day trip instead of a carefully planned vacation. We bought a house built in 1929 by the same developer who created Westwood Village. Two miles north is UCLA, where my mother was among the first students on the Westwood campus when it opened, the same year our house was built.

I became a Dodgers fan, although my loyalties were torn when they played the A's, the team from my hometown of Oakland, in the 1988 World Series. We found a favorite market, Gelson's in Century City, and a favorite fish market, Santa Monica Seafood. We learned to enjoy living in a place where movies open before they are shown just about anywhere else. I even got used to the monotonously temperate weather. It means that on most Sundays, I can make the 10-minute drive to the beach, dive into the surf, and then go to a coffeehouse and read the Sunday papers.

A daughter married and had a baby. She and her family live in a nearby neighborhood, Pico-Robertson, and we often baby-sit. Our house is packed with relatives and friends on holidays. At a certain point, it all had become very familiar and comfortable. L.A., this sprawling city of many faces, is now home.

Clark Kent may have made the news super at the fictional *Daily Planet*, but when it comes to real-life coverage, Bill Boyarsky is the mild-mannered city editor for the *Los Angeles Times*. In the 1930s, the newspaper located its headquarters in the Times Mirror Building on West First Street (OPPOSITE), conveniently a stone's throw from City Hall.

OPENS DEC. 15

I n the old navy port that became Long Beach Harbor, the 80,000-ton *Queen Mary*, one of the largest passenger ships ever built, has been converted into a hotel and several restaurants. Launched in 1934, the luxury liner features an art deco interior with nickel- and silver-plated hand-rails as well as hand-cut glass. Purchased by the city of Long Beach in 1967, the ship is a major tourist draw.

High flying takes on many forms in L.A., where hitching a ride with Bertie Duffy will result in an unobstructed aerial tour of the city (OPPOSITE). In bygone days, Fokker monoplanes provided a bird's-eye view of the still-growing metropolis. But look! Up in the sky, there's always Superman.

LOS ANGELES

Los Angeles' corridors of power refuse to limit themselves to one location. Wilshire Boulevard begins at the coast and sweeps past the Nobel laureates at UCLA, the financiers of Beverly Hills, and the film magnates of Hollywood before making its way downtown to the city's state-of-the-art convention center. The jet set, meanwhile, travel a path at loftier heights (pages 42 and 43).

Built in 1932, the 28-story Spanish renaissance-style City Hall stood for years as the tallest building in Los Angeles. Those who work among its hallowed halls today shepherd a city of nearly 4 million people.

The energy of Los Angeles and its people is proudly displayed in its public art—the headlong rush to success in downtown (OPPOSITE), the imposing "work" ethic in the offices of Sony Studios (TOP), and the head-banging stress of the daily grind at Citicorp Plaza.

f rom jumbo pocket knives to Jonathan Borofsky's celebrated 1991 *Molecule Man*, public art of all varieties dominates the urban landscape of L.A.'s downtown core.

Art and architecture often form a perfect marriage in L.A. Arched walkways welcome concert- and theatergoers to the Orange County Performing Arts Center (OPPOSITE TOP). The 28-story Home Savings of America Tower, completed in 1989, is a postmodernist dream come true (OPPOSITE, BOTTOM RIGHT). Members of the Los Angeles Chamber Orchestra grace the facade of a simple urban parking structure (OPPOSITE, BOTTOM LEFT), while abstract sculptures present a visual counterpoint to the stark outlines of downtown L.A. skyscrapers.

What would L.A. be without its palm trees? From the Los Angeles Convention Center (TOP) to Arco Plaza (BOTTOM) to the Wells Fargo Building (OPPOSITE), the classic foliage appears throughout the area.

To paraphrase words spoken about former U.S. President Ronald Reagan, who did pretty well here, "You just have to let L.A. be L.A." When you do, there are times when the sheer beauty of the city is almost overwhelming.

Among those pushing L.A.'s architectural envelope are Alfred Frey, father of 1950s Palm Springs kitsch and creator of his own modernist residence there (TOP LEFT AND RIGHT). Sony Music headquarters, another of the area's structural marvels, is the creation of Steven Erlich (BOTTOM LEFT). For a decidedly unorthodox design, Angelenos turn to Brian Alfred Murphy (BOTTOM RIGHT), who includes among his repertoire a home exterior covered in graffiti.

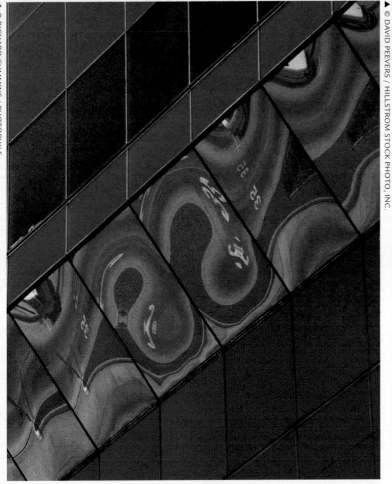

The architectural palette of L.A. is prominently displayed in the beach homes of Venice, located between Santa Monica and Marina del Rey (OPPOSITE). Also associated with its exterior color, the

Pacific Design Center (TOP AND BOTTOM LEFT) is often referred to as the Blue Whale. Packing some structural punch of their own are Santa Monica College (TOP RIGHT) and the uniquely Californian—and

Frank Gehry designed—Edgemar complex (BOTTOM RIGHT), a shopping mecca packed with clothing stores, restaurants, bookstores, and myriad art and photo galleries.

Many of L.A.'s public spaces bear the stamp of renowned design. The new, postmodern Getty Center (OPPOSITE, TOP LEFT) is the vision of famed architect Richard Meier. The facility's gardens, with their winding groves of trees and bougainvillea, are themselves works of beauty in the hands of landscape artist Robert Irwin (ABOVE). Prior to the center's opening in 1997, the J. Paul Getty Museum in Malibu housed the entire art collection of its oil billionaire namesake (OPPOSITE, BOTTOM RIGHT). The Museum of Tolerance in Beverly Hills uses the latest interactive technology and ancient symbols—like this stylized Menorah—to teach about racism and bigotry (OPPOSITE, TOP RIGHT). And the Mark Taper Forum downtown (OPPOSITE, BOTTOM LEFT) is home to a respected theater troupe whose high-caliber productions of new plays—among them *Angels in America* and *Children of a Lesser God*—often go on to Broadway, and then to win Tony and Pulitzer honors.

A cathedral could be defined as a place where devout people gather to share a common bond. In Orange County's Crystal Cathedral—a shimmering architectural marvel designed by Philip Johnson—the connection is obviously religion, while in the "cathedral" of the downtown library (BOTTOM RIGHT), the unifying force is literacy.

I n the circa 1921 Hollyhock House, the devoted gather to pay homage to the first Los Angeles project of famed architect Frank Lloyd Wright (TOP). Built in 1893, the Bradbury Building—with its interior atrium courtyard—is a frequent set for movies and a constant reminder of Victorian-era commercial architecture (BOTTOM).

The art deco roofline of the former Pan Pacific Auditorium (TOP LEFT) is no more, but the architectural embellishments of the Griffith Park Observatory endure (TOP RIGHT). An Assyrian facade fronts the Citadel, which today houses an outlet shopping mall. In the past, architectural treasures too often met with the wrecking ball. But now, through efforts of groups like the Los Angeles Conservancy, such downtown art deco icons as the majestic Eastern Columbia Building are being preserved.

© NIK WHEELER

The homes of the city are as varied as the hues in a Pacific sunset. They can be reminiscent of early California (OPPOSITE), whimsical—as in Beverly Hills' famed Spadena House, also known as the Witch's House (TOP RIGHT)—or stately studies in Victoriana.

The movies have a way of influencing all aspects of L.A. life—its architecture, its fashion, even its food. Steven Spielberg and Jeffrey Katzenberg's Dive! restaurant invokes a playful "Yellow Submarine" from the 1960s (RIGHT), and downtown's aged streamline moderne Coca-Cola bottling plant sports a facade that is positively "Titanic" (OPPOSITE TOP). Call it art deco or kitsch, but wacky over-designing in Los Angeles finds a way to justify itself and enlighten the spirit, as in Busby Berkeley's classic "By a Waterfall" segment in the 1933 film *Footlight Parade* (OPPOSITE BOTTOM).

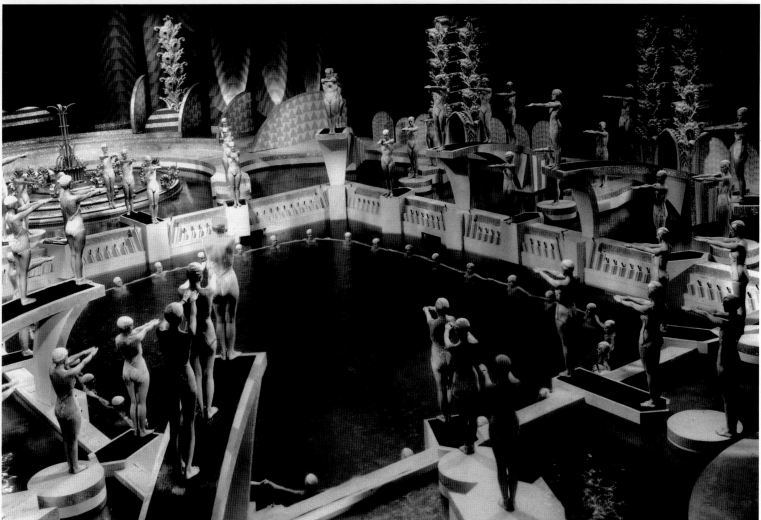

LOS ANGELES

L ike the palm tree, the swimming pool
is a symbol of the good life in Southern
California, dotting the landscape of
Beverly Hills and other affluent enclaves.
To be without it is a sign that you haven't
quite made it; clearly, L.A. artist Billy Al
Bengston has (OPPOSITE, BOTTOM RIGHT).

The population explosion that hit L.A. in the aftermath of World War II paved the way for tract housing and suburbia. As the construction of the area's freeway system began in earnest in 1947, vast expanses of land were opened up for development.

The seasons change, albeit slightly, in the Mediterranean climate of Los Angeles. But when the Christmas holidays roll around, the occasional irreverent image reminds us that somewhere, far, far away, people are deep in snow and shivering from the cold.

LOS ANGELES

When the Asian exodus to the California coast began in the 1800s, it brought with it centuries of heritage, helping to redefine the city's architecture and its culture through events such as the Chinese New Year parade (ABOVE). Since then, Asian landmarks including Echo Park—site of the annual Lotus Festival (OPPOSITE, TOP LEFT)—and the Wat Thai temple (OPPOSITE, TOP RIGHT) have become an integral part of the Los Angeles fabric.

The rich multiethnic tapestry of Los Angeles weaves a path throughout the city, from the ceremonial gateways and the colorful storefronts of Chinatown (OPPOSITE TOP), to the Vietnamese influences of Little Saigon (OPPOSITE BOTTOM), to the porcelain-like presence of a young Japanese girl costumed for a play (LEFT).

The serene simplicity of the Japanese house at San Marino's Huntington Library (OPPOSITE) reflects the careful study and preservation of Asian culture that is prevalent in the L.A. area. The aesthetic continues in the city's luscious outdoor gardens and artful bonsai and ikebana arrangements.

In Chinatown's traditional herbal apothecaries (TOP AND BOTTOM) or in the ceremonial gardens at Elixir Tonics & Teas (OPPOSITE), centuries-old traditions are routinely honored in daily life.

The very origins of Los Angeles lie in the rancho culture of the Mexican people who tamed the land. Today, the spirit of Mexico infuses every aspect of Angeleno life, especially its food and music. Indeed, roughly 35 percent of the city population is of Latino descent. And Spanish, while still the unofficial second language in newspapers, TV, and radio, is the mother tongue of nearly 70 percent of children enrolled in the city's school system.

ortraits of an enduring and creative spirit typify L.A.'s African-American population. Among its many accomplishments is the 10-member company of the Lula Washington Contemporary Dance Theatre, which has garnered critical praise for its celebratory cultural productions (TOP).

In 1965, L.A.'s Watts riots forever changed the face of the city—and the nation, as well. The area today is a center for African-American community activism, publicly honored via places like the Alma Reaves Woods Watts Library, named for the selfless woman who provided books to the facility after it was damaged in the riots (TOP). Message-oriented murals tell the story of the everyday challenges and conflicts facing the area's inner-city youth.

Beneath the Crossroads of the World tower, a colorful local character known as Mars makes a bold, if not fashionable, statement on Sunset Boulevard (TOP). Another crossroads of sorts can be found at the Watts Towers (BOTTOM). This amazing folk art creation, built over the course of 35 years by Italian immigrant laborer Simon Rodia, stands as testament to what vision and sheer determination can accomplish. Completed in 1954, the nearly 100-foot-tall structures are made of found objects, including bed frames, broken bottles, china cups, and thousands of seashells.

© JONATHAN POSTAL / TOWERY PUBLISHING, INC.

In spite of the city's well-publicized troubles over the years, the shapes, sizes, and cultures that form the core of Los Angeles quite often come together for one, unified message: "I love L.A."

Long before the ranchos dominated Southern California, this land belonged to the Native Americans. The Chumash, Shoshone, and Tataviam in Los Angeles still continue the fight to preserve their culture and heritage amid the succeeding influx of other populations.

The transcontinental rails arrived in Los Angeles in 1876, signaling an era of commerce for a city that, at the time, was a mere outpost. By the 1940s, new waves of immigrants, skilled laborers, and visionaries began pouring in, many of them arriving through the gates of historic Union Station (LEFT AND OPPOSITE, BOTTOM LEFT). The 1939 facility—built on the original site of Chinatown, which was, as a result, moved to its current location—brought together the three passenger railroads that served the area.

With the special-effects wizardry being churned out by Hollywood's movie studios, it's difficult to say whether life in L.A. imitates art or vice versa. At the California Science Center, interactive exhibits keep the kids busy and the adults entertained (OPPOSITE, LEFT AND TOP RIGHT). Over at Universal Studios, the characters from Star Trek have for years been transporting fans into a fictionalized outer space via both the big and the little screen. And Los Angeles International Airport—more commonly known as LAX—often features its own galaxy of traveling "stars" among the millions who land there each year.

Stars—celestial and earthbound—are a fixation in L.A. Two of the area's great spots for gazing heavenward are the open spaces of Santa Clarita Valley's Vasquez Rocks, located north of the city (OPPOSITE TOP), and the Griffith Park Observatory and Planetarium, with its giant, free-to-the-public telescope (LEFT). But if Mother Nature's offerings leave you feeling slightly, well, alienated, check out the terra firma festivities likely to draw the rich and famous—such as *X-Files* celebrities Gillian Anderson and David Duchovny (OPPOSITE, BOTTOM LEFT)—or those wacky martian types on Venice Beach.

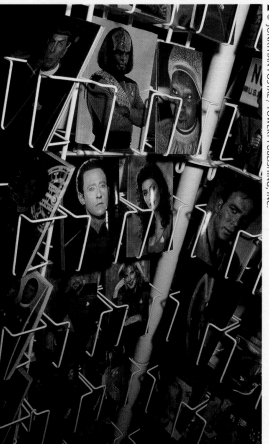

When the Griffith Park Observatory and Planetarium was built on a southern slope of Mount Hollywood in 1935, it was hailed as a major step in humankind's quest to come to terms with the universe. Part of the 4,000-acre Griffith Park, which is also home to the Los Angeles Zoo, the facility was built by mining tycoon Griffith J. Griffith, who said, "If every person could look through that telescope, it would revolutionize the world." Immortalized in the classic James Dean movie *Rebel without a Cause*, the site looms as a stunning focal point for the city at night (PAGES 100 AND 103).

LOS ANGELES

Beneath the moon and the snowcapped massif of the San Gabriel Mountains, the sheer beauty of Los Angeles glimmers majestically.

t falls to folks like Dr. George Fishbeck, former weatherman and noted television personality, to forewarn Angelenos of impending—not to mention spectacular—stormy skies.

The rains in L.A., when they come, are biblical—severe enough to turn inland valleys into overflowing lakes. And when the fierce Santa Ana winds howl down through parched canyons, the best-trained emergency response teams are often at a loss as the entire earth becomes their adversary. As if the wind, rain, and fires aren't enough, the area also has its infamous California earthquakes to contend with, making everyday life a very shaky proposition.

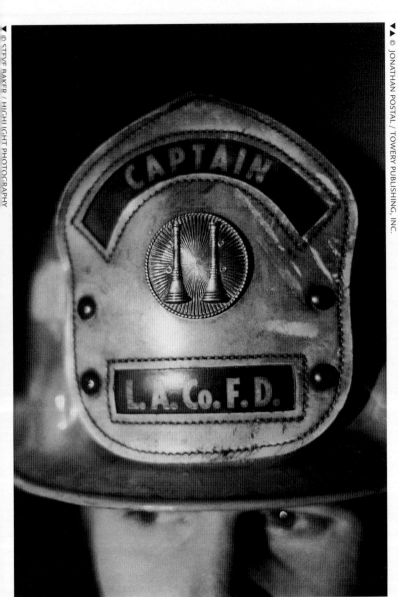

t's no coincidence that a CalTech Nobel laureate named Charles F. Richter invented the scale by which the world measures earthquakes. Straddling an intricate network of fault lines, the soil beneath L.A. has the fragility of an eggshell. But the mobilization of the city in times of disaster is a proud testament to the resilience of its people.

As destructive as the ever threatening earthquakes may be, their power can also serve as inspiration for some striking works of art.

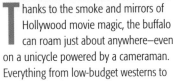

Thanks to the smoke and mirrors of Hollywood movie magic, the buffalo can roam just about anywhere—even on a unicycle powered by a cameraman. Everything from low-budget westerns to major releases, like the action-packed *Waterworld* (OPPOSITE), owe a great debt to the stunt doubles and special effects technicians whose feats of daredevilry thrill audiences near and far.

Hollywood might be the best public relations agent a city could ever have. When it produces another block-buster—à la Steven Spielberg's *Jurassic Park*—venues such as the Ripley's Believe It or Not museum (OPPOSITE, TOP LEFT) and even the Natural History Museum of Los Angeles County (OPPOSITE BOTTOM) reap the benefits. Universal Studios' Marvel Comics superheroes (OPPOSITE, TOP RIGHT) are taking note and getting their own piece of the action.

In the world-renowned La Brea Tar Pits in Hancock Park, animals still rule the earth. Researchers have learned much about prehistoric times from the ongoing excavation of this rich repository of oozing tar. Since 1906, the pits have yielded more than a million fossilized skeleton parts, including those of long-extinct mammals such as saber-toothed cats, ground sloths, mammoths, and mastodons.

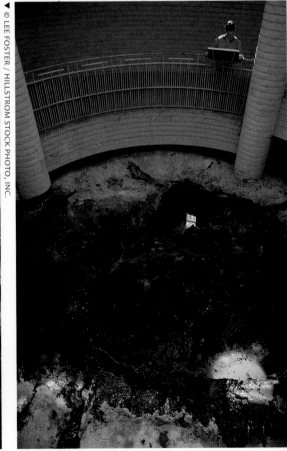

© LEE FOSTER / HILLSTROM STOCK PHOTO, INC.

In the great museums of Los Angeles, life is on display on the largest and the tiniest scales imaginable. Giant rulers of a bygone time still strike terrifying profiles at the Natural History Museum of Los Angeles County (TOP) and its satellite branch, the George C. Page Museum of La Brea Discoveries at the La Brea Tar Pits (BOTTOM RIGHT). At the California Science Center, the complex life of the interminable termite warrants a closer look (BOTTOM LEFT).

In sunset silhouettes, the oil wells and long-necked cranes off California's coastline loom as creatures of beauty. By day, they become the machinery that pumps the area's economy, bringing in much-needed fuel along Huntington Beach (OPPOSITE) or loading and off-loading cargo shipped from far and wide to the Port of Los Angeles (ABOVE).

LOS ANGELES

ollywood ships and make-believe storms (OPPOSITE, BOTTOM LEFT) don't hold much water compared to the real thing at the Port of Los Angeles. This vast network of docks, channels, and intermodal freight operations—once the scene of frantic preparation for World War II—is the single largest container port in the United States. To watch the gracefully gliding behemoths from Hong Kong, Bremerhaven, and Buenos Aires deliver their cargo is to observe a billion-ton ballet.

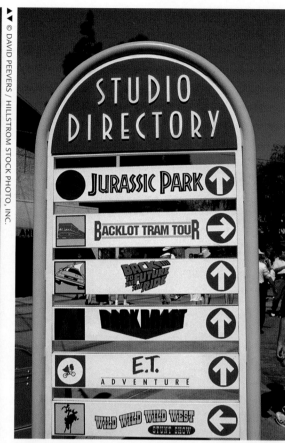

here else but at Universal Studios Hollywood can you whisk between the worlds of *E.T.*, *Jaws*, and *Jurassic Park*, and then wind up on an escalator with Lucy and Ethel? Even the atrium sky above Universal CityWalk is a piece of illusory engineering (OPPOSITE, BOTTOM LEFT).

SURFER

SEAL

LOS ANGELES

Beyond all else, it's the Pacific Ocean that unites much of Los Angeles. Surf culture has defined the city's image since the early 1960s craze kicked off by Jan and Dean and the Beach Boys. But the sea is a resource shared by all, including predators and their prey. That's one reason it's always wise to know how you look from below when surfing (OPPOSITE, BOTTOM RIGHT).

LOS ANGELES

Surfing is a sport that delights area youths and their adult counterparts. But even the land-bound in L.A. find outlets for their creativity. Afraid of the water? Try building a gigantic sculpture somewhere along the 50 miles of sand at your disposal.

Malibu and Laguna beaches are just two of the prime locations for making your mark on the surfing legacy that helps define L.A. Custom surfboard maker Dale Velzy (BOTTOM LEFT) has been refining his art for some 40 years now, and wave riders, such as Kelly Logan (PAGE 132) and Brenden Hearne (PAGE 133), do their part to keep the tradition afloat.

The Pacific locale of Los Angeles makes it ideal for more than just shipping and surfing. A mere 26 miles off the coast is Santa Catalina Island (TOP), a paradise for fishing, diving, and aquatic sports.

Visitors can also glimpse wandering herds of American bison, imported during the 1925 shooting of the *The Vanishing American* and left stranded on the island by the filmmakers.

Seafaring creatures are preserved, protected, and revered throughout the Los Angeles area in murals and tiles as well as in the spectacular Long Beach Aquarium of the Pacific (BOTTOM AND OPPOSITE BOTTOM), a new $117 million facility that houses 17 major living habitats, making it one of the largest aquariums in the United States.

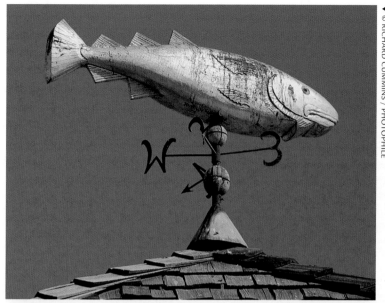

The mariner's life: From weather vanes to decorative sculpture, the elements of earth and sea constitute an integral part of daily life in greater Los Angeles.

Any exploration of the area should include a sea level voyage—whether it's a whale-watching cruise from Fisherman's Village in Marina del Rey (PAGE 138) or a gondola ride along the sinuous canals of Long Beach's Naples district (PAGE 139).

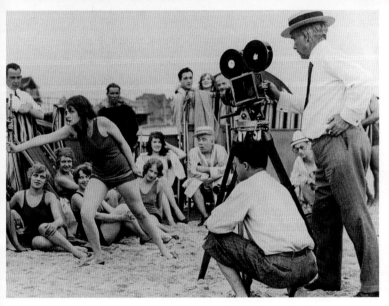

From mermaids to other beauties of the beach, Hollywood has capitalized on sex appeal to peddle its wares, one of the most recent being the buxom Pamela Anderson Lee (ABOVE RIGHT). Whatever your claim to fame, the richness of the area's shores provides a magnificent backdrop (PAGES 142 AND 143).

Popular tourist spots like the nearly 100-year-old Santa Monica Pier offer a world of fun for visitors, including an 11-story Ferris wheel with a panoramic view of the coastline. One native who knows all too well the area's watery wonders is Jamie Brisick, former professional surfer and executive editor of *Surfing* magazine.

Lights, camera, action: Today's film-makers are attracted to the same natural beauty that helped bring a fledgling movie industry to Los Angeles in the early 20th century. Legendary cinematographer Stephen H. Burum has done his part to further the industry with some 30 films to his credit, including *Mission Impossible*; *Hoffa*; *He Said, She Said*; and *The Untouchables*.

The bright lights are always beaming in L.A., particularly at the gala affairs that draw the stars. Out for a night in the ever present public eye are (CLOCKWISE FROM TOP LEFT) Sharon Stone at an American Film Institute salute to Martin Scorsese; teenage heartthrob Leonardo DiCaprio at the premiere of *Titanic*; Ellen DeGeneres and partner Anne Heche at the Oscar night *Vanity Fair* party; and Tom Cruise and wife Nicole Kidman at the Golden Globe Awards.

A golden gentleman named Oscar has been the ultimate Hollywood power player since he came along in 1928, bringing millions in future earnings to his lucky—and usually talented—recipients. On Academy Award night, billions world-wide tune in to watch Hollywood's biggest party, when the glittering film industry honors itself. Among the lucky who have taken Oscar home: director James Cameron (TOP LEFT); Helen Hunt and Jack Nicholson (TOP RIGHT); and Kim Basinger and Robin Williams (BOTTOM LEFT). Eddie Murphy, alas, is still waiting (BOTTOM RIGHT).

Oscar's statuesque little sister at the Academy of Television Arts and Sciences is Emmy, and she is coveted by those who ply their trade on the small screen.

© GREG DEGUIRE / ZUMA

The forecourt of the lavish Mann's Chinese Theater in the heart of Hollywood is on the must-see list for most tourists who come to worship the luminaries of entertainment history and walk in the footsteps of today's celluloid heroes. Among the many to leave their marks: actor Michael Douglas (TOP).

Sometimes it seems as though anyone in Los Angeles can be a star. Angelyne (OPPOSITE), self-crowned Queen of Camp, is one of the city's most enigmatic icons, and she knows how to use provocation and "exposure" to capture people's minds and imaginations. Often seen tooling around Hollywood in her pink Corvette, she's best known for her billboard campaign, paid for by an enthusiastic fan club.

© JEAN FERRO

The entertainment legends depicted in a panoramic 1983 mural by Thomas Suriya have all swept audiences off their feet. Although many—like Marilyn Monroe and Roy Rogers—have since gone on to greener pastures, they are immortalized in their movies, our memories, and the stars on Hollywood's Walk of Fame. More than 2,000 marble and bronze stars have been added to the sidewalks along Hollywood Boulevard and Vine Street since the first eight were unveiled in 1960.

The looming white letters of the Hollywood sign let you know you're in the land of make-believe, where Michael Jackson look-alikes roam the boulevards and more than 200 other celebrities—including Judy and the gang from the 1939 classic *The Wizard of Oz*—patiently await your arrival at the Hollywood Wax Museum.

An advertising gimmick to drum up interest in a real estate development called Hollywoodland, the 1923 Hollywood sign has become L.A.'s most enduring and recognizable landmark. It has made headlines ever since the 1930s when a young actress, despondent over her failing career, leapt to her death from the letter "H." The sign has also been a favorite target of pranksters: Potheads turned it into "Hollyweed," and during the Iran-Contra hearings, it became—briefly— "Ollywood."

The metamorphosis of Santa Monica's Third Street Promenade from a collection of ramshackle buildings into one of L.A.'s premier entertainment destinations a much copied civic miracle. Every day thousands mill along this three-block-long walking mall, browsing in eccentric and classy shops, enjoying culinary indulgences in its restaurants, or flocking to movie theaters to take in the latest blockbuster

The Music Center in downtown Los Angeles is a temple for world-class theater and musical performances of all kinds. Completed in 1969, this elegant complex is comprised of three venues.

The 3,200-seat Dorothy Chandler Pavilion is home of the renowned Los Angeles Philharmonic Orchestra, the Los Angeles Opera, and the Los Angeles Master Chorale. The 2,100-seat Ahmanson Theater often

plays host to visiting Broadway musicals, while the 750-seat Mark Taper Forum presents top-flight original plays that often end up winning Tony awards or Pulitzer prizes.

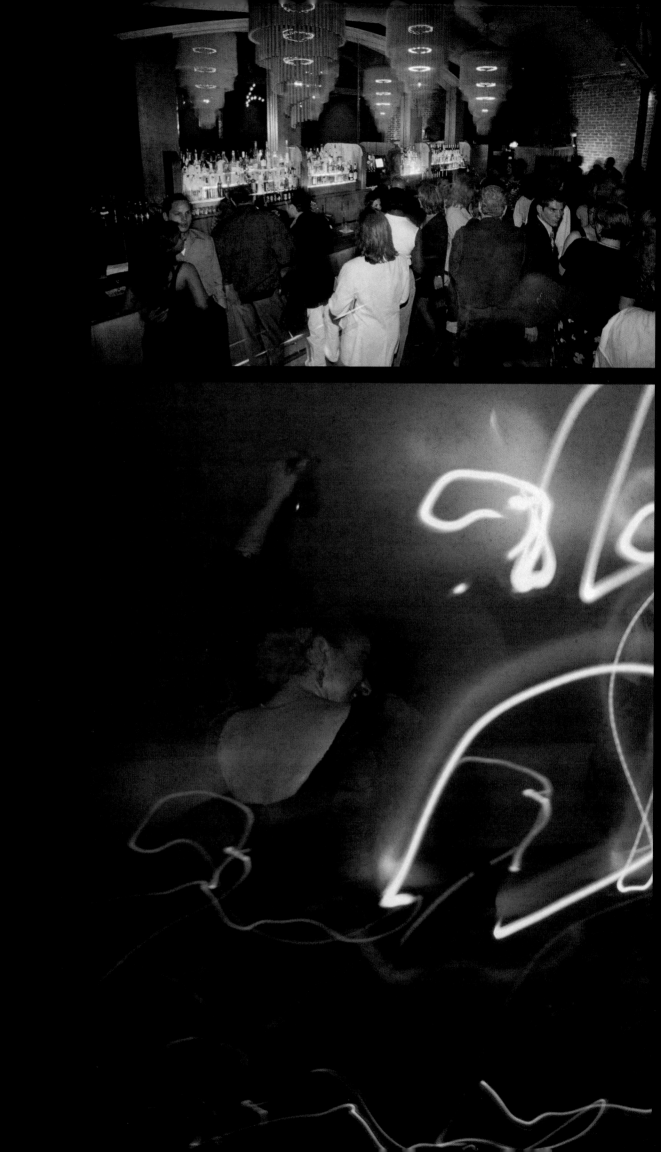

L.A.'s music scene is one of the liveliest in the country, catering to every taste. Ladies in spiky heels and nattily dressed gents writhe to the salsa beat at the stylish and trendy Conga Room in Hollywood (OPPOSITE TOP). Fierce flamenco dancers hold forth at Cava (OPPOSITE BOTTOM), while serious hepcats swing to the sounds of retro bands like Brian Setzer and his orchestra (BOTTOM). Classical music lovers, meanwhile, flock to the historic Hollywood Bowl, which echoes with some of the area's finest sounds. Opened in 1916, the venue is the summer home of the L.A. Philharmonic Orchestra.

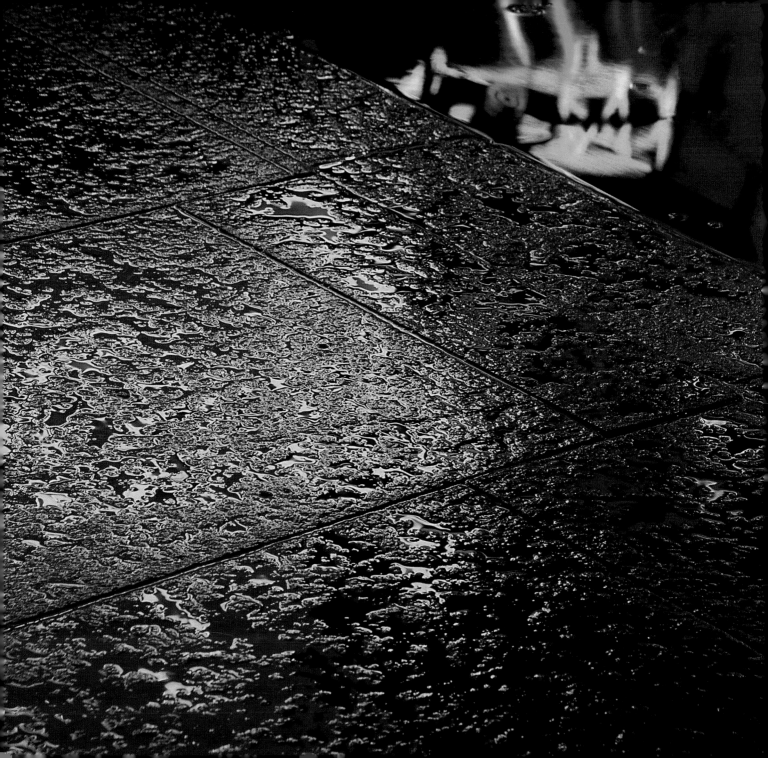

Adjoining the Universal Studios Hollywood theme park, Universal City Walk is a hugely popular outdoor mall with shops, restaurants, cinemas, and nightclubs. Plenty of inspiration, imagination, and innovation went into the critically acclaimed design, which is filled with whimsical visual surprises. At night, vibrant neon signs transform the promenade into a miniature Vegas-style strip.

CINEMA COLLECTORS
Movie Posters,
Photos & Books

Neon marquees brighten the Los Angeles landscape by night, whether they advertise the Guinness World of Records Museum in Hollywood (TOP LEFT), the Palace movie theater in the historic Broadway Theater District downtown (TOP RIGHT), or a movie collector's paradise (BOTTOM LEFT). Neon, electric, and kinetic arts are also the focus of downtown's Museum of Neon Art–MONA– the world's only permanent facility of its kind. The entrance is guarded by the museum's namesake, Mona Lisa (OPPOSITE), while a rocking Elvis is part of the collection inside (BOTTOM RIGHT).

MUSEUM OF NEON ART

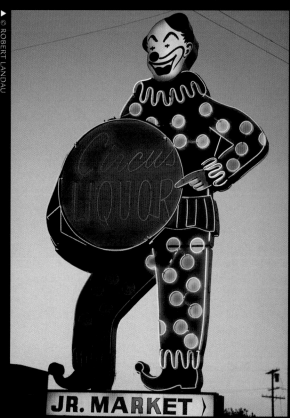

Circus LIQUOR

JR. MARKET ›

os Angeles loves the night. Saturday midnight screenings of the *Rocky Horror Picture Show* at the art house movie theater Nuart in West Los Angeles, and the periodic return of the Canadian avant-garde *Cirque du Soleil* to Santa Monica are embraced as traditions. Indeed, the night sky over L.A. has a distinctly circus atmosphere, which makes some cynics opine that La-La Land is more than just a little "wacko."

WACKO

In Los Angeles, the worlds of commercialism, art, and show business are often intertwined. Tom Patchett, producer of hit TV shows like *ALF*, is equally at home in his eclectic Track 16 Gallery in Santa Monica's Bergamot Station (OPPOSITE). There, he exhibits, publishes, buys, and sells both contemporary art and 20th-century Americana and collectibles, a unique combination that creates a vibrant and inspiring atmosphere.

From colorful baroque to angular ultra-modern, L.A. design styles run the gamut. In Venice Beach, artist Jonathan Borofsky has decorated the Renaissance Building with his 34-foot-tall *Ballerina Clown* (OPPOSITE TOP). And at Harvey's Antiques, retro is always in style with amoeba-shaped tables and couches (OPPOSITE BOTTOM).

The Capitol Records Tower on Vine Street in Hollywood is a clever example of symbolic architecture (PAGE 174). Designed by Welton Becket Associates in 1954, the 13-story circular structure is supposed to look like a stack of records topped by a stylus. Its rounded-at-the-edges approach to life may well have inspired the design of the Hanna-Barbera studio, known for its animated cartoons, in nearby Studio City (PAGE 175).

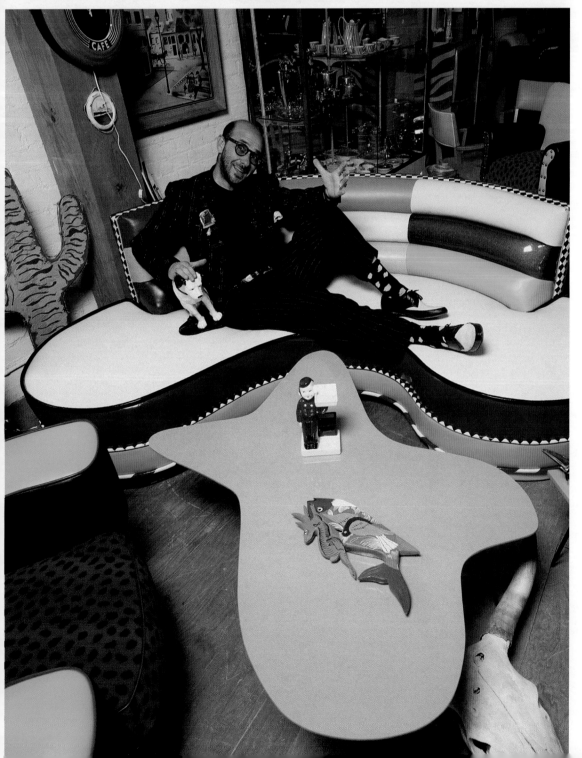

The influence of "the Industry" is felt in every aspect of L.A. life, including its architecture. This is especially true of Burbank, where major studios like Disney and Warner Brothers tout their unforgettable characters, such as Doc of the Seven Dwarfs and Bugs Bunny. Meanwhile, creative mind Dan Quarnstrom, director of Rhythm & Hues Studios, keeps company with characters from his video game, Eggs of Steel.

Imagination, pop culture, and food make for interesting combinations in the L.A. area. Santa Monica's larger-than-life waitress welcomes people to Bergamot Station. In Burbank, a cheeky character dishes out burgers and fries at Bob's Big Boy, a legendary 1940s coffee shop. With advertising like this, it's not hard to guess what's on the menu at the Donut Hole in the eastern suburb of La Puente, or from the roaming Oscar Mayer Wienermobile.

A love for things retro, like handmade cookies from milliner Drea Kadilak's shop on La Brea Avenue, forms a direct link with old-fashioned simplicity in this most complex and driven of American cities.

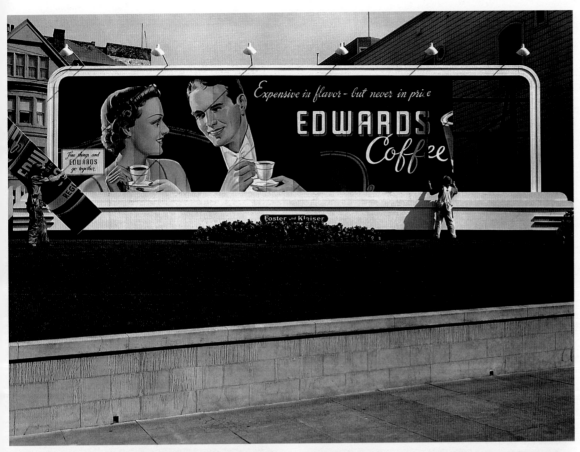

The appeal of Eisenhower-era comforts is an antidote to the stress and sheer velocity of living in L.A. Here, where the old Route 66 once thrived, the American diner is still a welcoming place to hunker down with the paper and a cuppa joe. (And perhaps be served a kind word and a winning smile, as well.)

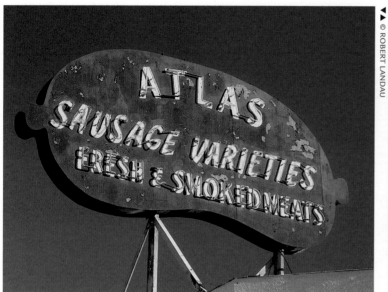

Hot dogs and hamburgers have always been the ultimate American comfort food, whether purchased at McDonald's, the well-known international chain founded in California, or local favorites like Fat Boy.

ndustrial Vernon is the home of the Farmer John sausage factory, a historical landmark known for the mural covering its facade. Tongue-in-cheek, yet macabre, it depicts a bucolic landscape inhabited by happy oinkers romping in the lush countryside, clearly oblivious to their future as pork rind.

food has come a long way since Libby's canned fruit cocktail was a dietary staple. Many experts regard L.A. as the culinary capital of the West Coast, due in part to the extraordinary innovation and creativity of its chefs. Mary Sue Milliken and Susan Feniger, owners of the trendy Border Grill in Santa Monica, use only top-quality ingredients when concocting mouthwatering Latin American dishes with a California twist (OPPOSITE). In South Central L.A., Vintress McCallum really puts the "Southern" in Southern California cuisine at his M&M Soul Food restaurant (CENTER). The area's fresh produce, especially during the three-week Los Angeles County Fair in Pomona, makes all the fine cooking feasible.

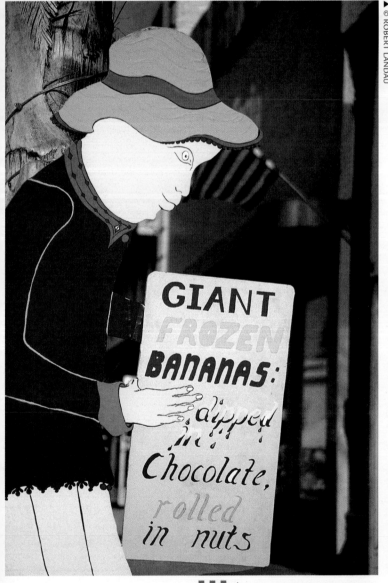

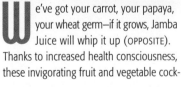

GIANT FROZEN BANANAS: dipped in Chocolate, rolled in nuts

We've got your carrot, your papaya, your wheat germ—if it grows, Jamba Juice will whip it up (OPPOSITE). Thanks to increased health consciousness, these invigorating fruit and vegetable cock-tails are now part of the daily diet of many Angelenos. Others also stock up on fresh produce at neighborhood farmers' markets (TOP LEFT), on Mexican *especialidades* at the Central Market downtown (TOP RIGHT), or on a wiggly catch in Newport Beach (BOTTOM RIGHT)—topped off with a tasty dessert.

The glass and steel towers of downtown L.A. now stand on land once lush with grapes. In 1917, the year Italian immigrant Santo Cambianica founded San Antonio Winery, L.A. had nearly 100 such facilities, providing the germ cell for California's fecund wine industry. Today, only San Antonio remains. Owner Steve Riboli (TOP) and his staff uphold family tradition, producing prize-winning wines from grapes grown in Northern California. Their winery and tasting room in an industrial section downtown is one of L.A.'s best kept secrets.

Long before cigars became a fashion statement, there was La Plata, L.A.'s only handmade cigar factory. The family-owned business has used charm, quality tobacco, and the deft fingers of Cuban-born cigar rollers to survive and thrive for more than half a century. To smoke a La Plata—or to watch one being made in the diminutive back room—is to steep yourself in tradition, craftsmanship, and tobacco lore.

olfgang Puck, chef to the stars, is very much a celebrity in his own right. Puck not only helped define California cuisine but also invented the Jewish pizza—topped with cream cheese, lox, and caviar—which has become his trademark. Wife Barbara Lazaroff designs the restaurants and industry insiders love his flagship location, Spago, where who-sits-where is a gauge of current power and status.

The local menu of culinary choices would sate even the appetites of a Hemingway. Cutting-edge dining in Los Angeles is an art: At celebrity-heavy Matsuhisa, located along Beverly Hills' historic Restaurant Row on La Cienega Boulevard (BOTTOM), chef Nobu Matsuhisa is as deft with a knife as he is at conceiving creative seafood dishes.

I n L.A., it don't mean a thing if it ain't got that swing! Elsewhere the swing era may have ended in the 1940s, but locally, things are just getting started. Dancers Jenny Nissenson and Paul Mojica do the lindy at the historic El Rey Theater, a 1928 art deco gem, now a frequent venue for swing parties.

Swing is once again king, and groups such as the Jumpin' Jimes Band have been booked solid since the swing revival shimmied into Los Angeles in the mid-1990s (OPPOSITE). At L.A. nightspots like Silver Lake's Derby—as seen in the hit film *Swingers*—sharply dressed young couples are doing the lindy and the jitterbug, proving, if nothing else, that everything old is new.

Almost every L.A. nightclub with a dance floor now hosts swing nights, including the Viper Room on the glitzy Sunset Strip in West Hollywood, where Dean Miller emcees wildly popular Thursday night blowouts (OPPOSITE). A mobster lounge back in the 1940s, the Viper Room is now co-owned by heartthrob actor Johnny Depp (BOTTOM), and it gained some unwanted notoriety in 1993 when the young actor River Phoenix fatally overdosed there.

f orward into the past: Johnny Boyd and his Indigo Swing band are the future of L.A.'s retro swing trend (OPPOSITE). And while the sounds may be the same, this isn't the 1940s—as proven by the tattooed denizens of the nightclub scene, who blend punk-rock style with thrift-store chic. Even in the imaginary barrooms of Disneyland and Carole and Barry Kaye's Museum of Miniatures, romance, as always, is on tap.

creen queens like Faye Dunaway (top) project a timeless glamour that helps define the appeal of Hollywood. Care to see what's underneath all that star power? At the Frederick's of Hollywood Celebrity Lingerie Hall of Fame, garments such as a tasseled bustier worn by Madonna, a billowy underskirt from Joan Crawford, and a pair of boxers once worn by Robert Redford are all on display—along with an oil painting of Mr. Frederick himself, fully attired, of course.

The performances of ace magician Billy McComb are as illusory as the postcard lures of L.A.'s beached beauties. A board member of the Academy of Magical Arts, Inc., McComb and his colleagues practice their craft at Hollywood's Magic Castle, a Victorian chateau that is a private club and showcase for the magical arts.

One of the city's acclaimed native sons, novelist James Ellroy (OPPOSITE BOTTOM) is known for works including *American Tabloid*, *White Jazz*, and *L.A. Confidential*, which became a critically lauded 1997 film that garnered an Oscar for actress Kim Basinger. Glorious architectural monuments to the age of art deco, such as the Argyle hotel on Sunset Boulevard and the Hollywood Park Casino, evoke the crime noir ambience of Ellroy's best-selling mysteries.

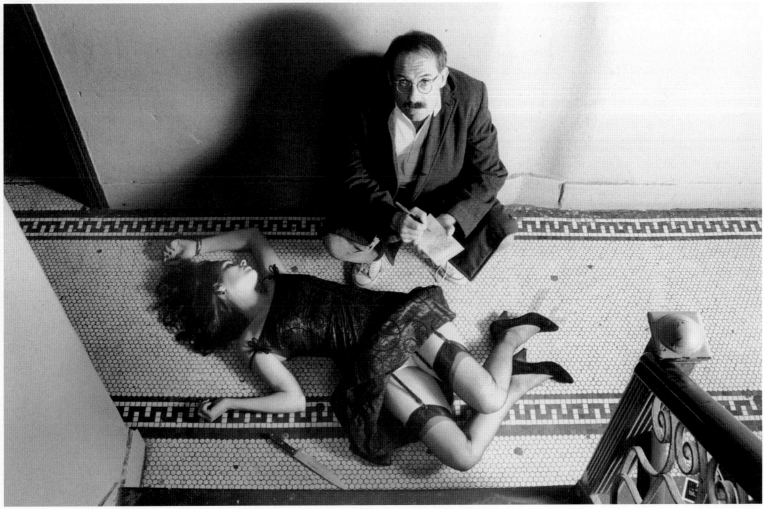

C.NICOLI

Although German Romantic writer Jean-Paul Richter never visited L.A., his heavenly sentiments seem to apply nonetheless: "The guardian angels of life sometimes fly so high as to be beyond our sight, but they are always looking down upon us" (PAGES 204-207).

The grim business of death is undercut on occasion with dark and often apt humor. Grave Line Tours will take you on a two-hour journey—in a swank hearse, no less—past the homes where numerous Hollywood icons met their makers. The inscription on the headstone of cartoon legend Mel Blanc, the voice of Bugs Bunny, Daffy Duck, and other Warner Brothers animated stars, says it best: "That's all folks."

For the world's shortest train ride, hop on Angels Flight, a rail system built in 1904 along a one-block stretch of Bunker Hill. Is it possible to make the trip in less than two minutes? As Groucho Marx would say, "You bet your life."

Come fly with me: Historically, L.A. signage has been rife with images of flight—no surprise, since the city's role as an aviation center stretches back to 1912, when Glenn L. Martin of Lockheed Martin fame opened his first company here. Nearly a century later, Santa Monica sculptor Michael C. McMillen takes measure of a decidedly smaller aerial construction.

© DAUNA WHITEHEAD

Sun City resident Lieutenant Colonel Charles M. Bussey flew on countless missions during World War II and the Korean War, earning seven service medals and 10 ribbons before his retirment (BOTTOM). On the civilian front, noted author Donald J. Waldie (OPPOSITE) found time while serving as Lakewood public information officer to pen its autobiography-cum-history. In the award-winning *Holy Land: A Suburban Memoir*, he tells the tale of the area's development as home to the battalions of local McDonnell-Douglas workers.

ichael Gregg Michaud is among the young lions of the Los Angeles literary community. The Maine transplant's poems, plays, and short stories—which include *The World of Mirth* and *The Sea Within*—have garnered considerable press praise. Michaud's performance piece *Flames of Hate in the City of Angels* offered nonflinching commentary on the 1992 L.A. riots.

f or close to 100 years, Dawson's Book Shop has kept Angeleno bookworms well fed with tomes covering Southern California's culture, politics, and arts scene. The North Larchmont Boulevard store was founded in 1905 by Ernest Dawson, and is currently overseen by his grandson, Michael.

Between creative genius and global megasuccess stand a small number of people with unusual powers of discernment. Script reader Roy Lee (OPPOSITE) submerges himself in his work, searching for the next big hit. Reprise Records President Howie Klein has been in the music industry for more than 20 years, and has been instrumental in the careers of artists ranging from Tom Petty and Neil Young to Madonna and Alanis Morissette.

cenes from the streets: Homelessness is one of the major problems plaguing Los Angeles, where it's estimated that between 68,000 and 177,000 call the concrete home.

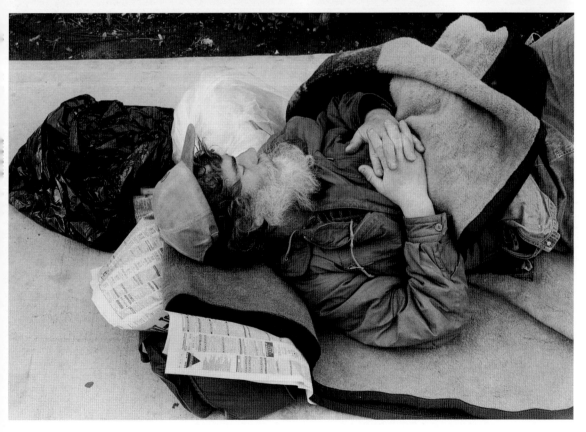

The Rose Bowl Flea Market is a favorite among Angeleno bargain hunters, who hit the city's largest such event as early as 6 a.m. on the second Sunday of every month in search of cast-off treasures.

With hundreds of bowling alleys located throughout Southern California, it's obvious that the fine art of knocking down the tenpins will always be in vogue. Boasting its own staying power is Pasadena's Rose Bowl Stadium, an L.A. fixture since the 1920s.

As old styles continually return to the fashion forefront, business always booms at vintage clothing stores such as L.A.'s Golyester Antiques, a shop on South LaBrea owned by Linda Davis (OPPOSITE). Among the old threads and knickknacks found at this retail time capsule are more than 150 pairs of vintage pajamas—Golyester's specialty.

Life can be a circus—or a party—for children in Los Angeles, the hometown of adolescent icons from Mickey Mouse to Howdy Doody. And remember, kids: If it's your party, you can cry if you want to.

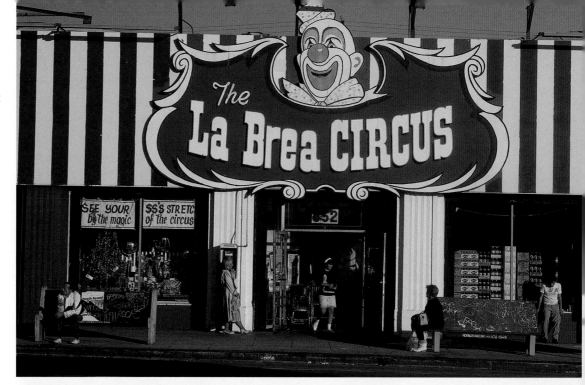

When the Persian Gulf War ended in early 1991, the city of Los Angeles threw a celebratory wingding for its local veterans along Sunset Boulevard, complete with a massive American flag. And as the adage goes, there's something about a man—or a G.I. Joe—in a uniform.

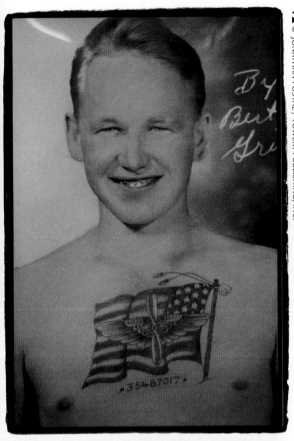

They've been inking human flesh for more than 70 years at Bert Grimm's World Famous Tattoo Studio in Long Beach, where, if you believe the stories, gangster toughs Bonnie Parker and Pretty Boy Floyd had their hides decorated. Amply emblazoned tattoo artist Rick Walters (OP-POSITE) carries on the tradition set by Grimm.

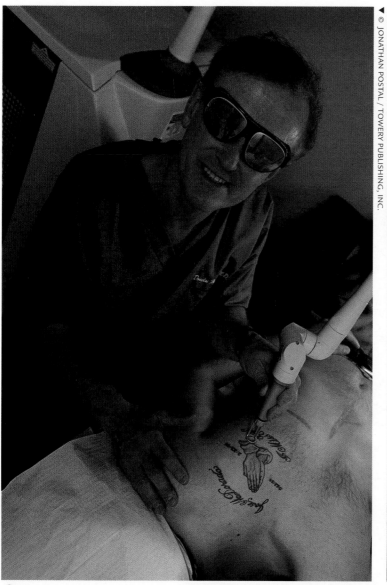

Although tattooing has become more and more acceptable, dermatologist Dr. Douglas Hamilton (LEFT) has also seen the removal business boom over the past few years. Some things, however, aren't so temporal, such as the ever growing popularity of the cowboy culture, nurtured in Hollywood through early television westerns like *The Lone Ranger* (RIGHT), and the gunslinging horse operas of action-flick titan Clint Eastwood (OPPOSITE).

Despite a reduction in violent crimes nationally, L.A. continues to grapple with the problems associated with gang violence. Each year, the sheriff's department spends more than $10 million to combat the growing urban threat.

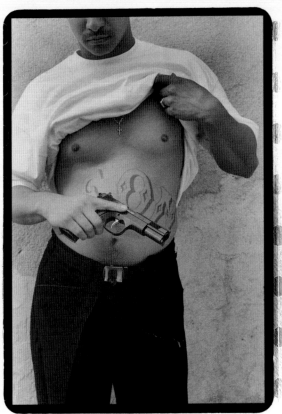

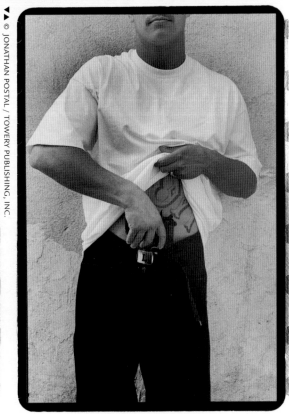

hat most of the world knows about how the West was won came via silver screen legends. From silhouetted statues of John Wayne (TOP) to the Roy Rogers-Dale Evans Museum (BOTTOM), memories abound. Strumming and smiling underneath his white hat, Rogers—along with his trusty horse, Trigger, and faithful dog, Bullet—puts the "good" in "good guys."

BULLET

▼▲ © BUD LEE / THE ARTISTS AND WRITERS GROUP

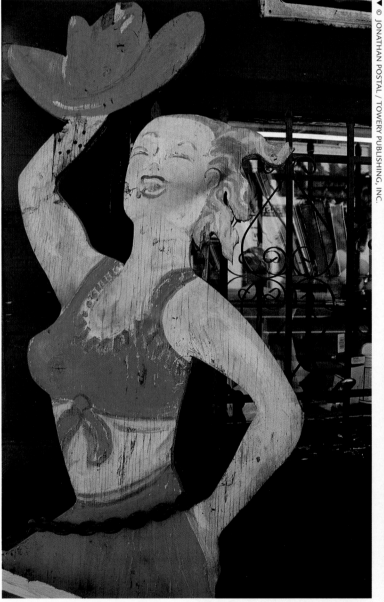

In neighboring Orange and Ventura counties, the cowboy legacy continues to thrive thanks to events such as the Police Rodeo in Huntington Beach (TOP LEFT) and Anaheim's aptly named Wild Bill's Extravaganza (TOP AND BOTTOM RIGHT), where the cowgirls handle a rope as well as Barbara Stanwyck did in the 1954 film *Cattle Queen of Montana.*

SHE STRIPS OFF HER PETTICOATS
...and straps on her guns!

BARBARA STANWYCK
woman of fire...in a land aflame!

RONALD REAGAN
dangerous friend...deadly foe!

CATTLE QUEEN
OF MONTANA

PRINT BY TECHNICOLOR

GENE EVANS · LANCE FULLER · Directed ALLAN DWAN · Screenplay ROBERT BLEES & HOWARD ESTABROOK · Produced BENEDICT BOGEAUS

opularized by the saloon showgirls of countless westerns, the dance hall tradition thrives in Lady Jane, a shining pearl on the Los Angeles burlesque revival scene.

BACK IN THE SADDLE AGAIN

With its artist studios in the old Paradox Iron building downtown (TOP), the Brewery Arts Complex hangs on to a piece of L.A.'s past. A significant portion of that rich history is musical legend Gene Autry, the "Singing Cowboy," whose Autry Museum of Western Heritage (OPPOSITE) has celebrated the growth of the area since opening in 1988. Another well-known site for remembering the old days is the ranch estate of humorist and actor Will Rogers (BOTTOM). And musician Paul Greenstein (CENTER) does his part to keep the memories alive through his unique brand of country swing.

The lure of motorcycle culture has captivated countless weekend warriors and nonconformists who prefer the open highway to any cubicle-bound desk job. The bad-boy image personified by Marlon Brando in the 1950s biker flick *The Wild One* appears to have struck a chord with Royal Crown Revue vocalist Eddie Nichols (OPPOSITE LEFT).

Los Angeles hot-rodders combine the mechanical passions of gearheads with a love of detailed artwork, as proven by the countless vintage-automobile hoods adorned with sprawling flames. Many of them are the creation of Hollywood car customizer/stunt driver Dean Jeffries, who's been at it for more than 35 years. Jeffries' work has been featured in films, such as *Who Framed Roger Rabbit*, and he was the creator of James Bond's famed Moon Buggy.

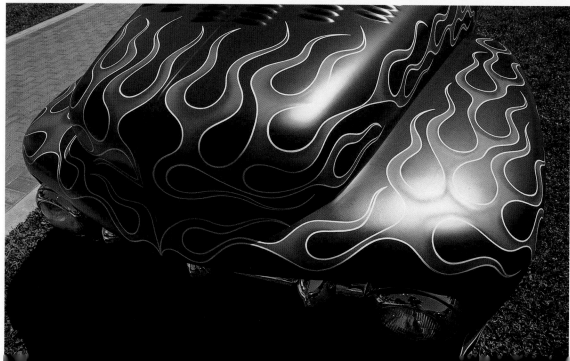

Though you could argue that almost all of Los Angeles is a car museum— witness the city's slew of bulbous lowrider classics (ABOVE)—the Petersen Automotive Museum in Hancock Park is the real thing (OPPOSITE, BOTTOM LEFT AND RIGHT). Among its host of spiffy vehicles are vintage Model-T Fords and Mercedes-Benz classics.

f New York is the city that never sleeps, L.A. has to be the city that never sits still—from the bicycle races and Grand Prix events in Malibu to the Los Angeles Marathon, which attracts 10,000 runners annually. Even the animals are in on the act, with pig races in the San Fernando Valley and horses galloping along the famed track at San Gabriel Valley's Arcadia.

T une up, fill up, and wake up: If you want to get ahead in Los Angeles, jumpstart the morning commute with a trip to the nearest gas station. But don't forget to rev up your own engine with a daily dose of everyone's favorite fuel—caffeine.

With 18 major freeways crisscrossing the city and millions of car-crazed denizens, it's likely you'll find a few casualties along the way.

The Los Angeles highway system is a necessary evil for those getting from point A to point B. It's also useful for anyone just wanting to get *away*, with the top down and the urban jungle disappearing in the rearview mirror.

L os Angeles is the western terminus of the legendary Route 66, which winds from Santa Monica through the city and east, all the way to the Great Lakes region. En route, the sights are quite spectacular, both natural and man-made.

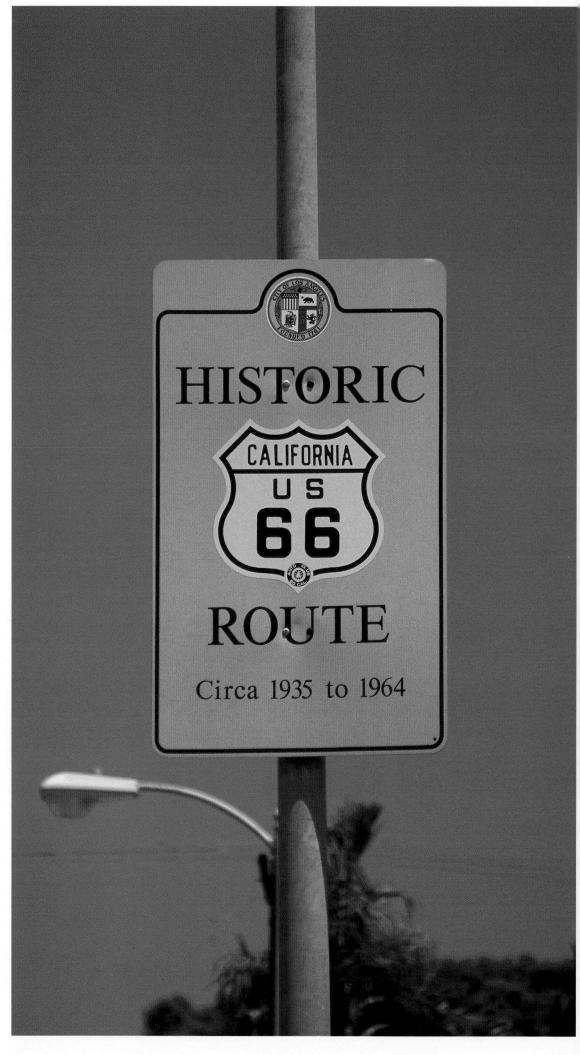

H eat notwithstanding, the desert is an arid seductress, with wide-open spaces, meditative tranquility, and seemingly endless vistas.

The land surrounding the Los Angeles area is rich in the flora and fauna of the desert. Streams flowing from the San Jacinto Mountains sustain a variety of plants in Andreas Canyon (OPPOSITE), an oasis near luscious Palm Springs. Eastward is Joshua Tree National Park, home to the tenacious Joshua tree and a prolific family of other bizarre cacti (TOP). The 12-acre Desert Garden at Pasadena's Henry E. Huntington Botanical Gardens brings an array of the prickly plants into a more urban locale (BOTTOM).

Phalanxes of whirling windmills harvest the dry, withering wind of the desert and deliver around-the-clock power to the city of Palm Springs.

need an umbrella? You could find plenty of them—1,760, to be exact—for a few weeks back in October 1991, when the famed artist Christo unveiled his aptly titled conceptual piece *The Umbrellas* in a valley among the hills of Tejon Pass. The two-prong presentation also included more than 1,300 umbrellas in Ibarak, Japan, that were opened simultaneously with their California counterparts.

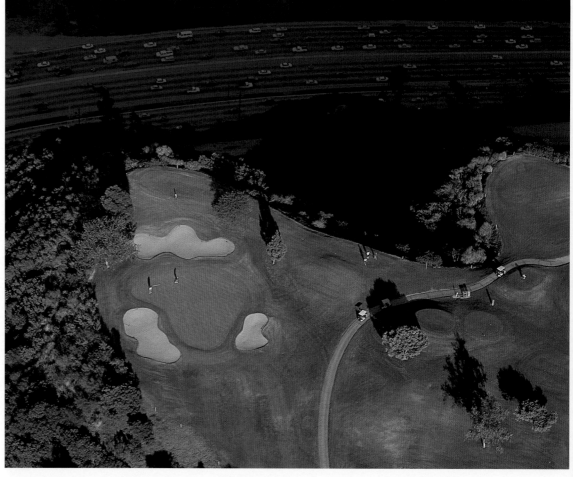

A mecca for too many celebrities to list—let alone name a street after—Palm Springs is also a haven for golf nuts, with some 80 courses regularly hosting major tournaments. Towering above Palm Springs are the San Jacinto Mountains (PAGES 270 AND 271), which jut skyward to elevations of more than 10,000 feet, offering a different climate and a seemingly different world.

ith its daunting 8,000-foot ridge, Big Bear Lake in the San Bernadino Mountains is a veritable hotbed for downhill skiing and snowboarding (RIGHT). Snow usually falls by mid-December and lasts until early spring, with machines providing supplementary powder when nature falls short. From the scorching heat of the desert floor to the snow-capped top of San Jacinto is only a matter of a brief ride on the Palm Springs Aerial Tramway (OPPOSITE TOP), where cable cars climb 6,000 vertical feet in just 14 minutes.

Outside of L.A. lie enough beauty and serenity to make for a perfect weekend getaway for locals. The snow-capped mountains and the area's numerous waterways stand in defiant contrast to the skyscrapers and bustle of the city.

LOS ANGELES

The Los Angeles River (BOTTOM) was the only source of water for the L.A. area until William Mulholland stepped in. It was Mulholland's idea to build a 250-mile-long aqueduct from the faraway Owens Valley, effectively bringing a second water source to the city. The aqueduct opened in 1913, and its water is stored throughout Southern California, including the scenic Hollywood Reservoir (TOP).

fitness is a central part of the L.A. life-style, which is no surprise given the beautiful natural surroundings and a climate that lends itself to outdoor exercise. Skiing, skateboarding, windsurfing, para-sailing, jogging, and biking all have a place in daily life (PAGES 278-281).

About 60 miles south of Los Angeles, in Orange County, is Mediterranean-flavored Laguna Beach, where splendid cliffside mansions are built right up to the edge of America (OPPOSITE). On Victoria Beach, one of Laguna's less crowded patches of sand, stands a Rapunzel-worthy French Norman tower. Built in 1926, its sole purpose is to provide private beach access from the house perched on the bluff above.

In Southern California, the life of birds has been an indicator of ecohealth since local Native Americans performed their rituals at Eagle Rock in nearby Topanga Canyon (OPPOSITE BOTTOM). Supporters of wetlands preservation and nesting issues have delayed numerous projects that would endanger such feathered friends as the great blue heron and the oddly noble pelican.

ot just a bastion for the young and trendy, Los Angeles holds sunny comforts and ample activities for its older citizens (and their feline friends).

Henry Moore
Reclining Figure, 1983
GIFT OF THE ANGELS OF THE ARTS
JUNE 11, 1984

MRS. ROBERT B. EGELIN
MRS. THOMAS J. MCGONIGLE

A formation of rocks at the Joshua Tree National Monument (ABOVE) seems to mimic one of the acclaimed *Reclining Figure* pieces by modernist sculptor Henry Moore, whose work graces the exterior of the Orange County Performing Arts Center in Costa Mesa.

from the mud baths at Glen Ivy Hot Springs to a boardwalk massage on Venice Beach to the R and R offered at the spa in Hotel Laguna, Southern California has a slew of ways to recover from the pressures of the day.

Everyone knows it's a dog-eat-dog world out there, so why not have a place for pooped pooches to unwind and take a load off? Welcome to the Los Angeles Kennel Club, where canines can relax, kick back with some restful television viewing, or go for a swim. After all, it *is* a dog's life.

© LISA ROMEREIN

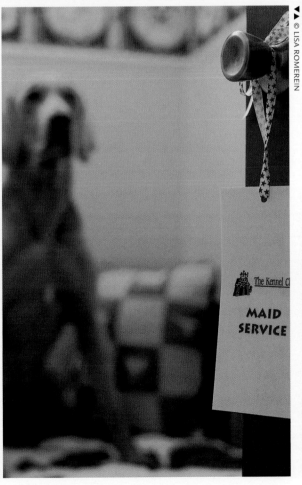

Some of Hollywood's biggest stars have been real dogs—from Lassie and Rin Tin Tin to *Frasier* scene-stealer Eddie. No surprise, then, that L.A. canines always try to look their best and show off their talents. As for Peabody the Chihuahua, he seldom leaves the shoulder of his owner, Hollywood agent Eddie Morris.

rom the Venice Boardwalk to the jam-packed Zuma Beach, it's always easy to get lost in a Southern California crowd.

Venice Beach founder Abbot Kinney originally envisioned a dream town that would become an intellectually stimulating center for the arts, music, and theater. Instead, it became a destination for oddball characters and the eccentric denizens of West Coast counterculture—from the Beats of the 1950s to the flower children of the 1960s to the guitar-playing Rollerbladers of today.

The L.A. area proved fertile stomping grounds for the counterculture of the 1960s, an era captured musically by groups such as the Mamas and the Papas, featuring the soothing alto of "Mama" Cass Elliot (CENTER). But California dreamin' isn't confined to bygone decades. Today's alternative generation gathers at shopping centers like Costa Mesa's LAB Anti Mall (BOTTOM), a self-described "iconoclast village of goods and consumables."

The Doors and their decadent, charismatic vocalist Jim Morrison helped to popularize the Sunset Strip during the 1960s with their faintly psychedelic pop. The group's fame lives on, as does the solo career of Doors keyboardist Ray Manzarek (BOTTOM RIGHT), who has produced several L.A. bands. And Morrison, in death as in life, remains an iconic sex symbol—and a source of inspiration for local muralists.

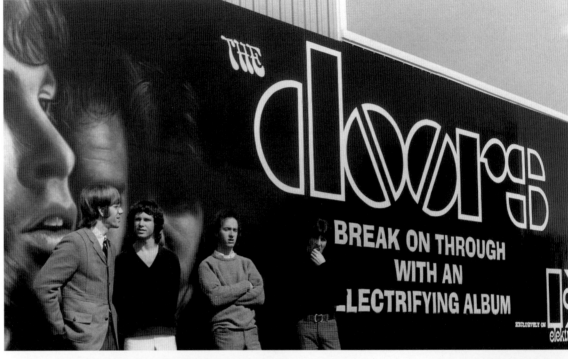

© STEVE BAKER / HIGHLIGHT PHOTOGRAPHY

ore than 30 years later, the work of '60s icons such as the Grateful Dead, Bob Dylan, and Joan Baez still reverberates through the consciousness of pop-music fans. The 1995 death of Dead leader Jerry Garcia sparked countless tributes across the globe, including one on Venice Beach (TOP).

How L.A. rocks today: the heavy-metal cool of Slash (opposite, top right), the alt-rock bizarreness depicted by Perry Farrell of Jane's Addiction (OPPOSITE, BOTTOM RIGHT), and the tattooed punk grimace of Social Distortion front man Mike Ness (LEFT).

f rom tarot cards to Hare Krishnas, from scientology to body piercing—name a fad and odds are it's flourishing somewhere in Los Angeles.

The birthplace of Los Angeles is the historic downtown district of El Pueblo and its commercial heart, Olvera Street. Established by the Spanish in 1781, the area is now the site of numerous Hispanic festivals, a treasure trove of historic architecture, and a tourist destination brimming with museums, restaurants, and shops.

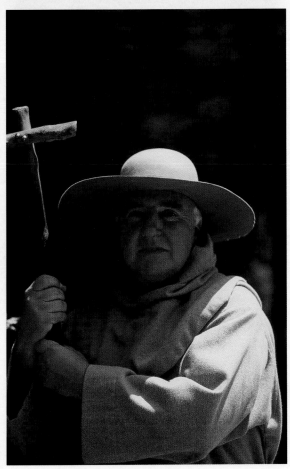

Since the 1700s, when the region's Native American tribes were Christianized by Father Junípero Serra, Catholicism has been a strong religious force in Los Angeles. Of the 21 missions established along El Camino Real (The King's Highway) between San Diego and Monterey, only a few remain—among them, the Mission San Fernando Rey de España, founded in 1797.

Originally a movie palace built in the late 1920s, the Mayan Theater in downtown Los Angeles is the embodiment of the Latino influence in the city's architecture. Warriors embedded in its ornate facade keep their eyes peeled, while inside, the theater houses a popular Latin-music dance club.

E ast L.A. abounds in colorful, artful images of religious inspiration, with murals and mosaics of the Virgin of Guadalupe seemingly everywhere (TOP LEFT). While the faithful attend services at the Mission San Fernando (TOP RIGHT), revelers and testifiers get decked out and take it to the street during the annual Day of the Dead celebration, a Mexican festivity honoring the deceased (BOTTOM).

There's an otherworldly atmosphere in L.A., where heaven and hell seem to pop up in some unexpected places.

The annual Doo Dah Parade is held the Sunday before Thanksgiving in Pasadena as both a riff on the Rose Parade and a slightly tongue-in-cheek attempt to call attention to relevant social issues. For matters of a more physical nature, Los Angeles acupuncturist Dr. Mao can get right to the point.

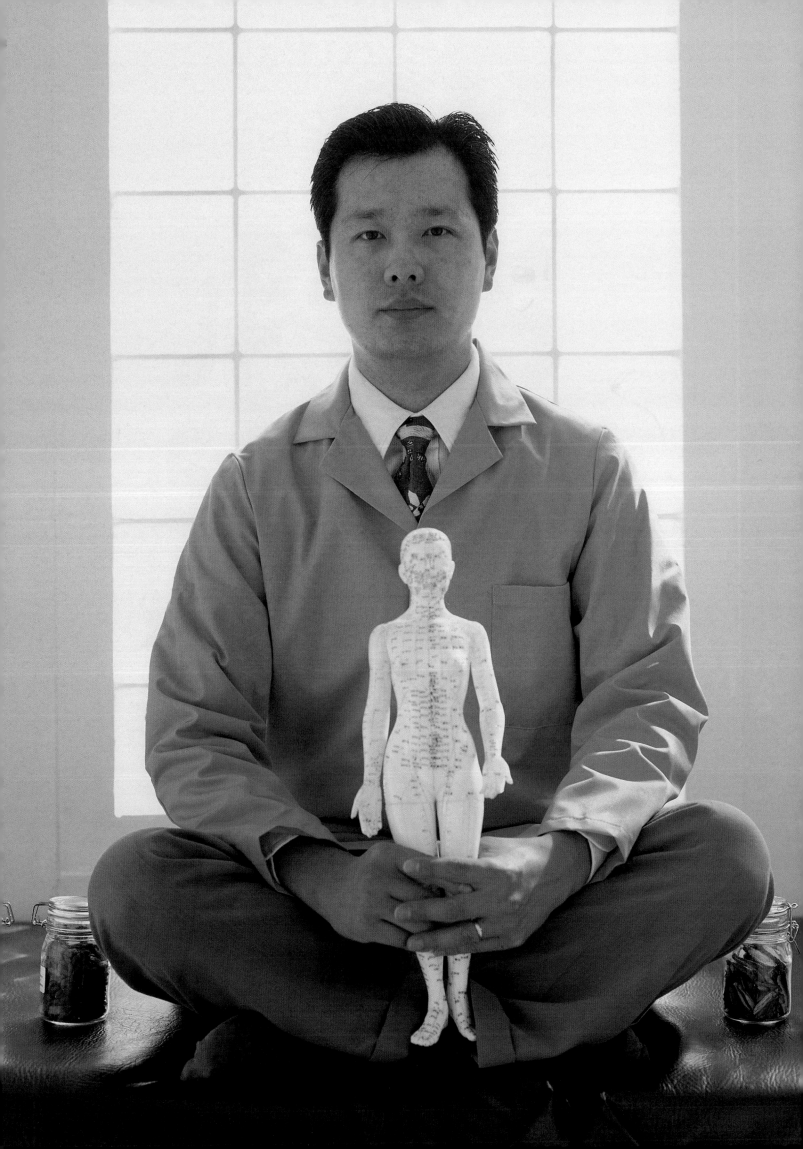

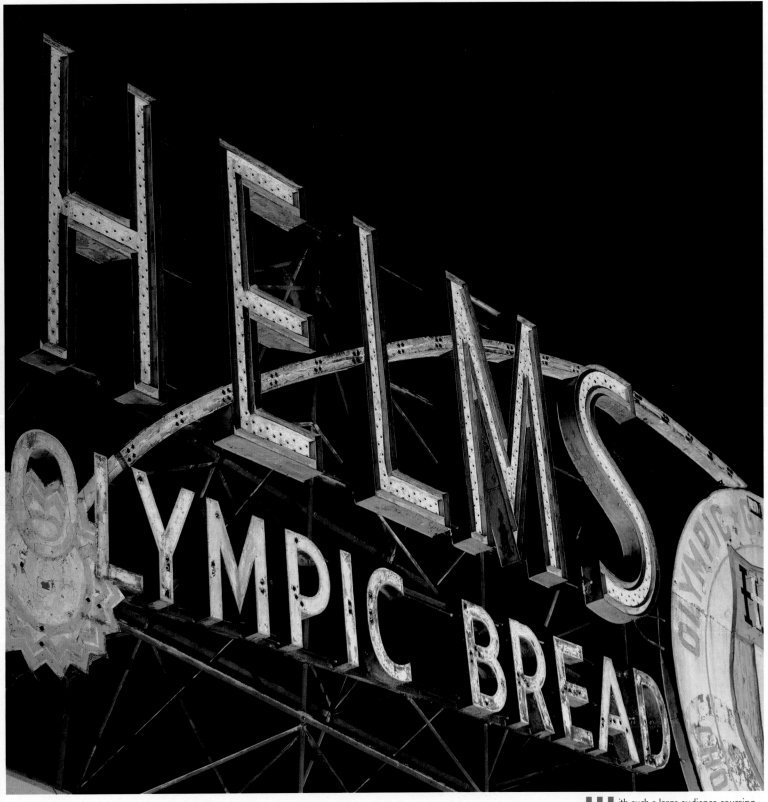

With such a large audience coursing its streets, Los Angeles is the perfect candidate for communicating via signage—whether the message regards salvation or sustenance.

A recent exhibit at the J. Paul Getty Museum looked beyond the mere beauty of Greek and Roman statues and architecture. Yet physical beauty itself is still a widely celebrated attribute, be it at a muscle competition on Venice Beach or in Los Angeles artist Robert Graham's curiously headless, bronzed bodies, which guard the entrance of the Memorial Coliseum in Exposition Park.

Rocky V™ - Rocky (Sylvester Stallone) rediscovers his roots in the fifth chapter this series. After returning home from his latest triumph, Rocky suffers seve financial losses and is forced to retire from boxing due to injuries. He and his far ily return to Philadelphia where Rocky trains a promising young boxer who rises t national prominence. When the young fighter turns against his mentor and publicl taunts him, Rocky knows he must fight once more to regain his dignity. This inspir ing film brings the saga full circle.

os Angeles is nothing if not a sports town. More than 10 college and professional teams call the area home, as does Sly Stallone of *Rocky* fame.

LOS ANGELES

Who knows how many hoop dreams began at the Los Angeles Forum, home of the world-champion Lakers. Team of choice over the years for Nick Van Exel (TOP), Rick Fox (BOTTOM RIGHT), and Kobe Bryant (BOTTOM LEFT), the Lakers are the winningest team in basketball and the second-winningest team in professional sports (after the New York Yankees).

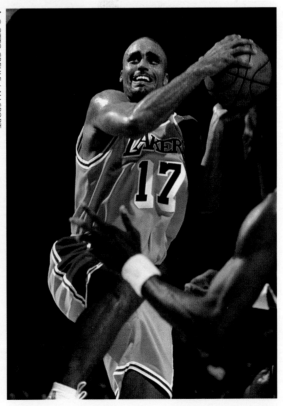

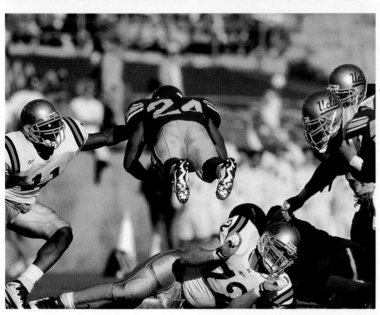

LOS ANGELES

hether it's basketball or football, whenever crosstown rivals at the University of Southern California (USC) and the University of California at Los Angeles (UCLA) square off, the city shuts down for the game. Fans of both teams have no problem filling the stands at the L.A. Memorial Coliseum, home of the USC Trojans (ABOVE).

LOS ANGELES

Every New Year's Day, Pasadena's 101,000-seat Rose Bowl is host to its namesake college football championship. Known as the granddaddy of all bowl games, the event pits the best Pac-10 (West Coast) university team against the best team from the Big Ten (Great Lakes region). The match is preceded by the Tournament of Roses Parade, a century-old event seen locally by about 1 million spectators and beamed via satellite to millions more in some 100 countries. Among the glitter and glitz of the Rose Parade's pageantry are the flower-laden floats—gigantic, ornately decorated vessels covered with as many as 100,000 blossoms.

LOS ANGELES

On a chaparral-cloaked hilltop overlooking downtown stands Dodger Stadium, home to the Los Angeles Dodgers. Among the most popular teams in major league baseball, the Dodgers moved to L.A. from Brooklyn in 1958 and settled into the 56,000-seat ballpark. Winners of seven National League pennants and four World Series titles, the Dodgers have included among their ranks some of the modern era's greatest players. South of L.A. in Orange County, the American League's Angels, a Southern California fixture since 1961, call Anaheim Stadium home.

The "old ball game" isn't necessarily confined to sold-out stadiums or sandy beaches, as proven at MacArthur Park (BOTTOM) and at the century-old Pershing Square, L.A.'s oldest public park (OPPOSITE).

In 1994, Pershing Square got a $14 million face-lift, accented by a 120-foot purple tower, fountains, and plenty of public art, including a pair of concrete spheres.

Amid the jubilation and joyous celebrations that are part of the L.A. lifestyle, the laughing Buddha seems to signal that all of life must not be suffering.

© JIM RUSSI

t takes just the right moves to keep the traffic flowing through the city's many busy intersections.

t's a well-known axiom that driving in Los Angeles isn't exactly easy, but apparently parking can be equally perilous (PAGES 336-339).

rom its trademark freeways to its stunning vistas dotted with palm trees, Los Angeles has captured the imaginations of countless romantics and visionaries, all of whom call this city of dreams their home.

PROFILES IN EXCELLENCE

A look at the corporations, businesses, professional groups, and community service organizations that have made this book possible. Their stories—offering an informal chronicle of the local business community—are arranged according to the date they were established in Los Angeles.

Allstate Insurance Company ☙ Alschuler Grossman Stein & Kahan LLP ☙ American Airlines ☙ Amptron International, Inc. ☙ Applause, Inc. ☙ ARCO ☙ Aref & Associates ☙ Arrowhead Mountain Spring Water ☙ Automobile Club of Southern California ☙ Baker & Hostetler LLP, Counsellors at Law ☙ Bank of America ☙ 92.3 The Beat ☙ The Boeing Company ☙ Bragman Nyman Cafarelli, Inc. ☙ Bugle Boy Industries, Inc. ☙ Capitol Records ☙ CB Richard Ellis ☙ Century 21 Real Estate Corporation ☙ Certified Grocers of California, Ltd. ☙ Childrens Hospital Los Angeles ☙ Compensation Resource Group, Inc. ☙ Daniel, Mann, Johnson, & Mendenhall ☙ Environmental Lighting for Architecture, Inc. ☙ Ernst & Young LLP, Entrepreneur Of The Year Program ☙ George D. Bjurman & Associates ☙ The Getty Center ☙ Hilton Los Angeles Airport ☙ HR Textron Inc. ☙ Hughes Electronics Corporation ☙ J & H Marsh & McLennan ☙ Katell Properties ☙ KCBS-TV ☙ Kingston Technology Company ☙ KLVE-FM, KSCA-FM, KTNQ-AM ☙ Koo Koo Roo, Inc. ☙ KTI Corporation ☙ Litton Industries, Inc. ☙ Lockheed Martin IMS ☙ Los Angeles Chamber of Commerce ☙ Los Angeles Community Colleges ☙ Los Angeles Department of Water and Power ☙ Los Angeles Times ☙ Los Angeles World Airports ☙ Majestic Realty Co. ☙ Marriott International ☙ McKesson Water Products Company ☙ McKinsey & Company, Inc. ☙ MediaOne ☙ Mercury Air Group, Inc. ☙ National Coatings Corporation ☙ Nelson Shelton & Associates ☙ Nestlé USA ☙ Northern Trust Bank of California ☙ O'Melveny & Myers LLP ☙ Pacific Bell ☙ Park Labrea ☙ Party Planners West, Inc. ☙ Providence Health System ☙ Public Storage, Inc. ☙ Rancho Los Amigos National Rehabilitation Center ☙ Raytheon ☙ Relaxor ☙ Romac International ☙ The Seiniger Advertising Group ☙ The Sheridan Group ☙ Southern California Gas Co. ☙ Southwest Airlines Co. ☙ State Farm Insurance Companies ☙ Textron Aerospace Fasteners ☙ Transamerica ☙ Troop Steuber Pasich Reddick & Tobey, LLP ☙ Turner Construction Company ☙ Tutor-Saliba Corporation ☙ University of California, Los Angeles ☙ Union Bank of California, N.A. ☙ United Airlines ☙ Universal Studios ☙ University of Phoenix ☙ University of Southern California ☙ ViewSonic Corporation ☙ Virco Mfg. Corporation ☙ Washington Mutual ☙ Watson Pharmaceuticals, Inc. ☙ Wells Fargo & Co. ☙ Westside Distributors ☙ Wyndham Checkers Hotel

1855 - 1933

1855 Wells Fargo & Co.

1867 Southern California Gas Co.

1880 University of Southern California

1881 Los Angeles Times

1885 O'Melveny & Myers LLP

1888 Los Angeles Chamber of Commerce

1888 Rancho Los Amigos National Rehabilitation Center

1894 Arrowhead Mountain Spring Water

1900 Automobile Club of Southern California

1901 Childrens Hospital Los Angeles

1902 Los Angeles Department of Water and Power

1906 Pacific Bell

1906 Transamerica

1912 Universal Studios

1913 Bank of America

1914 Union Bank of California, N.A.

1919 University of California, Los Angeles

1922 Certified Grocers of California, Ltd.

1922 KLVE-FM, KSCA-FM, KTNQ-AM

1923 J & H Marsh & McLennan

1924 CB Richard Ellis

1926 United Airlines

1927 Wyndham Checkers Hotel

1928 Los Angeles World Airports

1928 State Farm Insurance Companies

1929 Environmental Lighting for Architecture, Inc.

1930 American Airlines

1931 KCBS-TV

1932 Hughes Electronics Corporation

1933 HR Textron Inc.

Wells Fargo & Co.

Wells Fargo was synonymous with gold during the building of this nation's West, with fast delivery of banking assistance to pioneers through its legendary stagecoach service. Today, the assets behind Wells Fargo Bank remain its quick delivery of reliable, consistent, and efficient financial products and services provided to customers locally and worldwide. ♔ Henry Wells and William Fargo founded the company in San Francisco

in 1852. When Wells Fargo & Co. opened an express and banking office in Los Angeles on January 4, 1855, the company had already established a reputation as the main express office and banking house during the flurry of the northern California gold rush. Nearly a century and a half later, Wells Fargo & Co. boasts some $95 billion in assets, as well as more than 4,500 automated teller machines (ATMs) and nearly 2,000 locations throughout 10 states in the western United States.

"We are the right kind of corporate citizens," says Paul M. Watson, vice chair and senior officer in Los Angeles. "One of our goals is to create awareness of the

company: We are involved in all aspects of the community through the market. We are responsible to the businesses we serve in the communities we operate in. We always have been."

Fast Then, Fast Now

Wells Fargo's heritage is rooted in helping small-business owners grow. In fact, in the late 1850s, Wells Fargo helped a small saloon-keeper, Manuel Ravenna, prosper after its express service brought in the first ice shipped to Los Angeles for commercial purposes, according to Wells Fargo historian Beverly K. Smith. In the same tradition, today, Wells Fargo Bank provides a speedy

delivery of a broad array of products and services so customers can choose the options that are most convenient to their way of life.

Customers can access their account information any time of the day or night from practically anywhere in the world. Wells Fargo was the first bank in the country to offer on-line banking, which lets customers download their account information onto their personal software and conduct transactions using their personal computers. More than 470,000 customers do their banking on-line. By 1999, the bank expects to serve 1 million customers via the Internet.

For customers who choose the traditional method of banking, the bank has many strategically located branches with extended hours. Wells Fargo express ATMs located throughout the Southern California area make banking fast and easy. Bank by mail, telephone banking, the Internet, and branches inside supermarkets provide other convenient access points, supporting the bank's current philosophy of "anywhere, anytime banking."

The bank's uniform products and services provide customers the guarantee that they can count on Wells Fargo for the same quality banking support throughout its 10-state territory. Because Wells Fargo has streamlined its services over the years, customers can do their banking without waiting in line.

"This market is incredibly diverse, and because of that, it's very resilient," Watson says. "We serve a core base of businesses that are germane to the growth of the Southern California economy." In fact, Wells Fargo is one of the nation's leading small-business lenders. In addition, Wells Fargo has the West's largest private-client services trust and investment management group. Over time, the bank has acquired Crocker Bank and Bank of America's trust department.

Following a Tradition

By helping small businesses grow, Wells Fargo also helped the country grow. During World War I, the bank was forced to sell its express business to the government as a wartime measure, ending its presence in the Southland for half a century. In 1967,

Today, Wells Fargo & Co. boasts some $95 billion in assets, as well as more than 4,500 automated teller machines (ATMs) and nearly 2,000 locations throughout 10 states in the western United States.

Wells Fargo reopened a branch office in Los Angeles.

After purchasing Crocker Bank in 1986—a financial institution with deep roots in the Southland—Wells Fargo moved into Crocker's corporate offices in downtown Los Angeles across from the Los Angeles Museum of Contemporary Art. In addition, the company houses one of five Wells Fargo History Museums at the Grand Avenue building.

In 1996, Wells Fargo solidified its position as a banking leader in the nation when it acquired First Interstate Bank in what was then the largest merger in U.S. banking history. Today, the company is a financial institution offering a full range of banking services to individual, corporate, commercial, and real estate customers in Los Angeles and beyond.

Following in the tradition of its legendary frontier agents—celebrated for their integrity and enthusiasm in helping clients—Wells Fargo's personal bankers are dedicated to understanding their customers' needs and meeting them with state-of-the-art products and services.

"Our approach is to have speed and accuracy. We layer that in all of our business from lending to consumer banking," Watson says. "We create an expectation and make that deliverable."

Clockwise from top left:
In the 19th Century, Wells Fargo was famous for its legendary stagecoach delivery services to pioneers. Today, Wells Fargo Bank is among the leaders in its fast delivery of reliable, consistent, and efficient financial services to customers locally and worldwide.

By the time Wells Fargo & Co. opened an express and banking office in Los Angeles on January 4, 1855, the company had already established a legendary reputation in the gold areas of Northern California as an express office and banking house.

The company's offices in downtown Los Angeles also house one of five Wells Fargo History Museums in California.

The nation's largest natural gas distributor, Southern California Gas Co. serves 18 million people in 535 Central and Southern California communities, from San Luis Obispo on the north, to the Mexican border on the south. Not only does the company dominate the residential energy market—providing fuel for space heaters, water heaters, cooking appliances, and clothes dryers—but it also does its part to improve the environment and promote safety. On top of this, Southern California Gas Co. is the largest subsidiary of Sempra Energy, a San Diego-based, Fortune 500 energy services holding company with the nation's largest U.S. utility customer base, not to mention 12,000 employees and $10.8 billion in assets.

A History of Dependability and Service

Southern California Gas Co.'s rich heritage goes back to June 28, 1867, when a blacksmith, two partners in a sawmill, the town postmaster, and a gas engineer formed the Los Angeles Gas Company to serve the Southern California population of fewer than 50,000. In the four decades that followed, the company met the challenges of government ownership of utilities and cutthroat competition from other companies—including Thomas Edison's newly formed California Electric Light Company. Still, the company—now called Southern California Gas Co., thanks to the consolidation of several gas companies—became the largest in the nation, pioneering newly discovered, clean-burning natural gas. By the end of the 1930s, Southern Californians were using more gas and paying lower rates than anywhere in the United States.

Through World War II, the company enhanced its storage and delivery capabilities, as well as its energy conservation strategies. Because Southern California was connected to natural gas fields in Oklahoma and Texas by the largest long-distance gas pipeline built to that time—1,200 miles—gas promotion efforts were accelerated with an astounding success rate. By the end of the 1950s, 90 percent of all cooking ranges in Southern California were fueled by gas—six times the national rate in comparison to electric ranges. In addition, nearly 100 percent of the area's water heaters and home heating systems were fueled by natural gas.

During the oil shortages of the 1970s, Southern California Gas Co. encouraged more efficient gas use and developed conservation programs that promoted energy-saving features in new construction long before it was required to by law. Throughout the 1980s, use per meter went down continuously in Southern California, enabling residential customers to realize approximately $550 million in savings from lower energy bills. Innovative advertising campaigns encouraged consumer conservation and promoted the use of gas-efficient appliances and incentives for consumers to install insulation and solar energy systems. Today headquartered in downtown Los Angeles, the company has 4.8 million customers with a service territory of 23,000 square miles.

Community Involvement

Southern California Gas Co. is committed to being a responsible, involved corporate citizen. For example, after the Los Angeles riots broke out in 1992, the company pledged $40 million in cash and in-kind services to help Rebuild L.A. More than 350 company volunteers distributed food, removed graffiti, and found shelters for people displaced by the disturbances. Two years later, when a massive earthquake devastated parts of Los Angeles and the San Fernando, Simi, and Santa Clarita valleys, employees restored service to more than 150,000 customers and set up command centers within communities in the impacted area—which was the size of the sixth-largest city in the world. In addition, Southern California Gas Co. has a long history of civic involvement with initiatives such as the community advisory panels that regularly discuss emerging issues and trends with various community leaders.

The company depends on the strength of its more than 5,500 employees. That's why it is committed to maintaining a diverse workforce that represents and reflects the communities it serves. Through the company-sponsored volunteer incentive program, employees provide human and financial resources to nonprofit groups of their choice. Whether it's assisting in a low-income housing unit in Koreatown, helping a clothing designer's expansion to create 800 new inner-city jobs, adopting schools,

Southern California Gas Co.'s headquarters is located in downtown Los Angeles in the Gas Company Tower.

In the 1920s the company, then called the Los Angeles Gas and Electric Corporation, was head-quartered at 7th and Flower streets. The company used these early service trucks, which had a top speed of around 12 miles per hour and motors that had to be overhauled nearly every day.

or contributing computers to the South Central Los Angeles-based African American Unity Center so students can develop work skills, the company continues to establish deep roots in its communities.

Thanks to dramatic changes in the utilities industry—from government restructuring of the electric industry to such competitors as interstate pipelines and municipalities—Southern California Gas Co. has maintained a competitive edge by developing new strategies in order to keep prices low while maintaining high levels of customer service. Southern California Gas Co., under the leadership of Sempra Energy, will meet the challenges that the next century brings, drawing from its deeply rooted service to all those who call Southern California home.

In the 1930s, the company—now called Southern California Gas Co., thanks to the consolidation of several gas companies—became the largest in the nation, pioneering newly discovered, clean-burning natural gas.

Today, the company is still the nation's largest natural gas distributor, with 4.8 million customers and a service territory of 23,000 square miles.

University of Southern California

Located in the heart of Los Angeles—in close proximity to downtown's skyscrapers and museums—the University of Southern California (USC) has maintained a symbiotic relationship with the city since its founding in 1880. As the only major comprehensive university in Southern California for nearly 50 years, USC was called upon to provide the knowledge and training for a burgeoning region. By 1930, most of the Southland's doctors, lawyers, judges, teachers, dentists, pharmacists, urban planners, and government officials were USC trained. The nation's first schools in international relations and cinema were established at USC.

Today, USC is the oldest and largest private research university in the American West, ranked among the top 10 private universities in sponsored research and development, and the largest private employer in Los Angeles. Through the years, USC has played an important role in improving the quality of life in Los Angeles and continues to strengthen Southern California's economy through such innovative resources as the Integrated Media Systems Center, the Annenberg Center for Communication, and the Marshall School of Business.

Integrated Media Systems Center

Established in 1996, USC's Integrated Media Systems Center (IMSC) was founded to define and advance new media technology, foster the development of emerging technology, and discover applications for it in business, education, and entertainment. The IMSC is the nation's only National Science Foundation Engineering Research Center in multimedia, and serves as a unique clearinghouse for multimedia research and education for Los Angeles and the nation.

In just two years, IMSC has contributed to the creation of two start-up companies, nine new technology applications for the center's business partners, and the retraining of 150 dislocated workers (many from aerospace) prepared to work in new media.

Annenberg Center for Communication

Los Angeles, the world capital of the entertainment industry and a leader in information science, presents the perfect setting for USC's Annenberg Center for Communication. Established in 1993 as the result of a world-record $120 million contribution by Ambassador Walter H. Annenberg, the center draws upon the strengths of three of USC's top-rated professional schools—engineering, cinema-television, and journalism/communication. The result is a communications powerhouse that provides an inter-disciplinary forum for practical research, scholarly theory, and multimedia advancements.

Marshall School of Business

Now more than ever, Los Angeles is seen as the gateway to the Pacific Rim and emerging markets in both Asia and Latin America. To that end, USC's Marshall School of Business teaches students about the increasingly global nature of business. The Marshall School is the first business school in the world to require all of its MBA students to study abroad as part of its Pacific Rim education program. Students have traveled to China, Japan, and Mexico to study how business is conducted in other parts of the world and to contribute their own expertise to international companies.

By recognizing and taking advantage of the resources Los Angeles offers as one of the most dynamic and diverse cities in the world, USC has enriched the experience of its international student body, and has developed innovations and provided resources that improve the lives of those who live and work in Los Angeles.

Clockwise from top:
The second-oldest school structure in use in California, Widney Alumni House was the University of Southern California's first campus building.

Since its unveiling in 1930, the statue of the bronzed Trojan warrior has served as a popular meeting place for students on campus.

Modeled after a medieval monastery in Tuscany, Italy, Mudd Hall of Philosophy is now a city historical landmark.

ounded in 1885, O'Melveny & Myers LLP is the oldest and largest law firm in Los Angeles. Its ranks include attorneys who have international and national reputations—including Warren Christopher, who returned to the firm after serving as U.S. secretary of state, and Walter Dellinger, who served as President Clinton's acting solicitor general. O'Melveny & Myers has combined the values of a traditional law practice with entrepreneurial drive, verve, and talent to become one of the nation's leading law firms.

O'Melveny & Myers' nearly 700 attorneys in 10 offices across the globe represent businesses, governments, nonprofits, and individuals in nearly every area of the law. O'Melveny is consistently ranked first among the city's largest law firms and among the nation's top 15.

Growing with Los Angeles

The firm's growth has paralleled that of Los Angeles. When founder Henry O'Melveny started his practice, Los Angeles was a small frontier town. In a city now known for its plethora of cell phones, O'Melveny, in a quote from the book *Recollections*, illustrates the city's incredible growth: "I remember that in '85, when we began, there was no telephone, but we got the third telephone put up in this city, so we were Number 3 on the list."

By 1927, former California Chief Justice Louis Myers had joined the firm, eventually adding his name to the practice's shingle. Jack O'Melveny, Henry's son, joined the firm shortly thereafter and handled several major breakthrough cases for clients in the nascent Hollywood film industry. In fact, by the start of the sound motion picture era, the firm was known as "the law firm that Hollywood can talk to"— a reputation that remains unchanged.

Today, the firm is organized along traditional legal disciplines, including corporations, labor and employment, litigation, real estate, tax, and bankruptcy law. O'Melveny & Myers also has distinguished strategic practices—such as entertainment, health care, project finance, and intellectual property—that cut across department lines. This market-driven structure enables O'Melveny to handle matters that require expertise in multiple areas—such as providing corporate, real estate, environmental, tax, and bond counsel for the $2.4 billion Alameda Corridor, one of the largest infrastructure projects undertaken in the United States, which will link both ports in the city to rail lines, ensuring uninterrupted traffic flow of goods through Los Angeles.

Serving Those in Need

O'Melveny & Myers' commitment as a corporate citizen extends to causes both

within and beyond the Los Angeles community. For instance, the firm provides pro bono legal aid to the indigent, numerous nonprofit groups, school boards, and to a group of major cities and states supporting the use of statistical sampling in the 2000 census plan. In addition, the firm established the Christopher Scholarship program, which gives grants to 10th-grade students from the Los Angeles Unified School District. These scholarships, worth $16,000 to each recipient, are intended to encourage promising, financially needy students to remain in school, with the assurance that

they will receive scholarship funds to attend college upon graduation.

Like Los Angeles, O'Melveny attorneys embody a diversity of backgrounds and experiences, representing countries around the globe. While the firm has been at the forefront of the Los Angeles legal community for more than 110 years, it is not content to rest on its reputation. Through strategic planning and its commitment to providing unsurpassed intellectual capital and innovative counsel, O'Melveny & Myers continues to position itself for the legal challenges of the 21st century.

Founded in 1885, O'Melveny & Myers LLP is the oldest law firm in Los Angeles. Its first office was located on Spring Street near First Street (largest building shown above).

n today's media market, where substantive news is often supplanted by tabloid journalism, the *Los Angeles Times* thrives as a compelling source of in-depth, responsible reporting, analysis, and commentary. *The Times* is one of the most respected newspapers of the 20th century. One of the fastest-growing papers in the United States, in 1998 *The Times* recorded its fourth consecutive year-over-year daily circulation gain and its second Sunday gain. With a daily circulation of more than 1,095,000—and 1,385,373 on Sundays—*The Times* is the

second-largest metropolitan newspaper in the country and the largest newspaper in the West. The newspaper serves the vast Southern California market with four daily regional editions, each providing readers with a comprehensive package of local, regional, state, national, and international news and features.

A Growing City and Its Paper

In 1881, Civil War General Harrison Gray Otis bought the *Los Angeles Daily Times*, a fledgling four-page paper on the verge of bankruptcy. While Otis built up the paper's reputation, his future son-in-law Harry Chandler built its circulation routes.

Chandler became publisher in 1917, and led the newspaper to new records in circulation and advertising growth. Meanwhile, he helped shape the future of Southern California with a pro-growth editorial stance. *The Times* received its first Pulitzer Prize in 1942 for editorials supporting freedom of the press.

The paper continued to be published by the Chandler family, passing from Harry Chandler to his son, Norman Chandler, in 1944, and then to Norman's oldest son, Otis Chandler, in 1960. When Otis took over, *The Times* was stronger financially than any other newspaper in the United States. Otis shifted from the paper's conservative bias, increased the number of domestic and foreign bureaus from two to 31, hired top writers, and garnered seven more Pulitzer Prizes.

Into the Next Century

Today, the *Los Angeles Times* is considered one of the nation's most influential newspapers and serves a region that is one of the world's leading economic centers. Given changing global economic and regional business trends, *The Times* is poised to be what Editor Michael Parks calls "the newspaper for the capital of the 21st century."

Winner of 22 Pulitzer Prizes, *The Times* has one of the largest editorial departments in the nation, with more than 1,000 staff members. *The Times'* 27 foreign bureaus and 15 domestic bureaus are staffed by some of the world's most experienced and respected journalists.

Editorial innovation has driven many changes at *The Times* in recent years. New sections and features have been launched to enhance the paper's relevancy and appeal, including Monday's Health section, Thursday's Calendar Weekend, Sports Weekend on Fridays, a revamped Wednesday Food section, and a new Southern California Living section that reflects the rich and diverse lives of Southern Californians. *The Times'* award-winning Business section has launched an array of new features, including weekly sections focusing on personal finance, the impact of technology on daily life, small business—to serve the small business capital of the nation—and commercial real estate.

The Times runs more color than any other U.S. newspaper. Coupled with sophisticated graphics, called "info-graphics," color

has made the paper more vibrant and provided new ways of illustrating the news. The newspaper's computerized news editing system, one of the largest in the world, on average processes more than 10 million words a day for the next day's paper.

Serving the large Southern California region requires elaborate production and distribution systems: *The Times* offers home delivery of the newspaper from Santa Barbara to the Mexican border—a 45,000-square-mile-area, larger than the state of Ohio. *The Times* is one of very few metropolitan newspapers to be published out of three satellite printing facilities, which are in Orange County, downtown Los Angeles, and the San Fernando Valley.

On-line Ventures

The *Los Angeles Times'* Web site, latimes.com, is one way the newspaper is extending the role it plays as the leading source of infor-

Clockwise from top:
Mark Willes is the eighth publisher at the *Los Angeles Times* since it began publishing in 1881.

The Los Angeles Times Festival of Books has become a community event of epic proportions. Each year, more than 100,000 people of all backgrounds attend this two-day festival; meet more than 150 of the world's most popular and diverse authors; and attend book signings, author panel discussions, poetry readings, and a variety of activities for children.

The *Times* has grown steadily since its founding, and, in its early years, was a strong pro-growth proponent for Southern California. As the paper began to draw national attention, it received its first Pulitzer Prize in 1942 for editorials supporting freedom of the press.

Times staff in the San Fernando Valley celebrate the 1998 Pulitzer Prize for team coverage of the North Hollywood shoot-out. Since 1942, the *Times* has won 22 Pulitzer Prizes (left).

One of the fastest-growing newspapers in the country, the *Los Angeles Times* was founded in 1881 (right).

mation for and about Southern California. The site has more than 44,000 content pages and more than 25,000 stories every day. It was recently inducted into *PC Magazine*'s Hall of Fame for making the magazine's Top 100 Web sites list all five times that the list has been published.

The *Times*' expanding family of on-line ventures also includes Hollywood Online, ListingLink, and affiliations with CareerPath.com and Classified Ventures.

Community Outreach

The Times has extensive community out-reach programs that support education, literacy, journalism, youth organizations, and the arts. Founded in 1944, the Los Angeles Times Fund is targeted toward helping underprivileged youth in Southern California lead better, more productive lives. In addition to the many grants pro-vided to various organizations, The Times Fund built, and continues to support, the Los Angeles and Watts/Willowbrook Boys and Girls Clubs. The Times Summer Camp Fund, which has raised $20 million through the generosity of *Times* readers, has en-abled more than 350,000 needy children to experience summer camps since its inception in 1954.

The Times has also launched an am-bitious, five-year program called Reading by 9 that seeks to improve the reading skills of Southland children by the time they reach the age of nine. Extensive edito-rial coverage is focusing attention on the problem of child illiteracy and possible solutions. For the non-editorial aspect of the program, *The Times* is forming partner-ships with organizations in the public and private sector in what *Times* Publisher Mark Willes calls "an urgent and massive effort to improve our children's reading skills and improve their—and our—chances for future success." Reading by 9 involves virtually every division of *The Times*, which has made a commitment of cash and resources of more than $5 million to the project. Corporate sponsors are also donating to the program, which will train volunteer reading tutors for classrooms, fund and expand existing reading programs, set literacy achievement standards, and provide books for schools and libraries.

Founded in 1983, the *Los Angeles Times*' Minority Editorial Training Program (METPRO) has trained more than 100 Afri-can Americans, Asian Americans, Latinos, and Native Americans for jobs at daily newspapers. This idea was expanded in 1998 with the founding of METPRO.biz, designed to develop the business leaders of tomorrow.

As it works to better the community that it serves, *The Times* continues to fulfill the legacy begun more than a century ago: the pursuit of journalistic excellence.

latimes.com is recognized as one of the Internet's leading Web sites, both for its award-winning editorial content and for its comprehensive user services. The site features daily content from the paper, continuous news updates, access to archives of past articles, and a wide range of other infor-mation for and about Southern California. Lycos, one of the Internet's most popular search engines, rated latimes.com the best news site on the Internet.

LOS ANGELES AREA CHAMBER OF COMMERCE

The huge metropolitan area that is today Los Angeles began as a small Spanish settlement of fewer than 50 people. Founded in 1781, Los Angeles grew slowly, becoming first an area of large "ranchos," and later, after California was admitted as the 31st state in the Union, a Wild-West town with few amenities. But by the late 1880s, amid a local real estate boom, the huge ranchos of Southern California's sunny desert were being transformed into communities. At the same time,

the Southern Pacific Railroad continued to gain steam, bringing new people and resources to the underpopulated region, while helping foster the fledgling industries of export agriculture and tourism. But the area still needed more economic stability—and more people.

Founded in 1888, the Los Angeles Area Chamber of Commerce stepped in to help propel the city toward its current status as the second-largest urban area in the United States. Today, the chamber's 1,500 members are spread throughout Los Angeles, Orange, Riverside, San Bernardino, and Ventura counties. Although their diversity is as broad as the region they call home, their mission is the same: to strengthen the economy and communities of Greater Los Angeles.

A Growth-Oriented Approach

Transforming Southern California from ranch land into a thriving network of communities was an enormous task at the turn of the century, but chamber members were convinced early on that Los Angeles could become one of the world's great cities. Time proved them right.

Although many people were already traveling through Los Angeles, the chamber focused on promoting the region's mild climate and on generating jobs, services, and customers as a way to entice newcomers to stay. Creative advertising lured thousands of new residents, who went on to cultivate a citrus-producing empire and a vibrant business community. Chamber members worked with other groups that

helped build the area, including the railroad, local governments, and the Automobile Club of Southern California. During those early years, the chamber also did its part to secure a stable supply of water and a network of roads that is still expanding today.

Beginning in 1923, chamber photographers amassed a huge archive of 50,000 images to promote the region. The photos touted the city's favorable climate and helped convince the nation to make Southern California the aeronautics capital of the country. The area's agricultural and manufacturing bases also began to grow, and local industry was nourished by the chamber's work in converting the mudflats of San Pedro into the largest man-made harbor in the nation.

An Advocate for Business

As one of the most influential organizations in Southern California, the chamber is no less active today in bolstering the Greater Los Angeles business climate. Members range from individual entrepreneurs to multinational conglomerates, in addition to nonprofit associations, hospitals, schools, and individual members, making the chamber representative of the total business community.

Today's chamber has six standing committees: International Commerce; Business and Regional Development; Governance, Finance & Justice; Human Resources; Natural Resources and the Environment; and Transportation and In-

Conveniently located downtown, the chamber offers everything needed for a successful meeting. A variety of rooms are equipped with state-of-the-art audio and video systems, including teleconferencing. The chamber is the place for everything from an intimate gathering to a full-day training seminar, with several rooms for breakout sessions. There is also an impressive boardroom and a beautiful outdoor terrace for private receptions (top and bottom left).

The mission of the Los Angeles Area Chamber of Commerce reads: "Working to ensure the success of commerce and industry in the Southern California Region." Toward that mission, the chamber has chosen education and workforce development as one of its priority issues. The chamber is working with existing school-to-career programs and has expanded its political role in fighting for more accountability and tougher standards in the public schools (bottom right).

frastructure. Chamber directors are deeply involved in shaping public policy. Welfare-to-work initiatives and proposed reforms to the city's charter are just a few of the issues driving the organization today.

In addition, priority-issue task forces are appointed each year to supplement the ongoing efforts of the six standing committees, and are responsible for the development of general policy and advocacy. The task forces have tackled such issues as local government reform, transportation funding, and water availability and reliability.

A major priority task force in 1998 was the Welfare-to-Work subcommittee, which is working to increase access to jobs and reduce welfare dependency for Southern Californians on public assistance. The chamber, in coalition with other business groups, has formulated a detailed plan to further this mission. Additional areas of interest to the chamber are the Year 2000 computer problem and the promotion of international trade for its members.

The chamber also offers an ever growing list of services to members—all geared toward helping each business achieve its goals. With offices in the downtown area just west of the Harbor Freeway, the chamber is an excellent location for businesses to hold power breakfasts, all-day training seminars, and luncheons for as many as 300 guests. A variety of meet-

ing rooms are available, with a warming kitchen, outdoor terrace, teleconferencing, and other audiovisual resources.

One of the largest networking organizations in the nation, the chamber provides members with invaluable resources, such as the *Southern California Business Directory & Buyers Guide*, group health benefits, free counseling, seminars, and workshops that run year-round. The chamber also offers in-depth information on its programs on its Web site at www. lachamber.com.

With roots extending from the dusty cow town that was once Los Angeles to the business epicenter it is today, the chamber remains a vital force in the City of Angels.

The chamber's standing committee on Transportation and Infrastructure works to shape public policy. Through involvement in freeway system improvements, Metro Rail projects, and the expansion of Los Angeles International Airport, the chamber seeks to alleviate the region's traffic congestion, meet air quality standards, and remain competitive in the global economy. In 1912, the chamber lobbied tirelessly for federal assistance in dredging the largest man-made harbor in the world out of the mud-flats at San Pedro, which was a key step in developing Los Angeles into a port city.

Rancho Los Amigos National Rehabilitation Center

Rancho Los Amigos National Rehabilitation Center is, in the eyes of many, a place where miracles happen every day. Rancho is an internationally recognized medical center that helps rehabilitate individuals who have suffered catastrophic spinal cord injuries, traumatic brain injuries, strokes, and other disabling injuries and illnesses. Its work begins when patients arrive for their initial evaluation and treatment, and extends all the way through reintegrating them into the community

at their highest possible level of functioning. Rancho's staff assists patients with every aspect of their recovery—physical, mental, emotional, and spiritual.

"Our focus is not solely on rehabilitating the body," says Consuelo C. Diaz, Rancho's chief executive officer, "but also on motivating the soul and fanning the fires of hope."

More Than a Century of Service

Rancho Los Amigos National Rehabilitation Center was established in 1888 on a vast, 220-acre, California-Spanish ranch-style campus located southeast of downtown Los Angeles in Downey. For more than a century, it has offered the best rehabilitative care in the state, and among the finest in the country. In 1998, Rancho was ranked in the top 10 on *U.S. News & World Report*'s list of the best rehabilitation centers in the United States, the only facility in California to achieve that distinction.

Patients come to Rancho from all over the world and range in age from infants to seniors. As a Los Angeles County Department of Health Services facility, Rancho provides care to the county's indigent and uninsured

populations, as well as to individuals with health care coverage from throughout the world. Members of its staff have won numerous awards for their groundbreaking work in treating and rehabilitating patients with a variety of catastrophic illnesses and injuries.

Rancho has long been in the forefront of innovative rehabilitation techniques and surgical procedures. Rancho's Los Amigos Research and Educational Institute (LAREI) has received more than $100 million in contracts and grants to continue its

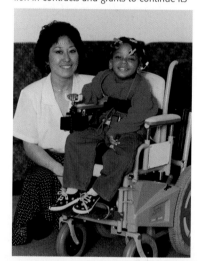

groundbreaking clinical research efforts. In addition, Rancho has the only federally funded Regional Spinal Cord Injury Service in Southern California.

Comprehensive Care

Through its more than 20 centers of excellence, Rancho's patients receive care that is unparalleled in Southern California. Those centers include Spinal Cord Injury, Stroke, Neurologic Disorders, Pediatric Program, Alzheimer's Disease Diagnostic and Treatment Center, Rancho Adult Day Services, Gerontology Program, Arthritis and Rheumatology Center, Pathokinesiology Lab, Diabetes/Limb Preservation and Amputation, Post-Polio Center, Pressure Ulcer Management, Liver Disease Center, Environmental Health Service Center, Dentistry for People with Disabilities, Center for Applied Rehabilitation Technology, Seating Center, Driver Training Center, and Vocational Services.

Rancho's Center for Applied Rehabilitation Technology focuses on integrating assistive technology with everyday living activities, thus enabling patients to achieve independence through the use of computers, augmentative communication devices,

Rancho Los Amigos National Rehabilitation Center, an internationally recognized medical center, helps rehabilitate individuals who have suffered catastrophic spinal cord injuries, traumatic brain injuries, strokes, and other disabling injuries and illnesses (top).

Rancho maintains its administrative offices in the historic Harriman Building (bottom).

and environmental control units. Rancho also provides pre-driving screening and behind-the-wheel driving evaluation and training. Rancho's facilities include a free-standing model home that assists patients in their transition back into independent living, and a low-cost housing facility with 10 luxury suites that allow a patient's family or significant others to be near their loved one to receive instruction, comfort, and support during the rehabilitation program.

Rancho provides on-site surgery and has a highly customized dentistry facility that accommodates patients with severe physical disabilities. Its internationally recognized Pathokinesiology Lab is noted for its evaluation and diagnosis of abnormal joint motion and muscle activity patterns related to walking and upper extremity function. Additionally, the Rancho Adult

Day Services program provides care to persons diagnosed with Alzheimer's.

Rancho also shares its knowledge and expertise with care providers beyond its own staff. As a teaching hospital, it trains thousands of physicians, nurses, therapists, and other health care professionals through its affiliations with medical schools and universities across the country.

Focused on a Bright Future

No matter how serious an illness or injury might be, Rancho remains focused on ensuring the brightest possible future for every individual it serves. Rancho's spirit of hope, its clinical innovation, and its compassionate treatment ensure that victims of catastrophic injury and illness are provided with the best possible chance to build their own bridges to independence.

Clockwise from top:
Fidel Valenzuela, a former Rancho patient, counsels young people on the center's campus.

Consuelo C. Diaz, chief executive officer, Rancho Los Amigos National Rehabilitation Center

Through its more than 20 centers of excellence, Rancho provides unparalleled care to Southern Californians. Pictured is Rancho's new Jacquelin Perry Institute.

Rancho's staff assists patients with every aspect of their recovery—physical, mental, emotional, and spiritual. "Our focus is not solely on rehabilitating the body," says Diaz "but also on motivating the soul and fanning the fires of hope."

ARROWHEAD MOUNTAIN SPRING WATER CO.

As the nation becomes more and more health conscious and increasingly particular about water quality, Southern California supermarkets are stocking their aisles with a growing array of bottled waters. One label that stands out is Arrowhead Mountain Spring Water, one of California's oldest and most popular bottled waters. ⚊ Nestled high in the San Bernardino Mountains is the natural landmark that gives the water its name: a gigantic stone in the shape of an arrowhead, which

points to the site of California's oldest known springs. Originally mentioned in records left by priests stationed at the San Gabriel Mission in 1774, David Noble Smith constructed the first permanent building at Arrowhead Springs in 1857, and opened a retreat for city dwellers seeking the benefits of pure water and clean mountain air. Visitors enjoyed both hot and cold springs and natural steam baths created by the hot springs that released steam into the caves. In 1885, the first of a series of hotels was built at Arrowhead to accommodate travelers from all over the United States who were drawn to the springs in the hope that drinking the water would cure their ailments. In 1894, Arrowhead Mountain Spring Water was first bottled for visitors to carry home.

Originally, Arrowhead's water was shipped in bottles made of vegetable fiber and sealed with pitch. By 1905, Arrowhead Water was being placed on water trains—which looked much like modern-day petroleum train cars—for delivery to both San Bernardino and Los Angeles. The first bottling plant for Arrowhead was built in Los Angeles in 1915, with the water delivered via water trains until 1960, when the construction of the Los Angeles freeway system made tanker trucks the preferred mode of transportation.

Arrowhead today bottles a variety of waters, including mountain spring water, sparkling mountain spring water, distilled water, and fluoridated water, all of which are shipped throughout California and Arizona in containers ranging in size from the sprightly half-pint bottles to the five-gallon jugs found in many offices and kitchens.

From Spa to Shelf

While the fashion of "taking the waters" for one's health faded many decades ago, the demand for safe, controlled sources of drinking water still survives. Bottled water has become the choice for all-natural refreshment, with so many people attuned to healthy living, and others who dislike the taste of tap water or who worry about the threat of lead, cryptosporidium, or chlorine by-products in some water systems.

Arrowhead carefully controls how it gathers, bottles, and transports its spring water, and vigilantly protects its pristine water sources in California and Arizona. The company also invests in state-of-the-art monitoring equipment and high-tech bottling systems to safeguard its water with a multiple barrier approach from source to table. A case in point is Arrowhead's superior microfiltration system, which is an absolute barrier against cryptosporidium and other impurities.

Arrowhead surpasses the guidelines established by the U.S. Food and Drug Administration (FDA), which regulates bottled water as a food, imposing strict standards for quality, record keeping, sanitation, and even the types of bottle caps the company can use. In 1996, the FDA adopted even tougher industry definitions and quality guidelines, which the firm strongly advocated. Arrowhead also plays an active role in the International Bottled Water Association.

Times may have changed over the last century, but Arrowhead Mountain Spring Water remains as pure as when it was first discovered.

Arrowhead today bottles a variety of waters, including mountain spring water, sparkling mountain spring water, distilled water, and fluoridated water, all of which are shipped throughout California and Arizona in containers ranging in size from the sprightly half-pint bottles to the five-gallon jugs found in many offices and kitchens.

Arrowhead is guided by the philosophy that the company cannot afford to be any less meticulous in protecting the purity of its water, because of the trust consumers place in its product and in the firm. The company's strength as the industry leader gives it the backing to be dedicated to the best. This attention to detail has proved successful for Arrowhead. What began in the late 1800s with the popularity of spas has grown into a $250 million-a-year business that commands a leading percentage of the California market. The business today is headquartered in Brea, and is a division of Greenwich, Connecticut-based The Perrier Group.

Commitment to Customers and Community

Since 1995, Arrowhead has been the title sponsor of the Arrowhead Pond, home of the Mighty Ducks, and a sponsor of the Anaheim Angels. Fans can enjoy an Arrowhead Mountain Spring Water at both the Arrowhead Pond and Edison Field. In keeping with Arrowhead's commitment to preserving the environment, the company is also a sponsor of the San Bernardino National Forrest Association.

Arrowhead places a great emphasis on its commitment to its customers, and to providing pure, high-quality water and superior service. The company regularly ships supplies of water to the sites of earthquakes and other natural disasters when clean drinking water is needed. It has a strong commitment to environmental stewardship and is respectful of the conditions in nature that yield its fine spring water. Times may have changed, but the taste of Arrowhead Mountain Spring Water remains the same as when it was first discovered centuries ago.

Automobile Club of Southern California

Automobiles have long played a central role in the lives of Southern Californians, who are dependent on their cars to accomplish such daily tasks as getting to work, and then use them during their spare time to get away from it all. The Automobile Club of Southern California has been offering motorists a variety of services for nearly a century. ▼ The Auto Club was founded in 1900, when 10 owners of horseless carriages met in a lawyer's office in the

Stimson Building to form a club for people who owned or were interested in owning motorized vehicles. The meeting was inspired by the experience of one automobile owner whose car stopped running 10 miles from downtown Los Angeles. Apparently, his pilot light, located under the rear seat, had gone out. When the repairman arrived two hours later, he simply lit a match to reignite the pilot, and the car was on its way. Three days

later, the owner received a $15 repair bill—a large sum of money at the time.

In light of this experience, the club's primary mission became to provide motorists with reliable and inexpensive roadside service. Today, the Auto Club responds to a call for emergency help every 11 seconds, and it has whittled its response time down to an average of 25 minutes. The response times are even quicker in extreme emergency cases, such

as when a driver inadvertently locks a child or a pet inside a car.

Making Automobile Travel Safer

Shortly after the Auto Club was formed, the group became active in public service by promoting the need for good roads, suitable signs on principal highways, and accurate maps—all innovations that would make road travel safer.

From 1905 to the 1940s, Auto Club explorers charted dozens of national and international routes and posted thousands of directional signs on roads to make cross country and international road travel easier. By 1915, some 7,000 miles of Southern California highways carried the Auto Club's directional signs.

The Auto Club also had a hand in developing many of the laws and standards of road travel. In addition to creating a highway service entity that grew into the California Highway Patrol, the group helped the state of California develop its vehicle code. When governments were making decisions about the width of roads and the need for stop signs, many of them consulted with the Auto Club. Car man-

◄ MARC GEWERTZ

The Auto Club works with the National Hot Rod Association (NHRA) and Funny Car driver Gary Densham to develop education programs that emphasize safe driving and encourage teens to consider an automotive career.

Cruises, tours, airline reservations, and international travel plans can be made at any one of the Auto Club's 45 full-service AAA Travel Agency offices.

A toll-free, 24-hour insurance claims hot line and technology such as CD-ROM laptop computers for claims adjusters help to get cars repaired faster, with more convenience to the policyholder.

ufacturers, too, have sought the Auto Club's advice about how to make cars safer.

The Auto Club remains actively involved in urban planning issues and automobile safety issues across Southern California, advising government agencies about transportation and road planning, and lobbying on behalf of motorists' interests. In addition, it has sponsored public service announcements, in English and Spanish, reminding drivers of the perils of drinking and driving. More recently, the Auto Club sponsored legislation requiring teen drivers to have more driving experience before they can become fully licensed. Called the Graduated License Program, the law went into effect in California in July 1998.

Listening to Customers' Concerns

Making travel easier and more enjoyable remains one of the Auto Club's core missions. Its 4.5 million members can pick up maps and tour books, as well as hotel information for all kinds of trips in the United States and abroad, by visiting any one of dozens of Auto Club offices in Southern California.

In its efforts to improve and expand its services, the Auto Club relies on its customers to tell them what they want the club to provide. As a result, the organization has expanded its operations to provide members with airline and cruise reservations; auto, home owner, and watercraft insurance; and auto loans and leasing. And, much

Members receive added value through Show Your Card & Save discounts used on everyday purchases, including eyeglasses.

to the relief of those who dislike the long lines at the Department of Motor Vehicles, members can take care of their auto registration at Auto Club offices.

"We continue to ask what it is that members want and expect from their Auto Club," says Steve Lenzi, vice president of public affairs. "One of the things we have learned is that people's needs are always changing."

Modern Services for Modern Times

Recognizing that most people have little spare time, the Auto Club has sought ways to make its services more accessible to members. The organization recently established a site on the Internet so members

can get some of their services at home. The club also established a telephone service center to provide members with access to service without having to visit a local district office.

To make buying a car more convenient, the club has pioneered a service that finds the best deals in the shortest amount of time. More than 150 dealerships have agreed to sell cars for fixed prices to Auto Club members, who can get a computer printout of the prices and dealers from the Auto Club.

As long as cars are a fact of life in Southern California, the Auto Club will be there as an advocate for drivers, helping to make road travel safer, more convenient, and more enjoyable.

t's a given that providing even routine health care for children calls for specialized capabilities and training—but when a child's illness or injury is complex, traumatic, or rare, his or her needs expand exponentially. That fact is not lost on Childrens Hospital Los Angeles, a state-of-the-art health care provider that has earned an international reputation for the highest level of care and research by the best pediatric practitioners in the medical field. ⚓ With four beds in a converted, two-story private

home, Childrens Hospital Los Angeles began in 1901 as the first medical facility in California to care for children. Today, the hospital has grown to become a world leader for advanced pediatric care, research, and physician education, with 30 specialties and 31 specially focused services. Each year, the nonprofit, 330-bed hospital sees nearly 200,000 visits from children—ranging from newborns to 18-year-olds—who hail from Los Angeles and beyond, including several foreign countries.

The hospital houses the Heart Institute and the Childrens Center for Cancer & Blood

Diseases. The Heart Institute is the only pediatric facility in Southern California that performs heart, lung, and heart-lung transplantation. The Childrens Center for Cancer & Blood Diseases is the largest pediatric cancer center in the West, and the second largest in the United States.

Childrens Hospital Los Angeles also houses an internationally recognized research program focused on seven major pediatric areas: AIDS and host defense; cancer; endocrinology and metabolism; blood diseases and immunology; cell and developmental biology; gene therapy; and

community health promotion, disease prevention, and pediatric outcomes. And since 1932, the hospital has trained pediatric specialists through its affiliation with the University of Southern California School of Medicine.

A Gateway to Health

The level of specialized, multidisciplinary care in pediatric and adolescent medicine found at Childrens Hospital Los Angeles is rare at the community hospital level. Over the years, the organization has been fortunate to assemble a remarkable team of surgeons representing numerous specialties, including cardiothoracic transplantation, plastic and reconstructive, and orthopedic surgery. To keep pace with rapid advancements in these and other areas, the hospital will expand and reconfigure its surgical space. In fact, the volume of surgical cases is increasing an average of 5 percent annually, from just over 8,000 procedures in 1993 to nearly 10,000 today, requiring more than 19,000 surgical hours each year. What's more, Childrens Hospital Los Angeles performs more than twice the number of complex pediatric surgical procedures as any other hospital in Southern California, and boasts the area's only anesthesia staff with a pediatric specialty.

Even as adult and community hospitals curtail pediatric services, Childrens

Clockwise from top:
Dr. Stuart Siegel, director of the Childrens Center for Cancer & Blood Diseases, explains his pin collection to one of his patients.

The Research Institute at Childrens Hospital Los Angeles is one of the top five pediatric research facilities in terms of NIH grants every year.

A heart transplant was the ultimate Christmas gift for Alex Aguilar Jr. from Dr. Vaughn Starnes and his Heart Institute team: the gift of life.

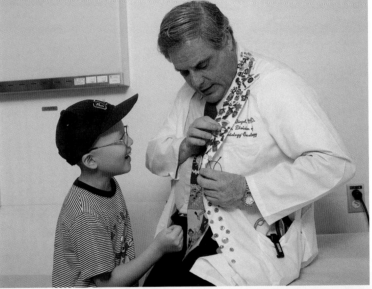
RANDY HARMON

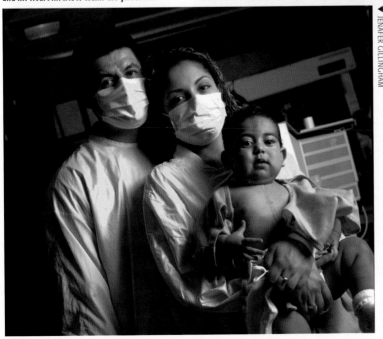
JENAFER GILLINGHAM

TIM STREET-PORTER

Childrens Hospital Los Angeles has been ranked among the top five pediatric medical facilities in the nation by *U.S. News & World Report* every year since the magazine began ranking hospitals in 1990 (left).

Pictured is an artist's rendition of the new Gateway Building, which will link Childrens Hospital Los Angeles with the 21st century (below).

Hospital Los Angeles has confronted the increased demand on its surgery space head-on. In preparation for the 21st century, the hospital raised some $55 million to build a new surgical center and operations plant on its nine-acre site on Sunset Boulevard. Thanks to the philanthropy of individuals, corporations, and foundations, the new building, known as The Gateway Building and Surgery Center, enhances the hospital's ability to treat sick and injured children effectively.

The Gateway Building includes a main lobby, admitting area, and blood-draw and blood-donor rooms, as well as a new central operations plant. The second floor features 14 state-of-the-art operating rooms and support facilities, a preoperative testing area, patient and family waiting rooms, and direct access to the existing intensive care and cardiac care units.

The building also houses the Associates' Center for Minimally Invasive Surgery, one of the only pediatric facilities devoted to minimizing surgical impact on young bodies. A decade ago, very little minimally invasive surgery was performed on children. Now, the approach is more prevalent, and by the turn of the century, approximately 40 percent of all surgical procedures will rely on this technique. Minimally invasive procedures mean less time, smaller incisions, less pain, faster recovery, and reduced costs.

Thanks to these and other ongoing efforts at Childrens Hospital Los Angeles, *U.S. News & World Report* has continually named the hospital the best pediatric medical facility in the western United States, and has ranked it among the top five in the nation since 1990.

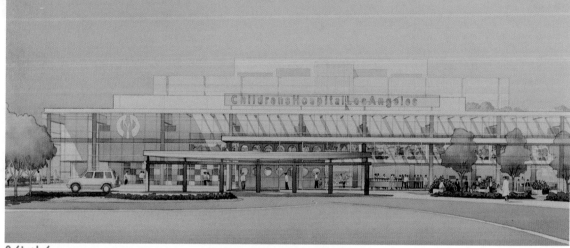

A Sixth Sense

An important part of the hospital's mission is to advance the health and well-being of children and adolescents in an atmosphere of love, compassion, and respect. At Childrens Hospital Los Angeles, considerable emphasis is placed on what the hospital calls the "environment of care."

All staff members—including more than 600 physicians, nearly 700 nurses, and hundreds of dedicated volunteers—are sensitive to what children go through when visiting the hospital. The people of Childrens Hospital Los Angeles know the importance of addressing patient needs in a child's terms. Without this sixth sense that comes from treating only children, the hospital experience itself could become confusing and traumatic.

Hospitalized children are allowed to continue their home routines as much as is possible and safe at Childrens Hospital Los Angeles. Visitation policies are extremely liberal for family members, and there is plenty of playtime with other children in

colorful playrooms staffed by Child Life specialists and recreation therapists. In addition, Los Angeles Unified School District teachers provide that most routine experience of all—school. Even children who profess not to like school take comfort in its familiarity when they are hospitalized.

These and many other experiences at Childrens Hospital Los Angeles are carefully geared toward child development. While most hospitalized patients are working to regain lost abilities, children also need to continue developing, growing, and learning. That's why the toys, video games, sports paraphernalia, art and poetry programs, and visits by famous celebrities and cartoon characters are treated as another kind of medicine at Childrens Hospital Los Angeles.

Building on nearly 100 years of solving the puzzles of childhood illness, Childrens Hospital Los Angeles, in partnership with the philanthropic community, will continue to be on the leading edge of modern pediatric medicine for years to come.

Los Angeles Department of Water and Power

I f not for the ingenuity of William Mulholland, the first superintendent of the city's new municipal water department, the diminutive Southern California desert community of Los Angeles may have remained just that. Fortunately, progress and innovation have been among the Los Angeles Department of Water and Power's (DWP) hallmarks since it was established in 1902. ⚜ That was also the year Mulholland, an Irish immigrant, completely restructured Los Angeles' means of water supply. The city had been drawing

As the Los Angeles Department of Water and Power (DWP) prepares for competition, it continues to provide customers with reliable energy at rates that are 10 to 15 percent lower than its nearest competitor (left).

DWP has a dedicated staff to address the Y2K issue. Through a series of tests, monitoring, and remediation, technologists are working to make sure the water will flow and the lights will stay on when the new millennium begins (right).

the much-needed precious liquid from the meager Los Angeles River since the first Spanish pueblo was built in the city in 1781. Instead, Mulholland designed and oversaw the construction of a 233-mile aqueduct that brought water to the city from the watershed of the eastern Sierra Nevada. Thus, the growth boom enjoyed by the city near the turn of the century—from a population of 5,728 in 1870 to 102,479 in 1900—was allowed to continue.

The ensuing decades have seen the expansion of Mulholland's original plans to supply water to a rapidly growing population, as more and more people are drawn to Los Angeles and its aerospace, oil, railroad, agriculture, and entertainment industries. In 1917, the DWP began supplying power to Los Angeles, a natural complement to water, since water flowing down

the mountains to Los Angeles at sea level creates hydroelectric energy in the process. By 1939, the DWP was the sole generator of electricity for the city. Today, the DWP supplies water and electricity to more than 3.6 million people in a 464-square-mile area.

A Model for the Nation's Utility Companies

With a workforce of more than 6,500 employees, the DWP delivers about 580 million gallons of water to Los Angeles' residents each day. Seventy percent of the city's water begins as snow in the eastern Sierra, while sources for the other 30 percent include the San Fernando Valley Groundwater Basin. Twelve reservoirs along the aqueduct and within Los Angeles store the city's water, which is piped into homes and

businesses through more than 7,000 miles of water mains. The DWP's 1997-1998 water revenues were $425.1 million.

The DWP promotes water conservation through a number of programs, enabling the city to make the best use of this valuable commodity. Eleven power plants along the aqueduct system currently provide more than 200 million megawatt hours of electricity annually. Power-generating stations as far away as Arizona, Utah, and northern Oregon also supply electricity for use in Los Angeles. The DWP's 1997-1998 revenues for energy were close to $2.6 billion.

Facing New Challenges

Deregulation is the DWP's next big challenge, for it is forcing the utility to devise creative solutions so that it can compete

against some of the most aggressive utilities in the United States. The DWP's ambitious outline of goals as it moves into the 21st century includes introducing a green power program, streamlining debt, and eliminating excessive layers of management. It is also committed to freezing rates until 2002, decreasing costs for residential customers (whose rates are already 10 to 15 percent lower than those offered by its nearest competitor), and making major cuts to business rates in order to meet or beat those of other energy providers. And it supports and promotes energy-efficient investments and technologies to help reduce the bills paid by its customers.

In fiscal year 1997-1998 alone, the DWP reduced its generation debt by $500 million, and is well on its way to achieving its goal of being debt-free by 2003. In the same fiscal year, it also realized a savings of $48 million through a variety of other means, from hiring freezes and the reduction of consultant contracts to decreasing the amount spent on materials and other nonlabor budget items. And the DWP has created new sources of revenue that are generating millions of dollars that will go toward debt reduction, including sales of real estate and other surplus property.

The rest of the United States typically looks to trend-setting California to see how the state handles its challenges. The Los Angeles Department of Water and Power, the country's largest municipally owned utility, sits squarely in the national spotlight, as it builds an agenda to help it not only survive but thrive in a new era of deregulation. After nearly 100 years of operation, the DWP looks forward to continuing the tradition of meeting the utility needs of Los Angeles.

Clockwise from top left:
The delivery of water to Los Angeles has spurred and maintained the growth of the city. DWP utilizes state-of-the-art treatment technologies to ensure a safe drinking water supply.

DWP customers will be able to capture the power of the sun by allowing DWP to install photovoltaic panels on their rooftops as a means to help the environment by developing clean, renewable energy sources.

The DWP is the largest municipal utility in the nation, serving water and electricity to more than 3.6 million customers in a 464-square-mile region.

The first telephone appeared in Los Angeles in 1877, just one year after Thomas A. Watson sat in a Boston boardinghouse and listened with amazement to Alexander Graham Bell's command, "Mr. Watson, please come here; I want you," over the wires of the prototype of the modern telephone. When the Pacific Bell Telephone Company was established a mere three years later on the opposite coast, Los Angeles was a sleepy little hamlet of orange groves and ranches with just seven telephones. In 1882,

the *Los Angeles Evening Herald* reported, "The telephone is becoming a necessity with our business men. The system in this city is largely patronized and now has 70 members." Telephone service in Los Angeles grew rapidly as phone installers made their rounds on bicycles with telephones strapped to their backs and tools tied around their waists.

Today, Pacific Bell is the largest player in the telecommunications game in Los Angeles. Servicing more than 17 million lines in the state of California, Pacific Bell in its current incarnation is the result of the 1997 merger of Pacific Telesis and Southwestern Bell Communications (SBC). This merger has produced a telecommunications company that is unrivaled in its range of services and in its dedication to the residents of California. Parent company SBC has been ranked by *Fortune* magazine as the most admired telecommunications company in the world.

Not Just Bigger

What sets Pacific Bell apart from the competition is not merely its size, but the breadth and quality of its service. In fact,

many of its competitors are able to do business only by buying Pacific Bell's services in bulk and then reselling them to their own customers.

The company has a tradition of working hard to meet the needs of its customers. In 1896, the Pacific company began what was known as "kitchen telephone service," through which housewives could

order their kitchen supplies by telephone for 50 cents a month. A century later, Pacific Bell continues to develop new technology and provide the products that consumers need for both business and personal use. It has evolved from simply being a provider of telephone service into offering a much more sophisticated array of services, including both regular telephone service and wireless service, Internet service, and custom-made services such as caller ID and three-way calling.

Acquiring economies of scale enables Pacific Bell to offer customers quality services at reasonable prices. For instance, Pacific Bell can deploy high-speed data transmission—called a digital subscriber line—on a large scale to people, thus bringing down the price of what would otherwise be a very costly service. And in less than two years' time, the company went from zero wireless customers to some 500,000 after it established wireless service in 1997. Pacific Bell continues to devise better ways to serve the public through improvements in high-speed data transmission and fiber optics, as well as through the merging of technologies such as the

By 1948, the region's landscape hadn't gotten any easier to navigate, but Pacific Bell's equipment and technology were always improving.

Pacific Bell has roots in the Los Angeles area that date back to 1880, just four years after the invention of the telephone. In 1913, the pride of Pacific's fleet was this Brush truck, a chain drive installation truck that was not noted for its smooth ride.

telephone and Internet. The company currently invests $2 billion each year in network infrastructure improvements.

Spirit of Community in California

Pacific Bell is a California institution that takes its dedication to the community seriously. Its 53,000 employees volunteer to participate in programs that enrich the lives of Californians and provide telecommunication support in times of emergency. Not only does the company provide monetary help when needed, but its employees get out, roll up their sleeves, and pitch in to help, whether or not those chores are listed in their job descriptions.

For example, Pacific Bell partnered with several other organizations after a flood in 1998 and contributed $250,000 for relief work in the state. Employees slogged through mud and floodwater to repair fallen lines and restore phone service, with some working 36-hour shifts in hazardous conditions to get the job done as quickly as possible. They also visited evacuation centers and shelters, delivering free calling cards, telephones, and services to assist those displaced by the disaster.

Other ways in which Pacific Bell employees have served their individual communities include building or repairing youth baseball fields, participating in AIDS awareness and prevention projects, and repairing a school that had been vandalized. The company's educational efforts include providing teachers with computer and technology training, and active involvement with youth in educational and self-improvement projects. Pacific Bell also provides technology for senior centers, schools, police departments, job training centers, and hospitals in rural areas. And the company works through a number of programs to encourage economic development in communities throughout the state.

Pacific Bell is an integral part of the nationwide Bell system, an American institution whose origins go back to Alexander Graham Bell, a man with a dream and a desire to help others. Like the company's founder and namesake, Pacific Bell is dedicated to helping improve the lives of those whom it serves and will serve for years to come.

Pacific Bell monitors its network statewide through two centers, including this one in San Diego, to ensure reliability and service.

TERRY LOWENTHAL

Pacific Bell has evolved from simply being a provider of telephone service into offering a much more sophisticated array of services. Today, the company is building the Advanced Communications network, a hybrid of optical fiber and coaxial cable that can carry voice, data, and video transmissions on the same line.

T ransamerica Pyramid, the world headquarters of Transamerica Corporation, is such a prominent and nationally known San Francisco landmark that few people realize the company traces its roots back to Los Angeles. In 1906, Karl K. Kennedy and 14 prominent Los Angelenos created Occidental Life Insurance Company—a bold endeavor. Not only was Occidental Life the first life insurance company in California, but at that time, Los Angeles was considered a remote city at the edge of the western frontier. Kennedy

and his associates saw the challenge many Californians faced getting insurance from companies in the east, and their vision paid off—Occidental was an almost immediate success.

Since its beginnings nearly a century ago, the company has continued to set its own traditions, capitalize on opportunities before others, and succeed. In 1930, Occidental merged with Transamerica Corporation, a San Francisco-based financial institution started by A.P. Giannini two years earlier. Giannini dreamed of branch services to help clients realize their financial goals. These plans matched well with the innovative insurance company in Los Angeles.

By 1936, Occidental Life was licensed to do business in 26 states. In 1959, it became the first company west of the Mississippi River to pass the $10 billion mark of insurance in force, accounting for nearly 80 percent of Transamerica Corporation's net income. In 1961, the company began construction on Occidental Center, later called Transamerica Center, which was the first high-rise office building in Los Angeles.

Transamerica has grown considerably since its founding, but its core mission

Transamerica Corporation traces its roots in Los Angeles back to 1906 (top).

Transamerica has grown considerably since its founding, but its core mission remains the same: to help its clients plan for their financial future and provide them with the services needed to accomplish their financial objectives (bottom).

remains the same: to help its clients plan for their financial future and provide them with the services needed to accomplish their financial objectives. "Our goal is to be the best at what we do—providing a range of financial services to help clients accumulate and protect assets," says Rudy Veerjee, president of Transamerica's insurance and investment group. "We have to

meet the demands of the marketplace more aggressively, in a more creative way than the competition." The company's largest division, the insurance and investment group, makes its home at Transamerica Center in downtown Los Angeles.

An Industry Pioneer

The company has always prided itself on being a pioneer in the industry. In the 1930s, Occidental became the first life insurance company to insure Asians at the same rates as Caucasians and to remove underwriting restrictions—a move that opened the door for selling life insurance in Asia. By 1937, Occidental was doing business in the Philippines, Hong Kong, China, and Canada.

At the same time, the company began offering term insurance—meeting a critical market need for affordable financial protection. This was a move many insurance companies were not willing to make, but which proved very successful. Today, these policies are widely accepted in financial planning and are offered by many companies.

In the 1950s, Occidental became the first life insurance company to issue policies by computer. In 1966, the company was chosen by the federal government to administer coverage of a new health care system, to be known as Medicare.

Transamerica is committed to hiring top talent and helping employees develop and grow professionally through ongoing training and education.

A Continuing Commitment

What is the cornerstone of Transamerica's success? "People are our biggest asset," answers Veerjee. "We have a team of innovative, talented, energetic people, all dedicated to delivering results and being the best." Transamerica is committed to hiring top talent and helping employees develop and grow professionally through ongoing training and education. Being based in the Los Angeles area and close to top universities helps attract superior talent at all levels. "One of our greatest strengths is the diversity of our employee base, which is enhanced by being located in the rich ethnic and cultural diversity of Los Angeles," notes Veerjee. Transamerica has deep roots in the Los Angeles community, with nearly a century of service in the area, and gives back to community through a wide range of corporate support and volunteer programs.

Transamerica continuously adds new products and innovations to keep ahead of customers' needs. The company recently began offering long-term care insurance policies to help cover nursing home or in-home nursing costs, which can drain a family's resources. For young people who are just starting to invest, the company established mutual funds with a $50 per month minimum—an easy way to start planning for the future.

Though best known for its life insurance, Transamerica offers a unique array

of financial services, including investment products like mutual funds and annuities and 401(k) programs, and insurance products, such as term, variable life, and long-term care insurance. Few companies provide this range of products and services. "Our customers may be saving for a new home, funding a college education, planning for retirement, or transferring wealth to their heirs," explains Veerjee. "We always strive to meet and exceed our customers'

needs at all stages of life, helping them meet their ever evolving financial goals."

For most of the 20th century, Transamerica has sought new opportunities and forged new industry traditions while helping people plan for their financial future. With these and other innovations on the horizon, Transamerica will continue to provide the products and services people need to accomplish their financial goals into the 21st century and beyond.

Transamerica offers a unique array of financial services, including investment products like mutual funds and annuities and 401(k) programs, and insurance products, such as term, variable life, and long-term care insurance.

Once a silent-film studio on a dusty ranch in north Los Angeles, Universal Studios is a worldwide leader in music, filmed, home-, and location-based entertainment. Universal's rich entertainment legacy can be traced back to 1912, when pioneer filmmaker Carl Laemmle, a Bavarian immigrant, founded the Chicago-based Universal Film Manufacturing Co. Three years later, Laemmle moved his company to Los Angeles and, on March 15, 1915, officially opened the gates of Universal

City on a 230-acre ranch. While producing a steady stream of silent films—including westerns, comedies, and action-adventures—Laemmle invited visitors to the property to observe, thereby establishing Universal's long-standing tradition of welcoming guests to enjoy the behind-the-scenes magic of moviemaking.

Over the years, Universal Pictures grew into a full-fledged movie studio and became a leader in motion picture production and distribution. In 1962, Universal merged with the Music Corporation of America (MCA), founded by Jules Stein in 1924 as a Chicago-based agency that booked bands into clubs and dance halls. With activities in television and motion picture production well in place in the early 1960s, the following years represented a period of growth and diversification for MCA/Universal.

In 1991, Matsushita Electric Industrial Co., Ltd. acquired MCA, and four years later, the Seagram Company Ltd. purchased a majority equity in MCA from Matsushita. On December 10, 1996, MCA Inc. was renamed Universal Studios.

Universal Studios' expansive back lot, the setting for many films and television shows over the years

An Entertainment Giant

Universal Studios' four main operating divisions are Universal Pictures, Universal Studios Recreation Group, Universal Music Group, and Universal Television & Networks Group.

The Universal Pictures business unit also includes Universal Studios Home Video, Universal Family & Home Entertainment, Universal Cartoon Studios, and Universal Pictures Animation and Visual Effects, as well as October Films, a leading producer and distributor for the ever growing specialty film market.

Universal Studios Recreation Group includes Universal Studios Hollywood and Universal CityWalk in Southern California, as well as Universal Studios Escape (featuring

One, two, three, and action! A production crew films a scene on the Universal back lot.

Clockwise from top left:
A view from above Universal City shows the Universal Studios Hollywood theme park, the Universal Amphitheatre concert facility, Universal CityWalk, production soundstages, and Universal's storied back lot.

Jurassic Park: The Ride thrills visitors to Universal Studios.

The Universal Studios Store features a wide array of Universal-branded consumer products.

Universal CityWalk, opened in 1993, hosts millions of guests yearly.

Universal Studios Florida and Universal Studios Islands of Adventure, opening in 1999) in Orlando, Florida; Universal Studios Japan, scheduled to open in Osaka in 2001; Universal Studios Experience in Beijing; and Port Aventura in Spain.

Under the Universal Music Group umbrella are labels such MCA Records, MCA Records Nashville, Universal Records, Geffen/DGC Records, Interscope Records, GRP Recording Company, and Hip-O Records, plus Universal Concerts, Univer-

sal Music Special Markets, MCA Music Publishing, and Universal Music & Video Distribution.

Universal Television & Networks Group is comprised of three distinct units to maximize product potential across all of its television businesses: worldwide television programming development, production, and distribution; domestic television distribution of Universal's feature film library in all forms of television; and networks, featuring Universal-

branded networks throughout the world.

Other product divisions include Universal Studios New Media Group, which develops and promotes Universal's properties for the global digital consumer market; Universal Studios Consumer Products Group, which licenses and markets retail items worldwide on behalf of Universal; and Spencer Gifts, a merchandise chain of more than 500 stores nationwide, featuring an array of trend-driven products.

BANK OF AMERICA

Bank of America has been doing business in Los Angeles for more than 85 years. During that time, the bank has met the financial needs of millions of local residents. It has underwritten a wide range of community improvements and helped fund the development of the area's leading industries—from agriculture and aerospace to energy and entertainment. ⚜ The Dodgers came to Los Angeles with Bank of America's help. And, local institutions such as The Walt Disney Company and

Mattel, Inc. were built with the bank's financing. In Hollywood, Bank of America became known as "the movie bank," lending money for thousands of films—from *Snow White and the Seven Dwarfs* and *Gone With the Wind* to *Lawrence of Arabia* and *It's a Wonderful Life*.

Today, Bank of America is one of the Southland's leading employers. In Los Angeles County, the bank delivers paychecks to more than 14,000 associates. In Southern California, it employs nearly 25,000.

Southern California remains Bank of America's largest and most profitable market. For the bank to thrive, Southern California must thrive. And, Bank of America has in place strong local leadership to help make that happen. Liam E. McGee, president of Bank of America, Southern California, and his management team have a unique understanding of this market's economic vitality and diversity, as well as the authority and responsibility to do what's right for their customers and communities.

Serving Local Clients of All Sizes

Millions of local individuals count on Bank of America when the time comes to purchase their homes, educate their children, or start their own businesses. The bank

serves two out of every three households in Southern California, providing access to a wide array of financial services through more than 650 banking centers and 2,200 automated teller machines.

At the same time, Bank of America enjoys relationships with just about every Fortune 500 company in the Southland, and is the region's leading provider of financial services to middle-market companies. It's also the largest Small Business Administration lender in Los Angeles and the number one small-business lender in the nation.

From helping Los Angeles resident Jose-Luis Saavedra build a new production facility for his family-owned Tapatío Hot Sauce-Salsa Picante company to financing the $350 million STAPLES Center in downtown Los Angeles, Bank of America continues to be a leading force in helping to shape the Southland's 21st century economy.

Promoting Community Investment

One of the most important ways in which any bank contributes to economic oppor-

Clockwise from top:
Bank of America's Southern California headquarters is located in downtown Los Angeles.

Bank of America helped Los Angeles resident Jose-Luis Saavedra build a new production facility for his family-owned firm—the Tapatío Hot Sauce-Salsa Picante company.

President Liam E. McGee, Bank of America, Southern California

tunity is through community development lending. Bank of America has consistently earned Community Reinvestment Act ratings of Outstanding for its work in meeting the credit needs of its communities.

Bank of America's Community Development Bank, created to provide financing for small business and affordable housing, is a recognized leader in community development in Los Angeles and throughout the United States. The construction of 14,000 affordable housing units in the Southland—including 100 households in a multiethnic community in Los Angeles known as Casa Heiwa—was made possible over the past decade with funding from the Community Development Bank. And, pioneering home loan programs featuring low or no down payment and flexible underwriting have helped Bank of America make home ownership a reality for more people in low-income areas of Southern California than any other commercial bank.

Bank of America's record is one of commitment—commitments made and commitments kept. In fact, the bank has pledged a record $350 billion over 10 years for community development lending and investment, including $180 billion for small businesses, $115 billion for affordable housing, $30 billion for consumer loans, and $25 billion for economic development. This pledge includes at least $70 billion for California. Bank of America will continue to work with local business leaders and community groups to make sure these resources are deployed where they are most needed.

Making Charitable Contributions

Another measure of the bank's commitment to Los Angeles is philanthropy. The Bank of America Foundation now operates with the largest philanthropic budget of any financial institution in the United States—$100 million in 1999. The bank

earmarked $18 million for the state of California, an increase of almost 30 percent over the 1998 California budget. More than half of this money will be distributed in Southern California to community groups and organizations that support economic development, education, and artistic achievement.

The bank's commitment to education recently was underscored with the announcement of a $2.5 million initiative to help improve child literacy in Southern California. The Bank of America Foundation has committed $1 million to support the Reading by 9 program launched by the *Los Angeles Times*, $1 million to support California Governor Gray Davis' teacher training initiative, and $500,000 to promote various literacy programs throughout the Southland.

Past initiatives have included a $5 million commitment to help build the Walt Disney Concert Hall, $1 million to build permanent housing for Los Angeles'

homeless, and $1 million to make quality child care more easily available throughout the county. Bank of America is the largest supporter of Junior Achievement of Southern California and, in recent years, has contributed more to local United Way chapters than any other company.

Making Banking Work Better Than Ever

Bank of America brings to Los Angeles the resources of the nation's largest bank—with $618 billion in assets, a global workforce of more than 180,000 associates, nearly 5,000 banking centers, and 14,000 ATMs—and delivers them in a way that makes banking work for its clients as it never has before.

Los Angeles' financial needs are enormous, and Bank of America intends to meet them. The bank has been an active member of this community for nearly a century, and looks forward to serving Los Angeles for a long time to come.

Clockwise from top left:
Bank of America operates more than 2,200 ATMs in the region.

For added customer convenience, Bank of America has more than 200 banking centers located in grocery stores throughout the Southland.

Bank of America serves two out of every three households in Southern California, through more than 650 local banking centers.

Union Bank of California, N.A.

The Southland roots of Union Bank of California, N.A. were planted in the 1890s when German immigrant Kaspare Cohn began acting as an unofficial banker to sheepherders of Basque descent in Los Angeles. The business was formalized in 1914, and later became known as Union Bank in the mid-1950s. Baby boomers may recall a Los Angeles skyline where the Union Bank building was the next-tallest structure in downtown, second only to City Hall. Today, the bank ranks as the second-largest commercial bank based in California, with assets of $32.3 billion. Union Bank of California has 245 full-service branches throughout the state, six offices in Oregon and Washington, and 18 international facilities, mostly along the Pacific Rim. The bank's majority owner, The Bank of Tokyo-Mitsubishi, Ltd., is among the largest financial institutions in the world, providing a global link to Union Bank of California's corporate and retail customers.

Strength through Diversification

"Union Bank of California's strength is our reputation for customer service and our diversification of products and services," says George Ramirez, senior vice president of the bank's Emerging Markets Division, which develops products and services tailored to Hispanic, African-American, and Asian populations. "These services and expertise span the market from small-business banking to retail, from international and trade finance to corporate and commercial banking, from trust and private banking to investment management services."

Ramirez adds that the new face of California consists of the rapidly growing Latino, Asian, and African-American markets. "The whole idea behind our Emerging Markets Division is to promote Union Bank of California as the bank of choice for these communities and growing markets. The key goal is to capture larger market share and to prepare ourselves for what is going to be the future and strength of the West Coast—a very diverse region with people from many different cultures."

Union Bank of California's century-old tradition as a banker responding to the evolutionary changes in Los Angeles positions the bank as uniquely capable of reacting to the financial needs of a new generation of Angelenos. The bank has been among the industry leaders in high-technology investments, most recently joining with IBM to create an advanced, on-line financial services system for conducting banking, investment, cash management, and other financial transactions. Meanwhile, customers requiring more specialized service—and who prefer the human touch—are welcome at all Union Bank of California offices.

Community Commitment

But like most successful corporations, the true value of a company is often measured by how it's perceived by its neighbors. In recent years, as banks and other industries have merged and relocated their headquarters out of state, Union Bank of California has stepped up its investments in the communities it serves by contributing to a wide range of nonprofit organizations.

In Greater Los Angeles, recipients have included Neighborhood Housing Services, Habitat for Humanity, the Economic Development Corporation, the Mexican American Legal Defense and Education Fund, Operation Hope, Women's Enterprise Development Corp., Carecen, Adelante Mujer Latina, and the I Have a Dream Foundation. In addition, Union Bank of California hosted a series of instructional seminars in Inglewood, Pasadena, and other communities for aspiring first-time home buyers.

The bank also has partnered with KCET-TV to underwrite a special programming feature honoring distinguished volunteers and activists from the Los Angeles Latino community during Hispanic Heritage Month. The feedback from the community prompted the bank and KCET to develop the program into an annual feature.

Along with a corporate financial commitment, Union Bank of California employees also volunteer thousands of hours of their own time, contributing significantly to the long-term health and vitality of the communities in which the bank does business.

Just as it did in the early days of the city's growth and development, Union Bank of California will continue providing the personal touch and corporate citizenship that have made it an integral part of the Los Angeles community.

Innovative, responsive, and customer oriented, Union Bank of California's team is ready to deliver superior resources and financially driven solutions to the diverse community of Los Angeles.

The bank has roots in Los Angeles that reach back for more than a century.

Nowhere in the world is the grocery business any greater than it is in Los Angeles. Each year, Los Angeles consumers spend nearly $20 billion on groceries, almost $4 billion more than shoppers in the second-largest grocery market area, New York. The totals are staggering; the growth, phenomenal. And more than any other organization in the state, Certified Grocers of California, Ltd. has been instrumental

in developing and shaping California's grocery industry.

Not surprisingly, California's grocery industry is the largest of its kind in the United States. In fact, one out of every $10 spent on groceries in America is spent in California.

The Largest Wholesale Grocer

Since its founding, Certified Grocers—the largest wholesale grocery company in California—has been dedicated to furnishing California grocers with the programs, products, and services they need to grow and succeed. For years on end, Certified has provided the economies of scale that have enabled its retail members to provide unique value to consumers, which, in turn, has led to the significant growth of the Los Angeles and California grocery industries.

Certified Grocers was formed in 1922, when 15 independent grocers from Los Angeles gathered at the Hotel Green in Pasadena to discuss how they could beat a new and growing form of competition—the chain store. Their solution was partnership. They reasoned that by combining their

individual talents and resources, they would be on the same playing field as the chain stores. They decided to form a cooperative, Certified Grocers of California, Ltd., which proved to be a solid business decision. In fact, what began with 15 grocers in Los Angeles now serves more than 2,700 stores. In recent years, Certified's annual

revenues have consistently approached $2 billion. Headquartered in Commerce, Certified has distribution centers in Commerce, Stockton, Santa Fe Springs, and Fresno, with manufacturing facilities in Los Angeles. The company employs more than 2,500 Californians, hundreds of whom call Los Angeles their home.

A Company in Motion

Despite its size, Certified Grocers is hardly a household name in California. Though Certified is widely known and well respected within the grocery industry, most consumers are unfamiliar with the wholesale company. Yet, most California shoppers are familiar with Springfield, Certified's comprehensive line of private label products. For more than 50 years, shoppers in grocery stores throughout the state have counted on the Springfield brand for quality and value. Equally popular with California's consumers are Certified's Golden Creme and Special Value private brand products.

Throughout Certified's 76-year history, one of the constants has been change—and Certified's ability to adapt to it. In the next millennium and beyond, change will again take center stage in the grocery industry. And Certified, as it has done since day one, will be on the cutting edge of that change, developing solutions that are ahead of their time and creating the programs, products, and services that California's grocers need to ensure their continued success.

The Apple Market banner adorns the front of grocery stores throughout California. Unlike chain grocery stores, Apple Markets are individually owned and operated. The Apple Market program is among the products, programs, and services that Certified Grocers of California provides (top left).

Each weekday in California, hundreds of trucks are loaded with grocery orders at Certified's warehouses in Commerce, Stockton, Santa Fe Springs, and Fresno, where Certified's drivers begin their deliveries to grocery stores throughout the state (top right).

For many California consumers, Springfield and Golden Creme are household names. These quality products are available exclusively at the member stores of Certified Grocers of California, Ltd.

University of California, Los Angeles

The University of California, Los Angeles, known worldwide as UCLA, is a youthful prodigy among the nation's academic elite. From standard-setting educational programs to world-changing research to inspired community service, UCLA has, in just 80 years, attained a stature to which most research universities can only aspire. With an enrollment of 35,000 spread among the College of Letters and Science and 11 professional schools, UCLA educates more students than any other university in California. A unique array of degree programs, along with innovative research and international studies opportunities, offer UCLA's student body a renowned academic foundation and the global perspective necessary for success in the new millennium.

UCLA's lofty standing among the nation's research universities attracts hundreds of millions of dollars in public and private funding. These financial partnerships help support the important work of distinguished and dedicated faculty, who are inventing the technologies of tomorrow and discovering new insights about our changing world.

Hundreds of thousands of Angelenos turn to UCLA each year for the best in medical care and continuing education. They also visit the campus to enjoy world-class performing artists and exhibits and dozens of architectural treasures situated on 419 wooded acres. At the same time, UCLA's many public service enterprises reach out to lend a hand to neighbors in need.

University of Big Ideas

UCLA research discoveries drive tomorrow's technology enterprise. One of the world's leading research institutions and birthplace of the Internet, UCLA advances knowledge in physical and life sciences, medicine, biotechnology, engineering, management, law, new media, communications, and the arts. Within this environment, multidisciplinary teams are assembled that provide unique value to industry. Successful collaborations involving UCLA research and intellectual property have been achieved with government agencies, industry leaders, and start-up companies. As California leads the way in moving toward a knowledge-based and information-driven economy, UCLA research provides high-impact solutions that generate economic growth and benefit the public.

Number One in the West

UCLA Medical Center offers the most advanced medical and surgical technologies available, cutting-edge clinical research trials, and the services of world-class physicians to more than 300,000 patients each year. Known worldwide for its pioneering technological contributions, including advancements in organ transplantation, artificial insemination, and ultrasound, UCLA Medical Center is consistently ranked number one in the West by *U.S. News & World Report*'s annual survey of America's best hospitals. Other factors that contribute to earning this top rating include specialized intensive care units, state-of-the-art inpatient and outpatient operating suites, a Level I trauma center, the latest diagnostic technology, and a high level of commitment from a dedicated and experienced staff of more than 1,000 physicians and 3,500 nurses, therapists, technologists, and support personnel.

A World Leader in Management Education

The UCLA Anderson Graduate School of Management has long been recognized as one of the world's leading management

Royce Hall, named for Josiah Royce, a leading philosopher of the time, is an architectural landmark of the University of California, Los Angeles and one of the original four buildings of the Westwood campus constructed in 1929 (top).

UCLA Extension sets the standard for lifelong learning. With more than 100,000 enrollments and 4,500 courses annually, UCLA Extension is the largest urban-based continuing education program in the United States, and the largest non-degree higher education provider in the world. Classes are offered on campus and in centers located throughout Greater Los Angeles—convenient to where people work and live (bottom).

educational institutions. Businesses from around the globe come to Anderson both to recruit some of the world's brightest and most talented MBA recipients and to secure the information and skills needed to meet critical management and organizational challenges. A vital part of the UCLA research tradition, Anderson faculty members create intellectual capital that is critical to today's business community.

The UCLA Anderson Business Forecast, one of the school's many research centers, provides a widely followed and often cited economic forecast for the nation and for the state. Other research centers and areas study and provide insight into finance, information systems, health services management, labor relations, international business, real estate, and entrepreneurial studies. In addition to a two-year, full-time MBA program, the school also provides lifelong learning opportunities for executives through seminars, short-term executive education programs, and part-time MBA programs.

An Education for All Seasons

UCLA Extension is the nation's largest urban-based continuing education program. More than 100,000 adult learners annually take part in some 4,500 UCLA Extension courses, seminars, and conferences on campus and at centers throughout Los Angeles County. Taught by leading experts from industry and academia, UCLA Extension programs combine hands-on experience with essential information. Each provides a one-of-a-kind opportunity to meet with fellow students and instructors—in both traditional classroom and on-line learning environments—for a rich exploration of knowledge and ideas.

Working professionals can stay abreast of new developments in their field or explore new career objectives, international students can improve their English and business skills, and anyone can indulge a favorite cultural or intellectual interest with courses that range from art and architecture to health and fitness to creative writing. In addition, the Custom Programs Unit can deliver most of Extension's existing courses to the workplace, as well as develop new programs to meet an organization's specific needs.

Continuing education also is available through UCLA Summer Sessions. An extraordinarily varied and extensive selection of classes is available to adult learners, as well as to high school, college, and university students. Summer courses are taught by regular UCLA faculty and outstanding visiting instructors.

As an educator, innovator, and partner, UCLA has a proud heritage, but it remains a work in progress. As long as there are mysteries to solve, communities to help, and frontiers to explore, UCLA will build on its tradition of excellence, striving for ever greater distinction.

Clockwise from top:
UCLA physics professor Walter Gekelman is making "strange electromagnetic weather" in a bottle. UCLA is among the nation's leading research universities and has 3,200 faculty members, all leaders in their fields of study.

Each year, more than 300,000 people from Los Angeles, from across the country, and from around the world come to the UCLA Medical Center to receive care from some of the world's best physicians and nurses. Thousands more receive care through UCLA's network of primary care offices and community outreach health programs.

The Anderson School at UCLA is recognized as the most technologically advanced management school in the world and is ranked among the nation's top 10 business schools. The entrepreneurial spirit of students and faculty has earned the school a reputation for innovation and cutting-edge research.

SETH JOEL PHOTOGRAPHY

MARK HARMEL

KLVE-FM, KSCA-FM, KTNQ-AM

With nearly 6 million Hispanic residents, Los Angeles is second only to Mexico City on the list of the world's largest Hispanic cities. And like no other community in the city, Hispanic Angelenos are bound together by radio. Of the eight Spanish-language radio stations broadcasting in the Los Angeles area, the three Heftel Broadcasting Corporation-managed stations—KLVE-FM, KSCA-FM, and KTNQ-AM—have become the region's leaders in providing news and

entertainment to this thriving Southern California market. Reaching the five-county area—Los Angeles, Orange, Riverside, San Bernardino, and Ventura—as well as the city of San Diego, the three radio stations have become a vital part of the daily lives of the area's Spanish speakers.

KLVE—K-Love (107.5 FM)—with its adult contemporary format, has become the nation's number one Hispanic FM radio station, and its sister station, 1020 AM, which has a news-talk format, is the most listened to Hispanic AM station in the United States. Meanwhile, the Mexican country-western music station KSCA—*La Nueva* (101.9 FM)—shares the top slot in the Los Angeles market with KLVE. The two stations account for 12 percent of the overall Los Angeles audience between 6 a.m. and midnight of listeners age 12 and over.

"We made L.A. radio history in this 80-plus radio station market by becoming the number one and number two radio stations in this market," says Richard Heftel, president and general manager of KLVE and KTNQ, as well as programming manager for KSCA. "Never before have the top two radio stations in L.A. been Spanish-

Maria Elena Nava, program director and midday host for KSCA, *La Nueva* (101.9 FM) (top)

Renan Almendarez Coello and his Tropa Loca lead the morning shows in Los Angeles (bottom).

language format. And never before have the top two stations been associated with one company."

Continual Growth in a Growing Market

KTNQ's roots go back to KPOP, which began operations in 1922 and later changed hands—and call letters—for the first time in 1959. Meanwhile, KLVE, which first broadcast in 1959, had been owned briefly by the now defunct Pacific Southwest Airlines (PSA). In 1978, the two stations changed ownership and formats when both began broadcasting in Spanish. KLVE was the first Spanish-language FM station in the continental United States.

Heftel Broadcasting Corporation (HBC), a publicly traded company that owns or operates 39 stations nationwide, is the largest Spanish-language radio broadcaster in the United States. In 1986, HBC acquired KLVE and KTNQ, and, although HBC doesn't own KSCA, it began managing the station's programming in 1997. Under Heftel's guidance, all three stations have skyrocketed on the ratings charts.

Listening to Listeners

"The success of the three stations is a result of responding to what listeners wanted," Heftel says. After extensive research for its Los Angeles-based stations, HBC took a risk in changing the format of 1020 AM from a Mexican-heritage-format station to a personality-driven, talk-radio format—the first in the western United States. The switch proved to be immensely successful, making 1020 AM the model for all of HBC's news-talk stations.

With a 50,000-watt signal, 1020 AM's 24-hour programming is carefully designed

JOHN MEJIA

More than 75,000 people gather at the annual fund-raiser the stations produce for the Los Angeles Police Department's Jeopardy program, which helps teach children to stay in school and out of gangs. The annual concerts have raised more than $1 million to aid youth at risk.

GEORGE RODRIGUEZ

to fully service the adult, 25- to 54-year-old market. Weekday mornings include entertainment, news, sports, and traffic. Midday and afternoon programs invite listener participation on subjects of community interest ranging from immigration and employment issues to consumer affairs and parenting to health and politics. *Sportstalk*, in the early evening, is dedicated to sports news, features, commentary, and listener reaction. Evening shows feature calls and interviews on relationship issues, while weekend programming revolves around advice shows and sports coverage.

During the highly competitive weekday morning drive time on the FM dial, from 6 to 10 a.m., *La Nueva*'s Renan Almendarez Coello, who was nominated

for the industry's prestigious 1998 Marconi Award, shares in the market's top ratings slot with K-Love's Pepe Barreto. Both Coello and Barreto combine their station's music format with provocative and entertaining talk radio. In 1997, K-Love was voted the best Spanish-language station in the nation by the National Association of Broadcasters, and it has been nominated many times as the best radio station in any language due to the strength of its Latin fare of mainstream pop, ballad, and tropical music.

The success of KSCA rests on providing the best mix of *norteña*, *banda*, and *grupo* music—known collectively as Mexican regional—to L.A.'s large, 18- to 34-year-old, adult Mexican population. Besides providing the newest music in this genre, *La Nueva* also dedicates programming to Hispanic oldies and *ranchera* music.

Fiestas for the Community

One way HBC's stations return the support they receive from the Hispanic community is by presenting outdoor music festivals. The HBC stations have hosted the West Coast's largest festivals celebrating Hispanic heritage. Drawing an average of 75,000 to 100,000 fans to its events, the radio stations bring the best family-oriented recording artists to perform for free at various locations throughout Los Angeles.

In addition, the stations host a yearly fund-raiser for the Jeopardy: Balancing the Odds program, which offers counseling, basketball programs, tutoring, acting and

JOHN MEJIA

dance classes, boxing instruction, and equestrian lessons to youths believed to be at risk for falling into crime or drug use. Developed in conjunction with the Los Angeles Police Department, the festival has raised nearly $1 million since it started in 1991.

The number of Hispanics in Los Angeles is projected to increase over the next 20 years from one-third to two-thirds of the population. As the new century begins, K-Love, *La Nueva*, and 1020 AM will continue to provide this growing market with the quality programming and community involvement that listeners have come to expect.

KLVE's morning drive host, Pepe Barreto

from the turn-of-the-century era of Yankee clipper ships to the millennium bug of the information age, only a handful of U.S. companies have a history as long or as rich as J&H Marsh & McLennan, now known as Marsh, Inc., which integrates the respected traditions of Marsh & McLennan, Johnson & Higgins, and Sedgwick. ▼ Today, as the world's leading risk and insurance services firm, Marsh combines the stability and tradition that come from a century of achievement with a commitment to breaking

new ground and creating new solutions to the risk challenges of its clients.

Marsh assists companies around the world in managing the growing range of risks they face as the global economy expands and becomes more complex. The firm's specialists serve such areas as arts and entertainment, aviation, marine and energy, financial services, high technology, real estate, and construction. Its consulting experts identify and quantify traditional and emerging risks for clients—and devise advanced structures for transferring and financing those risks.

The firm has 29,000 employees and serves clients in more than 100 countries. In addition to being a leader in meeting the risk and insurance challenges of the world's largest corporations, the firm has professionals in insurance brokerage, employee benefits services, and risk control consulting, who are dedicated to addressing the needs of mid-size businesses.

The firm's combination in 1998 with Sedgwick Group P.L.C. created the industry's leading global organization of owned and operated offices, giving clients access to enhanced service resources in the United Kingdom, Continental Europe,

the former Soviet Union, and the Asia-Pacific region. In the United States, the firm's more than 100 offices are organized so that companywide resources can be shared, and clients can tap into the exact expertise when and where they need it.

The firm first began doing business in the Los Angeles area in 1923. Now, with 600 employees situated in the CitiCorp Plaza in the main business district, the Los Angeles office serves clients in a broad array of industries, including aviation, health care, energy, and consumer goods, as well as providing property and casualty coverage for professional athletes and well-known entertainers.

According to Margaret Liptay, managing director responsible for the Los Angeles office, the firm has been in the forefront of product development and creative solutions for the industry, and is responsible for the release of some of the most innovative and important products to come along in the past 10 years. "We pride ourselves on the way our input helps create client solutions. It's part of the deep culture of the firm. We are always looking ahead. Now that it's 1999, we are already thinking years ahead, and

what we can do to meet the challenges that await us," Liptay explains.

Technology for Tomorrow

Marsh has been a leader in applying new technologies toward operations and service. Employees around the world are linked through a sophisticated, global computer information system that also gives employees instant access to hundreds of information resources and proprietary databases. The award-winning, on-line system enables employees to form virtual teams to help clients manage information and improve their ability to control risk and reduce costs.

The firm also has implemented a major initiative to help clients understand the myriad issues surrounding Y2K, or the millennium bug—which means that computer programs, if not corrected, will recognize the two-date digit of "00" not as the year 2000, but rather as 1900. Marsh is working with clients as they examine their Y2K risks and prepare for the millennium by helping them identify and prioritize key issues for their organizations—and then initiate effective action steps to head off

J&H Marsh & McLennan, now known as Marsh, first began doing business in the Los Angeles area in 1923, and now has some 600 employees serving clients in a broad array of industries, including aviation, health care, energy, and consumer goods, as well as providing property and casualty coverage for professional athletes and well-known entertainers.

John T. Sinnott (right), chairman and chief executive officer of Marsh, Inc., received the Japanese-American Cultural and Community Center of Los Angeles' Pacific Pioneer Award from Gerald Yoshitomi, executive director of the center, on June 11, 1998. The organization presented the award to recognize the firm for its role in helping Japanese businesses in the United States and for its leadership in supporting such organizations as the Japanese American National Museum, Keiro Services, and the Little Tokyo Service Center's Kansha Fund.

or at least mitigate any losses that might occur.

Corporate Citizen

A successful organization is not just concerned about business. Marsh also takes seriously its role as a corporate citizen, and for decades, employees of the firm have taken pride in their community leadership. Marsh provides opportunities for disadvantaged and handicapped children to visit zoos, science centers, nature centers, amusement parts, and sports arenas. Employees also donate time to spruce up camps, day care centers, playgrounds, and children's agencies.

Local offices lend their year-round support to numerous organizations, including the Boy Scouts of America, Big Brothers/ Big Sisters, March of Dimes, Easter Seals, United Way, the Red Cross, the Salvation Army, Junior Achievement, Habitat for Humanity, Head Start, Covenant House, Make-a-Wish Foundation, Ronald McDonald House, the YMCA and YWCA, and the Special Olympics. Marsh staff worldwide regularly raise funds to fight diseases such as multiple sclerosis, cystic fibrosis, Huntington's disease, and cancer, and to support AIDS research. The firm also lends support to schools, hospitals, cultural institutions, public television, and youth sport teams.

It is Marsh's long-standing heritage of community leadership, quality products, and exceptional client service that ensures

the company will remain the premier risk and insurance services firm.

Marsh is a major subsidiary of Marsh & McLennan Companies, Inc., a professional services firm that, in addition to risk and insurance services, provides investment management through Putnam Investments Inc., and human resources and manage-

ment consulting through Mercer Consulting Group. These capabilities are marshaled and mobilized through a Business in Combination initiative that assures its clients have access to the total spectrum of these resources. In 1998, Marsh & McLennan Companies, Inc. generated approximately $7 billion in annual revenue.

Marsh has been in the forefront of product development and creative solutions for the industry, and is responsible for the release of some of the most innovative and important products to come along in the past 10 years. Says Margaret Liptay, managing director responsible for the Los Angeles office, "We pride ourselves on the way our input helps create client solutions."

CB RICHARD ELLIS

Los Angeles is home to CB Richard Ellis, the world's leading commercial real estate services company. Responding to the evolving global marketplace, CB Richard Ellis was created by the 1998 merger of CB Commercial, one of the largest real estate services companies in the United States, and London-based REI Limited, an international real estate powerhouse that operated as Richard Ellis outside the United Kingdom. With more than 9,000 employees worldwide, CB Richard Ellis serves real estate owners, users, and occupiers

through more than 200 offices in 29 countries. The company's core services include property sales and leasing, property management, corporate advisory services and facilities management, mortgage banking, investment management, capital markets, appraisal/valuation, research, and consulting.

Navigating a New World

With global economic, political, and technological factors changing the world of real estate, CB Richard Ellis offers the industry's most talented, knowledgeable professionals to help its clients navigate through these changes—people with strong vision, fresh perspective, and proven ability.

With a diverse portfolio of real estate services, combined with extensive worldwide resources, market knowledge, and strategic expertise, CB Richard Ellis is able to create personalized solutions that make a tangible difference for each client. As the world navigator in real estate, CB Richard Ellis creates a powerful model that sets the new standard of excellence in service.

Recognizing that successful real estate ownership and investment in the 21st century will be based as much on the utilization of information and knowledge as examining locations and bricks and mortar, CB Richard Ellis is committed to providing clients with the market data and analysis they need to make successful

decisions. Through its Global Research and Consulting division, the company provides market information gathered locally through CB Richard Ellis' worldwide offices, assuring a consistency and uniformity of data that is unrivaled in the industry.

Founded in San Francisco in 1906 to help rebuild the city after a devastating earthquake, the company established its presence in the City of Angels in 1924. In 1968, the firm relocated its corporate headquarters to its current downtown Los Angeles location on South Fremont Avenue.

Nearly 200 CB Richard Ellis sales and leasing professionals serve the Los Angeles region from offices in downtown Los Angeles, Beverly Hills, Sherman Oaks, Torrance, and City of Industry.

CB Richard Ellis provides leasing and/or management services for a variety of prestigious buildings in the Los Angeles area, including (clockwise from top) 400 South Hope, Pacific Corporate Towers, and the Glendale City Center.

Recognized as one of the most widely diverse and capable motion controls companies in the industry, HR Textron Inc.'s product line offerings span the spectrum from space shuttle rocket-engine controls to complete robotic control systems for automatic passenger car refueling. Known today as "The Controls Company," HR Textron's broad capabilities provide its customers with advanced motion control products best matched to their needs.

Founded in 1933, the company was established in Southern California in order to capitalize on the region's rich pool of technical talent in the aerospace industry. In 1960, the firm became known as Hydraulic Research Textron, and in 1980, the name was shortened to HR Textron Inc., reflecting an evolution of the company and the industry from hydraulics to a more balanced product, including pneumatic and electromechanical solutions.

The company's headquarters, located in Santa Clarita in northern Los Angeles County, houses the executive facilities, research laboratories, and ISO 9001-certified manufacturing operations. The company also maintains manufacturing facilities in Pacoima, California, and Greenville, Ohio. A general service and repair facility is located in Cheltenham, England, along with worldwide product support facilities of its parent company, Textron Inc.

Capabilities and Products

HR Textron's capabilities include design, development, and manufacture of control actuation systems, fuel management systems, digital electronic controls, and such components as direct-drive valves, control valves, and actuators—all of which provide precise motion control. The company also has taken the industry lead in applying state-of-the-art aerospace technology to industrial and automotive applications. Examples of HR Textron's aerospace technology applied to commercial use can be observed at the Universal Studios parks in Orlando and Los Angeles, where HR supplies the direct-drive servovalves that control the robots from the *Terminator* movies. In addition, the company is currently developing an automatic refueling pump for automobiles. Called SmartPump™, the robotic system will be available at Shell gas stations and is being developed in conjunction with Shell Oil Company.

The roster of HR Textron clients includes some of the most distinguished and recognizable companies in the world. Among

them are Cessna Aircraft, Bell Helicopter, The Boeing Company, NASA, Delphi Automotive, General Motors, and Walt Disney Corporation.

The Future of Controls

The company's research and development programs are chosen to anticipate challenges and potential demands for future controls systems. HR Textron encourages personal growth and the free exchange of ideas in a multicultural and highly energized environment. In this setting, research and development professionals join the multidisciplinary teams to integrate a variety of controls-related technologies into techniques, processes, and products.

Current efforts include composite material actuators, fiber optics, digital motor controls, and self-monitoring control systems. These programs will enable HR Textron to make significant control system contributions to new generations of aerospace, industrial, and automotive motion-control system products.

Whether it's servovalves for the entertainment industry's animated figure displays, industrial valves for turbine engines, or automotive steering and suspension controls, HR Textron will continue to offer fully integrated systems to these rapidly growing industries well into the next millennium.

Recognized as one of the most widely diverse and capable motion controls companies in the industry, HR Textron Inc.'s product line offerings span the spectrum from space shuttle rocket-engine controls to complete robotic control systems for automatic passenger car refueling to the servovalves that control the robots from the *Terminator* movies.

UNITED AIRLINES

When the governor of California unveiled the state's new welfare reform law in 1997, he did it at the United Airlines Terminal in Los Angeles International Airport. United Airlines took a lead partnership role in the reform effort, because the world's largest employee-owned company knows about personal responsibility. Just ask any of the 90,000 baggage handlers, pilots, flight attendants, and ticket agents who

both own and run the largest airline in the West.

United has deep roots in Los Angeles, beginning in 1926, when its ancestor, Varney Airlines, first launched airmail service from Elko, Nevada, to Pasco, Washington. In 1931, Varney merged with United Aircraft and Transport Corporation—the holding company for Boeing Air Transport, Pacific Air Transport, and Pratt & Whitney—forming a company that employed nearly 13,000 people and served 78 cities in the United States and Canada.

Today, as the $15 billion company nears the 21st century, United Airlines transports 215,500 passengers on 2,200 flights a day to 139 destinations in 30 countries and two U.S. territories, and serves as the only true global carrier in the world.

An Alternate Business Model

But United's journey has included some growing pains. In 1994, the company made a key decision. Rather than downsize and break into several regional lines, employ-

ees came together and bought a majority share in the company, becoming an alternate model for businesses worldwide on how to turn adversity into triumph. The new owners immediately turned their attention to strengthening United's California base, and expanding this gateway to the Pacific Rim.

All employees, from baggage handlers on up, formed into teams and launched a new airline-within-an-airline, with the name Shuttle by United chosen out of 1,300 employee entries. Eventually, 366 Boeing 737s would launch from 12 western cities, offering United's "friendly skies" service on more frequent flights with economy and efficiency.

But employee ownership is not the only innovation in United's history. In 1930, the first professional flight attendants welcomed United passengers. Several years later, premier catering was whipped up in the world's first flight kitchen in Oakland. In 1987, first-class international travelers were treated to United's pioneering new concierge service. And employees and travelers together could rest easy when United became one of the first airlines to develop and install TCAS—the Traffic Alert and Collision Avoidance System—becoming one of the first airlines to carry the system on board its aircraft.

United Airlines is the world's largest employee-owned company, with some 90,000 baggage handlers, pilots, flight attendants, and ticket agents.

United has deep roots in Los Angeles that date back to 1926.

The largest airline in the West, United transports 215,500 passengers on 2,200 flights a day to 139 destinations in 30 countries and two U.S. territories.

This dedication to safety and innovation continues today. Passengers now enjoy paperless flights, from electronic ticketing to reservations made over the Internet. Shuttle by United offers self-service boarding in Los Angeles and San Francisco, and the company now has 24-hour customer service on its World Wide Web page, the Friendly Skyline.

The true test of excellence for passengers, though, comes on the flight itself—and delectable in-flight cuisine plays a major role in an enjoyable flight. United has worked in partnership with the Culinary Institute of America, HeartSmart Restaurants International, and various celebrity chefs to work up the most appetizing meals and snacks possible. In 1998, the airline and LSG/Sky Chefs linked up for the $1 Million Challenge, a strategic test to measure the value of in-flight foods to customers. Prestigious products such as Dom Perignon champagne, Starbucks coffee, Godiva chocolate, and Ben & Jerry's ice cream and frozen yogurt have made the skies not just friendly, but delightful for United passengers.

Delectable in-flight cuisine plays a major role in an enjoyable flight, and products such as Dom Perignon champagne, Starbucks coffee, Godiva chocolate, and Ben & Jerry's ice cream and frozen yogurt make the skies not just friendly, but delightful for United passengers.

United to Help Communities

Becoming their own bosses helped increase the dedication of United employees to improving the communities in which they live and serve. For example, they offered more than lip service to welfare reform, hiring more than 240 welfare recipients—94 of them in California—when the new reform program was launched in 1997.

United also makes contributions to charitable organizations in the area. The United Airlines Foundation was founded in 1952, first supporting the United Way and several smaller charitable organizations. That commitment has risen to take in more than 300 charitable groups around the globe, with some 2,000 United employees trained to serve as mentors to the world's youth. The company grants more than $4.6 million annually to endeavors such as Make-A-Wish, Habitat for Humanity, Inner-City Games, AIDS Memorial Quilt, and many national health organizations. By strengthening the education of the world's young, improving the quality of life in hometowns, and waging a worldwide battle against major health problems, employees help themselves and their neighbors.

This drive to make the world a better place also includes environmental concerns. United was one of the first airlines to establish corporatewide environmental standards and regulations. An integrated network of trained coordinators manages environmental issues at the local level, and the company's promotion of natural resource conservation means that many non-hazardous materials are widely recycled.

As an airline industry leader in quality service, an employee-owned business innovator, and a concerned corporate partner with the many communities in which it does business, United Airlines will continue making history for many years to come.

WYNDHAM CHECKERS HOTEL

n a city where the philosophy "bigger is better" reigns supreme, the Wyndham Checkers Hotel exemplifies the exception to the rule. By combining the stately elegance and amenities of a grand hotel with the intimacy of a private residence, the Wyndham Checkers has become an oasis amid the glass, concrete, and metal towers of Los Angeles. Wyndham Checkers was conceived with attention to detail and personalized service. With its exquisite furnishings that blend oriental and European antiques and contemporary California art, the 71-year-old hotel has the distinction of being the only small luxury hotel in the heart of downtown Los Angeles.

When it opened in December 1927 as the Mayflower Hotel, it was lauded as an enormous contribution to the city's blossoming business center. Today, the Wyndham Checkers is a world-class hotel and restaurant, and is one of the region's best-kept secrets among business professionals and Hollywood celebrities.

A Historic Monument

Although today's hotel is completely new on the inside, the exterior of the structure has maintained its original elaborate stonework facade: a modern Spanish-Moorish design, popular in Southern California in the 1920s. The hotel's authentic architecture and design make it a popular site for both Hollywood photo shoots and the film industry.

The hotel was completed in 1927 at a cost of $1 million, reaching the top of the era's 12-story height limit for downtown buildings. All of its original 348 rooms faced outside. After the Great Depression, the hotel passed through several owners, eventually becoming part of the Hilton chain in the early 1950s; it was then purchased by William A. Mallet and Monte L. Mallet, who operated it until May 1985, when it was sold to 535 South Grand Associates.

The hotel was then closed for a $49 million renovation. The number of rooms was reduced from 348 to 188, and only the exterior facade and columns were retained. It was reopened in 1989 as the Checkers Hotel, and, since April 1994, it has been known as the Wyndham Checkers Hotel under the management of Wyndham Hotels & Resorts.

Award-Winning Service

The Wyndham Checkers offers guests a wide choice of elegantly appointed rooms, including two penthouse suites. Each room, styled in ornate, 18th-century furnishings, offers complimentary coffee, three telephones, voice mail with two-line phone and fax capability, cotton robes, a minibar, a hair dryer, and an oversized marble writing table.

In addition, there is 24-hour concierge service, daily newspapers, and complimentary morning limousine service to downtown businesses. Guests may choose to use in-room irons and ironing boards or same-day professional laundry and dry-cleaning services.

A mezzanine level, with meeting rooms, executive offices, and a library, is designed to appeal to business travelers. The hotel's state-of-the-art rooftop spa, with a breathtaking view of downtown's skyscrapers, has a glass-fronted gym, saunas and locker rooms, an outdoor Jacuzzi, and a spa pool. Joggers are provided bottled Evian water and a terry towel by the doorman upon their return from exercise.

It is the hotel's policy to call guests five minutes after their arrival to confirm that they have found everything in top condition. "We find that if the first 15 minutes is a good experience for our guests, the rest of their stay goes swimmingly," says Joseph Mottershead, the hotel's general manager.

Although today's Wyndham Checkers Hotel is completely new on the inside, the exterior of the structure has maintained its original elaborate stonework facade: a modern Spanish-Moorish design, popular in Southern California in the 1920s (left).

With exquisite furnishings that blend oriental and European antiques and contemporary California art, the 71-year-old hotel has the distinction of being the only small luxury hotel in the heart of downtown Los Angeles (right).

The service and quiet elegance that the Wyndham Checkers extends to its guests has earned it AAA's four diamond award for 10 consecutive years.

A Place Where Everyone Knows Your Name

Because of its intimate, boutique style of hotel service, the Wyndham Checkers boasts a 40 percent repeat clientele. "Guests know how our hotel operates. They know our staff, and our staff knows them. It's a hotel where everyone knows your name, a major point of difference that larger hotels can't achieve," says Mottershead.

The hotel offers such personalized service to its guests that when the top brass of a company asks where to stay in downtown Los Angeles, the Wyndham Checkers is the answer. Presidents Richard Nixon and Jimmy Carter, as well as the former Soviet Union's head of state Mikhail Gorbachev, were regular guests of the hotel.

In the heart of Los Angeles' financial district, the Wyndham Checkers Hotel is within easy walking distance of leading economic centers, including the Pacific Stock Exchange, California Plaza, and Wells Fargo Center. Close by are some of the city's most prominent cultural landmarks, such as the Dorothy Chandler Pavilion, Ahmanson Theater, and Museum of Contemporary Art.

Tradition of Great Chefs

Nominated as chef of the year in 1995 by the California Restaurant Writers Association, Chef Tony Hodges is the latest in a long line of world-class chefs at the hotel's Checkers Restaurant, a posh, quiet dining room divided into intimate areas separated by columns and rose marble ledges.

Hodges' trademark is vertical dishes. "I believe that food should be as pleasing to the eye as to the palate," he says. As a result, his culinary towers complement the finely appointed tables. Besides adding a visual element to the restaurant's dishes, Hodges, who became Checkers' chef in fall 1997 after leaving West Hollywood's

Diaghilev Restaurant, has added a "martini and caviar" theme to the hotel's intimate cocktail lounge.

Recently named to *Gourmet* magazine's list of leading Los Angeles restaurants, Checkers Restaurant is open for breakfast, the ever important power lunch, and dinner. It is a favorite of Music Center patrons, with its pre-theater menu and complimentary round-trip limousine service to the Music Center.

Known for its grand style and sterling service, the Wyndham Checkers is recognized today by the Los Angeles Conservancy as a historic-cultural monument—further testament to the hotel's honored presence in the City of Angels.

Clockwise from top:
The hotel's state-of-the-art rooftop spa, with a breathtaking view of downtown's skyscrapers, has a glass-fronted gym, saunas and locker rooms, an outdoor Jacuzzi, and a spa pool.

The Wyndham Checkers offers guests a wide choice of elegantly appointed rooms, including two penthouse suites. Each room, styled in ornate, 18th-century furnishings, offers complimentary coffee, three telephones, voice mail with two-line phone and fax capability, cotton robes, a minibar, a hair dryer, and an oversized marble writing table.

Recently named to *Gourmet* magazine's list of leading Los Angeles restaurants, Checkers Restaurant is open for breakfast, the ever important power lunch, and dinner. Here, Chef Tony Hodges serves Joseph Mottershead, general manager of the hotel, one of his trademark vertical dishes.

I t is the most recognized airport in the world—and not simply because more than 200,000 passengers pass through its gates each day. The domed Theme Building at Los Angeles International Airport, bathed in a constantly changing, multihued palette of electric color, symbolizes the city it serves—a growing powerhouse at the crossroads of a global economy. ⬇ Flights began taking off from the runways of Los Angeles International Airport in 1928, and commercial aviation was launched in December 1946. At that time, five airlines served

only a million travelers and carried several hundred thousands of pounds of cargo each year. But, foreseeing the importance of air travel to its mobile and growing population, the City of Los Angeles established the Board of Airport Commissioners as a vital part of its charter to oversee the development of the city. The commissioners oversee a city department that is now known as Los Angeles World Airports (LAWA), which is responsible to the mayor, the city council, and, ultimately, the people of Los Angeles.

Today, Los Angeles International Airport is the linchpin in a system of airports that serve more than 66 million passengers each year, span Southern California, and include Ontario International, Van Nuys Airport, and Palmdale Regional Airport. Los Angeles International, the largest of the airports, is known worldwide simply as LAX. Like the region it serves, LAX has seen tremendous growth over the last 50 years, with passenger activity tripling since 1970. LAX is the second-busiest air cargo airport in the world, carrying 2.1 million tons a year and 25 percent of the nation's airborne trade with

Pacific Rim countries. All of this pales in comparison to the growth projected for 2020, when 94 million people are expected to travel through LAX. Air cargo will grow even faster, and is expected to reach 4.2 million tons of cargo each year.

Ontario International serves the fastest-growing region in Southern California. With two new terminals recently put on-line after a $270 million expansion project,

Ontario International expects to serve 10 million passengers each year. Ontario is likely to be the region's second most important airport by 2020, when it is projected to serve 15.3 million passengers a year.

Located in the San Fernando Valley, Van Nuys Airport, the nation's leader in general aviation, serves law enforcement agencies, air ambulance firms, and private and corporate travelers. Palmdale Regional Airport, an important asset for future passenger and air cargo service, is located 35 miles north of downtown Los Angeles. LAWA is seeking to establish passenger service at the airport to support regional needs.

Although a municipal department, LAWA operates as a proprietary agency, with 2,300 employees and $2.4 billion in assets. LAWA serves a five-county region that is home to 15 million diverse, active people. It contributes nearly $50 billion to the nation's economy and makes it possible for Los Angeles to be the largest international trading center in the United States, with more than $186 billion in global trade.

A Vital Link

LAX is the gateway to the Southland, which has the 12th-largest economy in the world. Air transportation is the region's second-largest industry, and LAX directly contributes $43.5 billion and 393,000 jobs into the Southland's economy every year. Passen-

Los Angeles International Airport served more than 61 million travelers and 2.1 million tons of air cargo in 1998. Officials predict the airport could serve 94 million passengers and handle 4.2 million tons of air cargo by 2020 (top).

The Los Angeles International Airport's unique Theme Building is one of the city's most recognizable landmarks (bottom).

gers at LAX fly on 112 airlines to U.S. destinations and more than 100 cities around the world, and 19 Asia-Pacific airlines recognized LAX as the premier entrance to the United States in 1998.

By the early 1990s, LAWA recognized that the airport system needed to expand its capacity to support the future economic role of the region. Decision makers determined that a key component in maintaining the infrastructure of the region as a global trading center would be the modernization and expansion of LAX.

A master plan for LAX calls for the investment of $8 billion to $12 billion. This infusion of funds will enhance airfield, passenger, and cargo capacity, with new runways and new terminals; add 2 million square feet of new and redeveloped air cargo space; and expand areas for U.S. Customs, inspections, and retail concessions. In addition, a limited-access ring road connecting the nearby freeways to terminals will greatly improve ground transportation and alleviate noise and pollution. The project will create 367,000

new jobs and generate an additional $37 billion for the economy.

Even with all the growth, LAWA has taken into consideration the airport's neighbors. Environmental mitigation is addressed in the master plan—from noise, traffic, and air quality to community beautification—and the expected growth will be accomplished with minimal expansion from the 3,600 acres on which LAX sits today. In addition, more than 9,000 homes closest to LAX and Ontario airports are receiving free soundproofing to reduce noise. The LAWA system has assumed the lead in reducing emissions by converting its fleet to alternative fuels, and the use of reclaimed wastewater has led to improved landscaping. These efforts have won the airports many local and national awards, including the Coalition for Clean Air's 1995 Clean Air Award.

A Global Marketplace

With all these changes, LAWA has not forgotten the basics: With so many passengers spending leisure time at airports,

the shops, restaurants, and concessions inside the terminals have taken on more importance. In 1994, LAWA adopted a concessions plan, committed to offering high-quality products, innovative retail shops, and diverse cuisine to air travelers. With the new program, the airport has increased sales from all concessions to $175 million in 1998.

In addition to quality passenger service, LAX enjoys an excellent reputation among shippers. Its customers in Asia voted LAX as the Best Cargo Airport in North America for the fifth straight year and voted LAX as the Best Terminal Operator in North America for the first time. The results are from the industry trade magazine *Cargonews Asia*, which conducted a poll of 13,000 air cargo managers and freight forwarders in 12 countries.

From its plans for major growth, carefully plotted to be sensitive to the environment, to its commitment to provide world-class air cargo service as well as comfort and convenience to every passenger, Los Angeles World Airports is truly a servant of the people who own it—the people of Los Angeles.

Clockwise from top:
The Tom Bradley International Terminal at LAX serves almost 8 million travelers annually and is home to a majority of the airport's foreign flag carriers.

Los Angeles World Airports increased the capacity of Ontario International Airport to 10 million passengers annually when it completed two new terminals in 1998 at a cost of $270 million.

Air cargo shipments attract more than $70 billion in imports and exports through Los Angeles annually.

STATE FARM
INSURANCE COMPANIES

In three quarters of a century, State Farm Insurance Companies has grown from a small farm mutual auto insurer to one of the world's largest financial institutions. But despite its growth, State Farm's original underlying philosophy has remained unchanged: insurance coverage at a fair price, coupled with fair claim settlement. The company's mission is reflected in its logo: "Like a good neighbor, State Farm is there." State Farm is the leading insurer of homes in the United States, and is also the

nation's largest auto insurer, with one out of every five cars on the road today covered by the company. In addition, State Farm is the nation's number one insurer of pleasure boats, with one of every 12 registered in the United States covered by the company.

"But our policyholders measure us not by our size," states Edward B. Rust Jr., president of State Farm Insurance Companies, "but by the personal, quality, one-on-one service we provide. Superior service is what sets us apart."

Rooted in Service

State Farm Insurance was the brainchild of George J. Mecherle, a farmer of 20 years who turned to selling insurance after moving to Bloomington, Illinois, due to his wife's failing health. As he began selling auto insurance, Mecherle suggested to his employer the idea of creating a rate system that would suit the needs of farmers, who drove less than people living in cities. When the idea was rejected, he left the company, and in 1922, started State Farm

as a mutual automobile insurance company owned by its policyholders.

By 1928, Mecherle, who served as president of State Farm Insurance until 1937, decided to decentralize the burgeoning firm. With a handful of employees from the Bloomington office and a few new hires, State Farm established its first branch office in Berkeley, California.

The original Berkeley office served all of California, including Los Angeles and the surrounding counties, until 1955, when State Farm opened additional offices in Orange County to serve the Southern California area. The tremendous growth in this area in the mid-1950s to mid-1960s led the company to split the Orange County office. In 1969, the company built offices in the

Clockwise from top:
One of State Farm Insurance Companies' 28 regional offices, the Westlake Village location services five metro counties in Southern California.

A State Farm volunteer teaches children the importance of calling 911.

State Farm associates volunteered more than 3,500 hours in 1998, participating in many different programs that give back to the Southland.

valley region of Los Angeles County. Today, the Westlake office is headquarters to the South Coast Region, which serves clients in Los Angeles, Orange, Riverside, San Bernardino, and parts of Ventura counties. All regional offices in California are overseen by an executive team led by Greg Jones, vice president of State Farm California.

Today, State Farm Companies has grown to 28 regional offices and more than 1,000 claim service centers across the nation, and has 69,000 employees and nearly 17,000 agents servicing 66.3 million policies in the United States and Canada. On average, the company pays more than $60 million on more than 35,000 claims every day.

The cornerstone of State Farm's success is a marketing partnership. State Farm agents are independent contractors who sell only State Farm products: automobile, health, property, home, and life insurance. In return, State Farm markets its products only through the State Farm agency force.

A Good Neighbor

State Farm was built on face-to-face service. Even though the firm today has more than 66 million policies, this tradition still sets it apart from other companies. More than a slogan, the firm's "like a good neighbor" commitment has meant being there when and where the firm is needed.

For instance, within 48 hours after the 1994 Northridge earthquake—the most financially devastating natural disaster the Los Angeles region has ever experienced— 600 State Farm employees from across the United States and Canada joined the local staff. Five mobile catastrophe offices handled more than 3,000 phone calls in the first two days of operation. Two months after the earthquake, the number of State Farm

employees still helping policyholders exceeded 1,600. More than 1,000 agents exclusively handled claims. By the time the dust settled, the firm's Corporate Call Center had received a total of 24,000 calls.

An Involved Citizen

Dedicated to supporting the communities it serves, State Farm's employees and agents from the five-county region pride themselves on participating in many different programs that give back to the Southland. These

programs include ones that donate goods to homeless shelters, beautify neighborhoods, work with local police departments on community events, and raise funds for nonprofit groups.

Whether by ensuring financial security or supporting charitable organizations, for more than 70 years, State Farm has displayed its commitment to being a good neighbor. Carrying on that commitment, the company stands ready to serve the Southland community into the next century.

Environmental Lighting for Architecture, Inc.

When hotels, restaurants, office buildings, municipalities, and residences need beautiful and unusual lighting fixtures and the highest-quality ambient lighting, the company they often turn to is Environmental Lighting for Architecture, Inc. (ELA). Established in Los Angeles in 1929, the company has earned a glowing reputation for its fine craftsmanship and ability to design and manufacture lighting in any style and any size. ▼ Originally

Established in Los Angeles in 1929, Environmental Lighting for Architecture, Inc. (ELA) has earned a glowing reputation for its fine craftsmanship and ability to design and manufacture lighting in any style and any size. Examples of ELA's work can be found all over Los Angeles, and include (clockwise from left) Home Savings of America Tower, MTA Gateway Plaza, and Ernest Borgnine's residence.

called the Hollywood Lighting Fixture Company, the company was founded by a small group of craftsmen who saw an opportunity to design custom lighting fixtures for Los Angeles' burgeoning film industry. They made their mark by being versatile, designing and manufacturing fixtures that reflected diverse architectural styles, such as art deco, western, and Victorian, and that enhanced the particular look of each movie set.

The company began creating residential fixtures at the request of a number of film stars and producers who admired the set lighting. One of the memorable periods in the company's history was when Alfred Hitchcock commissioned the business to design lighting for his home. Hitchcock often visited the Hollywood Lighting factory to oversee the work on his fixtures. In fact, company legend has it that he had to practically be dragged

out of the factory at the end of many workdays.

Lighting Up the Los Angeles Area

"We see examples of our work all over Los Angeles," says Elsie Dahlin, president of Environmental Lighting, whose craftsmanship is on display throughout the city— in the mayor's office, Pasadena Library, and Beverly Hills Hotel; in historic build-

Los Angeles Central Library, west lawn (left)
California State Capitol senate chamber (right)

ings on the UCLA campus; and in office complexes up and down the Wilshire Boulevard corridor. In addition, the company has created decorative street lighting for such nearby cities as West Covina and Anaheim, and fixtures from the company's residential line also light up homes and condominiums from Hollywood Hills to Beverly Hills to Malibu.

Decades of the company's glamorous work is still on display at its manufacturing plant and headquarters in City of Industry, where the firm relocated in 1982. There, fixture renderings drawn in the 1930s adorn the walls and thousands of decorative castings are on display, as are photographs of some of the company's most impressive work.

From Los Angeles to the World

In the years between its founding and the 1950s, Hollywood Lighting was sought out to manufacture lighting for commercial buildings by both architects and the city's growing hospitality industry. Soon, the company was creating chandeliers, wall sconces, and architectural lighting for office buildings, hotels, and other large commercial projects in Los Angeles. Many contractors chose Hollywood Lighting because its fixtures were very similar to those manufactured in Europe, but were much more accessible since they were produced locally.

Emerging markets provided opportunity for expansion. Hotels and casinos began sprouting up in the desert town of Las Vegas, and there was not a facility in those years where ELA's work was not dominant. The gaming industry expanded to Atlantic City, for which the company constructed its largest fixture, measuring 186 feet in length.

In the 1970s, Custom and Architectural Lighting, as Hollywood Lighting was then called, was merged with another Los Angeles-based quality lighting manufacturer, Environmental Lighting for Architecture. The ELA name was retained, as it depicted both future challenges and the dramatic increase in lighting services being provided, including historic restoration and replication such as that seen in the lighting of the California State Capitol and San Francisco Palace. Just as it adapted in the past 40 years to meet demands environmentally and in lighting, now with combined capabilities, the company continued to expand its business to meet new global demands.

As international markets opened in the 1980s to American lighting manufacturers, ELA took advantage. Now, the company has completed work for several prominent projects in such countries as Japan, Indonesia, China, Singapore, Saudi Arabia, Venezuela, Australia, and Canada. The company also participated in the manufacture of creative lighting for well-known theme parks in France and Tokyo.

Meeting New Challenges at Home

While Environmental Lighting's business began to thrive abroad, the company faced some unique challenges at home. As concern in Los Angeles grew over air and water quality, manufacturers were asked to help clean up the environment. In response, Environmental Lighting committed itself to addressing ecological concerns, investing extensively to perfect techniques for creating and finishing its products in a way that would decrease the emissions of particles into the air and contaminants into the water.

While the company completely changed the techniques that it had de-

veloped and perfected over decades of experimentation, it hasn't stopped creating the same look and quality that has been Environmental Lighting's trademark for some seven decades. And regardless of the changes the future might bring, the company intends to remain on the vanguard of architectural lighting, increase its international presence, and continue its leadership in creating ecology-friendly products for many years to come.

Clockwise from top left:
The Palace Hotel, Beverly Hills Hotel, and
MTA headquarters building

merican Airlines has long considered Los Angeles to be one of its homes away from home. Since American began serving Los Angeles on October 15, 1930, the relationship between the company and the city has grown and flourished. American currently employs more than 3,600 people in the Los Angeles area and offers more nonstop flights to the East Coast than any other airline. Just four years prior to American's arrival in Los Angeles, Charles A. Lindbergh took off from Chicago for

St. Louis with a single bag of mail, thus inaugurating the first regularly scheduled flight for what would later become American Airlines. Lindbergh was the chief pilot for Robertson Aircraft Corporation of Missouri, one of nearly 80 companies that merged in 1934 to become American Airlines. In the decades since that merger, American has faced and met the challenges of the ever changing airline industry and become a global leader in the process.

Originally headquartered in New York, American moved to the Dallas/Fort Worth area in 1979, and began developing its first hub at Dallas/Fort Worth International Airport two years later. In the years following the 1978 deregulation of the U.S. airline industry, American expanded greatly. Today, the airline and its regional partner American Eagle operate a fleet of more than 850 aircraft, employ more than 102,000 people, serve nearly 300 markets, and complete more than 4,000 daily flights throughout the world. On an average day, American handles 291,000 pieces of luggage, receives 354,000 reservation calls, and serves 194,000 in-flight meals and snacks.

An Industry Pioneer

Throughout its years of service, American has consistently led the industry with its innovative ideas and programs. In 1933, American was the first to introduce flight attendants. The following year, American originated an air traffic control system later adopted by all airlines and administered by the U.S. government. A mid-1930s collabo-

American Airlines began serving Los Angeles on October 15, 1930, and now offers more nonstop flights to the East Coast than any other airline. American has consistently led the industry with its innovative ideas and programs. In 1933, American was the first to introduce flight attendants.

ration with the Douglas Aircraft Company resulted in the development of the DC-3, one of the most famous commercial airplanes ever built. By 1937, the airline had celebrated carrying its 1 millionth passenger.

In 1953, American flew the first nonstop transcontinental route from Los Angeles to New York with the Douglas DC-7, and six years later, it was the first to upgrade this same route with the much faster Boeing 707. As those jets came on-line, American also introduced SABRE, the world's first computer reservations system, which today is used by thousands of travel agents in more than 70 countries.

By 1981, American had developed the AAdvantage Frequent Flyer Program, which marked a revolutionary new way to

attract and retain customers, and in 1992, American opened the Alliance Maintenance and Engineering Base, which was the first state-of-the-art airline maintenance facility to be built in the United States in more than 20 years.

A Promising Future

American's pioneering tradition continues as it charts new courses in Internet technology. As of 1996, customers could book travel on-line via American's AAccess page and by the following year, more than 1 million customers were receiving E-mail notices of discount fares through the NetSAAver program.

In addition, American is focused on expanding the breadth and depth of its

international network. At the beginning of 1998, the airline received permission to begin additional service to Japan, thereby strengthening American's presence in the Pacific Rim. American has also announced, and in some cases finalized, several code-sharing partnerships with Latin American carriers that will considerably enhance the airline's international system.

A large part of American's long-range plans revolves around its 20-year partnership with Boeing. In 1998, American began acquiring several new 767s, and a year later, added super-long-range 777s to its fleet. By 2002, American will have added more than 150 new aircraft to its system,

ensuring that the airline will continue to operate the youngest and most advanced fleet in the industry.

Serving the Community

An important part of American's leadership strategy is a strong commitment to the community. Throughout its history in the Los Angeles area, American has supported its employees and customers by being an active participant in several worthwhile causes and programs, including the Cystic Fibrosis Foundation, Los Angeles Philharmonic, Susan G. Komen Foundation, United Negro College Fund, and Universal Amphitheater. In addition to sponsoring

the Los Angeles Marathon, American has also been involved in the football and basketball programs for the University of Southern California and the University of California-Los Angeles.

Over the years, American has made it a priority to participate in programs that positively affect citizens and neighbors in every community it serves, proving that American strives to be something special in the air and on the ground. From the days of Lindbergh's mail route to today's increasingly global and technologically driven industry, one trend is clear: American has been, and will continue to be, a leader in its field.

One of the oldest and most respected purveyors of news and entertainment in the country, CBS2 (KCBS-TV) is a leader in local and national television programming. Reaching more than 15 million viewers in five counties, CBS2 delivers a balance of news, entertainment, sports, and special programming that is vital to a community as diverse as Metropolitan Los Angeles. CBS2 News is recognized locally and nationally for the quality and

substance of its coverage and for its on-air talent. Weeknight anchors Ann Martin and Michael Tuck have been an established presence in the Southern California market for more than 30 years collectively. Morning and noon news anchors Tritia Toyota and Paul Dandridge also enjoy a reputation as respected TV journalists, with a combined local on-air history spanning three decades. Linda Alvarez and Larry Carroll, co-anchors of *CBS2 News* at 5 p.m., are another highly recognizable pair of veterans, while newer additions to the talent roster include weekend evening anchors Gretchen Carr and Jonathan Elias.

Commitment to News Coverage

Broadcasting more than 30 hours of live local news and sports weekly, CBS2 has taken a leadership role in the community it serves, becoming a role model for its commitment to in-depth news coverage of issues that affect a wide audience. Addressing substantive issues that affect people's everyday lives, CBS2 News is the home of *Special Assignment*, a unique investigative reporting unit created in 1996 that has generated major consumer and legislative changes throughout Southern California and the state.

Special Assignment began largely because the station recognized that complex issues, especially in a market the size of Metropolitan Los Angeles, are best addressed by a thorough probe of key issues. Such hard-hitting reporting has uncovered issues like unsanitary restaurant conditions, phony doctors, car repair rip-offs, and a driver's license scam at the Department of Motor Vehicles. All of these reports resulted in prompt legislative action that improved the quality of life for Southern Californians.

What's Right: Good News

CBS2 News is the only station in the market to air the innovative *What's Right with Southern California*. The show is a campaign designed to highlight the positive achievements of ordinary citizens throughout Los Angeles' many diverse communities and cultures.

Weeknight anchors Ann Martin and Michael Tuck have been an established presence in the Southern California market for more than 30 years collectively.

As a growing part of its community affairs effort, the station annually honors 12 individuals who come from all walks of life and who personify the spirit of giving back to their community. These honorees are the focus of a 90-minute, prime-time special, on which they receive the CBS Annual What's Right with Southern California Community Service Award. The awards program has attracted the participation of many noted dignitaries and celebrities, including Hillary Rodham Clinton, Rob and Carl Reiner, Dan Rather, and CBS stars Della Reese and Candice Bergen.

Throughout the year, CBS2 also airs special *What's Right* programs that reinforce its long-standing interest in being a good corporate and community citizen. Recent programs have included Earthfest, an environmental celebration; the station's annual toy drive for needy children; an extensive behind-the-scenes look at the Getty Center, the region's newest art museum; and a multipart series on the Southland's financial rebound that focused on the economic boom throughout many Southern California industries.

Sports Central

Local and national sports are also a high priority at CBS2. The station's unique, two-hour weekend show, *Sports Central*, provides viewers with a comprehensive roundup of all of the major athletic events going on throughout the Southland. Hosted by sports anchor Jim Hill and longtime sportscaster Bret Lewis, the show covers everything from high school baseball to professional football. And with the return of the National Football League to CBS in 1998, the station is dedicated to using its *Sports Central* program as a vehicle to provide greatly expanded pre- and postgame commentary.

Origins of a TV Giant

Located on famed Sunset Boulevard in Hollywood, CBS2 is steeped in television history. The station was established at Columbia Broadcasting Company's historic Columbia Square in 1931 by Don Lee, Inc., which constructed all-electrical television equipment and succeeded in transmitting an image credited with being the official start of television in Los Angeles. The station first went on the air on December 23, 1931, providing one hour of programming six days a week. Because there were only five TV sets in Los Angeles that could receive a transmission, the station gave free demonstrations at the studio every day on how to operate televisions.

The station is known for many other broadcasting firsts. In 1933, it aired *The Crooked Circle*, the first full-length movie on television. That same month, in covering the Long Beach earthquake, it was first to broadcast rapid process film. TV's first soap opera debuted on CBS Channel 2 in 1938, and in 1940, the station aired the first live broadcast west of New York City with the celebrated Tournament of Roses Parade from Pasadena.

During World War II, the station's broadcasts were limited to civil defense bulletins and the promotion of war bond sales. The end of World War II signaled the beginning of the television boom—the number of TV sets in Los Angeles jumped from 400 in 1946 to 300,000 in 1950—allowing the station to grow dramatically. And in May 1948, the station gained full commercial status, taking the call letters KTSL-TV. In January 1951, Columbia Broadcasting System bought the station and changed the name to KNXT to emphasize the station's affiliation with CBS radio station KNX—which is still housed in the same building on Sunset Boulevard. To celebrate

CBS2 News is the home of *Special Assignment*, a unique investigative reporting unit created in 1996 that has generated major consumer and legislative changes throughout Southern California and the state.

The station's unique, two-hour weekend show, *Sports Central*, provides viewers with a comprehensive roundup of all the major athletic events going on throughout the Southland.

Clockwise from top left:
Anchor Ann Martin reported from England during Princess Diana's funeral.

I-Team reporter Joel Grover (right), conducted an interview for the investigation "Dirty Mechanics."

CBS2 News' reporters covered the disastrous effects of El Niño.

CBS2 News was on the scene for the opening of the J. Paul Getty Museum.

the CBS acquisition, entertainer Steve Allen hosted a 12-hour, live program, which included a live football game and a performance by famed actor Sir Lawrence Olivier.

As KNXT, the station continued to break new ground: *Panorama Pacific*, a live, two-hour talk series, established morning programming; *Ralph Story's Los Angeles* was the model for today's magazine shows; and years later, *2 on the Town* became the first local magazine series. In the early 1970s, the station also pioneered local public affairs programming with weekly shows, such as *Newsmakers* and *The Siesta is Over*. Hosted by Bob Navarro, *The Siesta is Over* was the first show in the United States to exclusively examine Latino issues. Navarro is now host of CBS2's Sunday morning public affairs program called *Bob Navarro's Journal*.

As the station has grown, its biggest contribution to Southern California's airwaves has been expanding local news programming. In 1960, KNXT created the country's first hour-long local news program, which expanded to two-and-a-half hours in 1976. In 1980, the station expanded its local magazine series *2 On The Town* to five nights a week, becoming the first network-owned and locally produced broadcast of its kind in the nation. KNXT also was a pioneer in switching from film to videotape, providing unprecedented on-the-scene news coverage.

Today, CBS2 is the second-largest CBS-owned and -operated affiliate in the United States, serving more than 15 million residents in Los Angeles, Orange, San Bernardino, Ventura, and Riverside counties. CBS2 airs news, entertainment, and community affairs programs 24 hours a day.

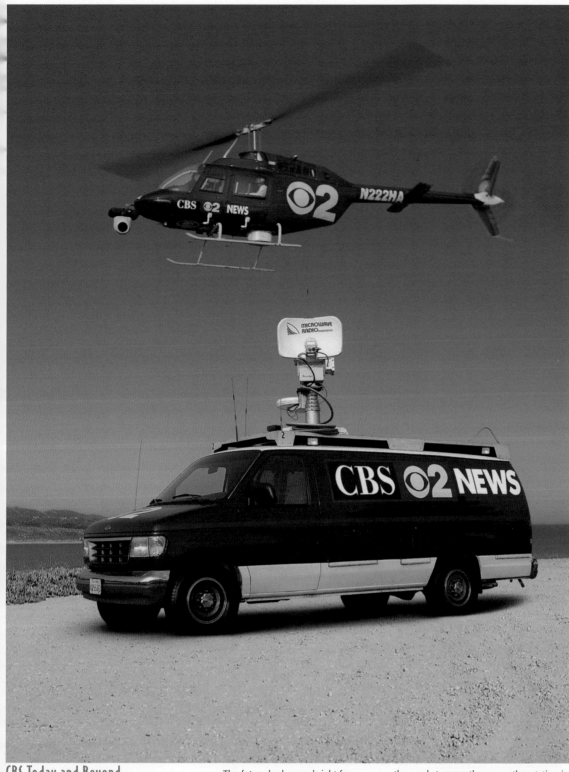

CBS2 News uses Chopper 2 and mobile vans to report live from the scene when news is breaking.

CBS Today and Beyond

The network boasts being home to several highly celebrated network shows. On the air for more than 20 years, *60 Minutes* is still among the highest-rated programs every week. Meanwhile, other shows that have strong household name recognition continue to flourish: *Late Night with David Letterman, Cosby, Candid Camera, Chicago Hope, Touched by an Angel,* and *Kids Say the Darndest Things.* Recent additions to the CBS2 afternoon lineup include a 1990s version of the popular *Hollywood Squares* and the *Match Game.*

The future looks very bright for CBS2. The station is carving a niche that has given it a distinctive look. With the advances of technology and new media, the station is the most comprehensive and interactive of any in the market. While offering enhanced coverage of broadcast stories, CBS's local Web site Channel 2000 (www.channel2000.com) generates fresh stories and provides a rapid-view response to all questions related to programs that the station airs.

CBS2 also has the unique advantage of having nine CBS sister radio stations in the market—more than any other station in Southern California and any other CBS affiliate in the country. This affords CBS2 much greater opportunity for visibility and synergy in disseminating timely information. With the advent of digital television, CBS2 is poised to be a leader in providing the most-advanced newscasts and programming available.

With its long and colorful history and a future that promises further innovations in the field of television, CBS Channel 2 continues to provide exciting broadcasting that puts the needs of its viewers first.

he surging demand of entertainment, business networking, Internet access, mobile telephony, and development of communications infrastructure has led businesses and consumers everywhere to turn to satellite and wireless technologies. Hughes Electronics Corporation is the market leader in four major industry segments that supply this demand—satellite manufacturing, satellite distribution services, telecommunications networks, and satellite television broadcast directly to the consumer.

Hughes Electronics was formed when General Motors acquired Hughes Aircraft Company from the Howard Hughes Medical Institute in 1985. Hughes Electronics now comprises Hughes Space and Communications Company, Hughes Network Systems, Inc., DIRECTV Global, and PanAmSat Corporation.

A Leader in Satellite Communications

In 1963, Hughes launched Syncom, the world's first geosynchronous communications satellite, a development that was to revolutionize communications worldwide. As satellite-borne information has become more common, Hughes' long history in the field has made it a natural leader in bringing satellite communication into homes and offices worldwide. From high above earth, satellites can relay signals to one-third of the globe. And unlike ground-based communications systems, there are no geographic barriers that impede the flow of information.

In the 35 years since Syncom was launched, Hughes has continued to improve satellite communication and make it accessible to more and more people. Today, Hughes Space and Communications Company, the recognized leader in the field of satellite technology and service, has built more than 131 communications satellites—some 40 percent of all active commercial communications satellites. The commercial communications satellites routinely relay digital communications, telephone calls, video conferences, television news reports, facsimiles, television programming, mobile communications, and direct-to-home entertainment—truly global communications.

Hughes Network Systems builds satellite-based communications networks and rural telephone systems worldwide using very small aperture terminals. It also provides wireless local loop telephone systems and mobile and PCS (personal communication system) cellular phone systems, as well as telecommunications equipment, satellite ground-based equipment, and subscriber equipment for reception of Hughes' digital direct-to-home television service, DIRECTV®.

Hughes' DIRECTV was launched in June 1994 and, with more than 4 million subscribers worldwide four years later, quickly became the leading satellite digital direct-to-home television service. DIRECTV is now in one of every 28 homes in the United States. DIRECTV, through an 18-inch satellite dish, beams 185 channels of programming to the United States, and is also

Broadcast operations supervisors monitor quality and continuity of signals for DIRECTV service to Latin America and the Caribbean, which originate from this broadcast operations control room in the California Broadcast Center in Long Beach.

PanAmSat Corporation's fleet of satellites, like this model built by Hughes Space and Communications Company, provides unparalleled satellite services worldwide. On any given day, PanAmSat satellites beam hundreds of television channels, thousands of data circuits, and billions of bits of digital information around the world for hundreds of international customers as diverse as Wal-Mart of the United States and Doordarshan, India's national network. PanAmSat is 81 percent owned by Hughes Electronics.

available to Latin America and the Caribbean through Galaxy Latin America and to Japan through the DIRECTV Japan Service.

Through its 16-satellite global fleet, PanAmSat Corporation provides satellite services to hundreds of cable TV programmers, television broadcasters, and direct-to-home television services. Worldwide, PanAmSat's satellites provide telecommunications services and Internet access to carriers and businesses worldwide. PanAmSat is a leader in both established and emerging markets.

Hughes' DirecPC service allows lightning-fast connections to the Internet for PC users at home or at the office. DirecPC connects users to the Web at Turbo Internet™ speeds—up to 400 kbps.

DirecPC offers more than just rapid Internet access—it lets the user surf the Web, send files, link remote offices together, and even manipulate data at speeds unheard of before. Thanks to advanced satellite technology, DirecPC avoids crowded computer networks and outmoded telephone systems, instead taking to the sky to transmit information.

For consumers who want their DIRECTV and DirecPC services using one satellite dish, Hughes offers DirecDuo™. With a single, 21-inch, elliptical satellite dish, DirecDuo brings the Internet and other data to users' personal computers, and DIRECTV to their television sets.

Hughes believes the demand for low-cost advanced communications will

continue to grow worldwide. Hughes is leveraging the company's leadership in designing and building satellite and wireless systems into delivering innovative communications services to businesses and homes.

DirecDuo allows users to receive both DIRECTV direct-to-home satellite television and DirecPC high-speed Internet services through a single, 21-inch, elliptical receiving dish. DirecDuo serves as the first true convergence platform (above).

With nearly 600,000 square feet of manufacturing space, the Integrated Satellite Factory of Hughes Space and Communications Company in El Segundo is the largest in the world. The latest addition is the 63,000-cubic-foot, dual-capacity, thermal vacuum chamber. The door alone weighs 105 tons (left).

1940 - 1975

1940	Textron Aerospace Fasteners
1942	Capitol Records
1943	Providence Health System
1944	Park Labrea
1947	Daniel, Mann, Johnson, & Mendenhall
1948	Majestic Realty Co.
1949	McKinsey & Company, Inc.
1950	Virco Mfg. Corporation
1952	Allstate Insurance Company
1952	Alschuler Grossman Stein & Kahan LLP
1953	Litton Industries, Inc.
1955	Lockheed Martin IMS
1956	Mercury Air Group, Inc.
1964	Turner Construction Company
1966	Applause, Inc.
1966	Romac International
1969	Los Angeles Community Colleges
1970	George D. Bjurman & Associates
1971	Century 21 Real Estate Corporation
1972	ARCO
1972	Public Storage, Inc.
1972	Tutor-Saliba Corporation
1973	Marriott International
1973	The Seiniger Advertising Group
1974	KTI Corporation
1974	Westside Distributors
1975	Troop Steuber Pasich Reddick & Tobey, LLP

TEXTRON AEROSPACE FASTENERS

Textron Aerospace Fasteners (TAF) is the world's leading manufacturer of aerospace blind rivet systems and tooling for the aerospace industry. From commercial transports and military aircraft to business jets and helicopters to general aviation aircraft and missiles, TAF fastening products are used on nearly all of today's aircraft. ⚉ Textron Aerospace Fasteners is a division of Textron Inc. Traded on the New York Stock Exchange as TXT, Textron Inc. is a $10.5 billion,

global, multi-industry company with market-leading operations in aircraft, automotive, industrial, and finance.

An Illustrious History

The firm was founded originally in Los Angeles as the Cherry Rivet Company in 1940 by Carl Cherry. His first blind fastener designs were used extensively on many of the Allied military aircraft in World War II. In 1952, the company moved to the current Santa Ana facility. Since that time, the company—which was purchased by the Townsend Company in 1951 and by Textron in 1959—has grown to be the leader in the design, manufacture, and sale of blind fasteners. Blind fasteners are primarily used where fastening can only be achieved from one side of the structure. They are typically installed on exterior aircraft areas, such as leading edges, trailing edges, limited access areas, and close-out areas.

In 1995, Textron Inc. acquired Avdel, a fastener manufacturing company based in Welwyn Garden City, England. The next year, Textron Inc. consolidated the aerospace operations of its Cherry and Avdel divisions to form Textron Aerospace Fasteners. TAF now maintains more than 320,000 square feet at two sites, with the global headquarters located in nearby Santa Ana and sales offices located in England and Beijing.

TAF has grown to supply the global aerospace industry with high-quality, efficient, and cost-effective blind rivet fastening systems, installation tools, blind bolts, shear pins, and specialty fasteners. The Cherry® and Avdel® brand names are recognized and used worldwide in a variety of applications. These are provided in a wide variety of materials, including titanium, stainless steel, and composite nonmetallics. TAF's product development and manufacturing techniques utilize modern technology, including computerized product design and statistical process control, as well as work cells and single-purpose factories. Certified testing facilities and sophisticated metallurgical laboratories assure that TAF products meet customer performance requirements and industry specifications.

TAF's global sales force and distribution network provide strong support for customers, covering both original aircraft manufacturing and repair markets. The company's technical service team helps solve design and application problems, and provides solutions for all customers worldwide. Every member of this team is a highly trained service engineer.

With state-of-the-art materials and methods, strategic expansion within its industry, and continued growth and success, Textron Aerospace Fasteners is ever allying itself with its longtime guiding principle: meeting customer needs with innovation. TAF is uniquely positioned to serve its broad range of customers "anytime, anywhere around the world."

Clockwise from top:
Textron Aerospace Fasteners (TAF) is a leading supplier of aerospace fastening systems for aircraft transports.

Certified testing facilities and sophisticated metallurgical laboratories assure that TAF products meet aircraft industry certifications and performance requirements.

A TAF manufacturing work cell producing aerospace tooling components

Whether representing a multinational corporation, a Fortune 500 company, a major player in the entertainment industry, or an emerging start-up, Alschuler Grossman Stein & Kahan LLP ensures that each of its clients receives all the expertise, personal attention, and skill the Century City-based law firm has to offer. Nationally recognized for its dynamic style of advocacy in complex business and entertainment litigation and in commercial transactions,

ALSCHULER GROSSMAN STEIN & KAHAN LLP

the firm has a proven track record of producing effective and efficient results for its clients.

Founded in 1952, the firm added name partner Marshall B. Grossman in 1964. A former member of the California Coastal Commission, Grossman is a renowned litigator of complex business cases. Burt Pines served two four-year terms as city attorney for Los Angeles before coming to the firm as a name partner in 1981, and he remains of counsel to the firm during his appointment as Governor Gray Davis' judicial appointments secretary. The firm recently doubled its capacity to serve its clients by combining with the equally highly regarded lawyers of Stein & Kahan, led by entertainment litigator Stanton L. "Larry" Stein and commercial lawyer Robert L. Kahan. The firm's key practice areas include administrative law, business law,

business litigation, employment law, entertainment litigation, financial institutions law, franchise law, insurance law, intellectual property and high-technology law, international law, mergers and acquisitions, professional liability defense, real estate and land use law, and securities litigation.

A founding member of the Association of Commercial Lawyers International, the firm has established relationships with leading law firms nationally and globally, allowing it to effectively assist its clients throughout the United States and abroad.

Alschuler Grossman Stein & Kahan LLP provides strategic and hands-on legal advice, using the latest technology systems to maximize efficiency. The firm recruits from the top ranks of the nation's finest law schools, and selects its attorneys on the basis of academic excellence, personal integrity, and commitment to excellence.

The firm's commitment to excellence in the practice of law is mirrored by its commitment to its profession and community. Since 1981, the firm's Charitable Foundation has provided material support to a variety of worthy causes. The firm's attorneys have a long history of commitment to social, political, and philanthropic endeavors, and have held leadership positions in a broad range of professional organizations, including the American Bar Association, Los Angeles Area Chamber of Commerce, Association of Business Trial Lawyers, Century City Bar Association, and community legal service providers such as Public Counsel, Legal Aid of Los Angeles, and Bet Tzedek Legal Services.

Alschuler Grossman Stein & Kahan's firm commitment is to excellence in the practice of law and to the betterment of the community of which it is an integral part.

The lawyers of Alschuler Grossman Stein & Kahan LLP include (standing from left) Johnnie A. James, Burt Pines, Gwyn Quillen, Robert L. Kahan, Michael J. Brill, (seated, from left) Marshall B. Grossman, Dana N. Levitt, and Stanton L. "Larry" Stein.

In a town filled with icons and legends, Capitol Records' legendary Tower stands not only as a symbol for H-O-L-L-Y-W-O-O-D (whose letters are blinked in Morse code from the beacon atop the building), but also for innovation, excellence, and quality in every aspect of the music business. Newly renovated as part of the revitalization of Hollywood, Capitol Records Tower remains as vital today as it was upon its completion as the world's first round office building and the first Los Angeles high-rise with air-

conditioning in 1956. Multiplatinum albums from Capitol's established stars such as Bonnie Raitt, Paul McCartney, Bob Seger, Garth Brooks, and the Beastie Boys line the lobby, mingling with newly minted platinum albums from some of today's hottest new artists—Radiohead, Foo Fighters, Everclear, Meredith Brooks, and Marcy Playground. Of the five albums nominated for the Grammy's® 1997 Album of the Year, two were on Capitol, which had an amazing 18 nominations in all.

Capitol's wide array of artists includes acclaimed singer/songwriters Rosanne Cash, Robbie Robertson, John Hiatt, and Jeb Loy Nichols. New artists like Sean Lennon, son of legendary Beatle John Lennon, and groups such as the Dandy Warhols, Supergrass, and Bran Van 3000 are critics' favorites, poised for more mainstream breakthroughs. Capitol has also found gold and platinum for the silver screen with a recent foray into movie sound tracks for *Hope Floats, Clueless, Trainspotting, Good Will Hunting* (nominated for an Academy Award for Best Original Song and Score), and the four-time platinum *Romeo + Juliet*. With the just-formed Java Records—run by famed Grammy-winning producer and songwriter Glenn Ballard—housed on Capitol's 12th floor and the Beastie Boys' growing Grand Royal label, Capitol is assured of continuing its place as one of the most storied, successful, and independent-minded of all music labels.

Nothing Is Impossible

The extraordinary Capitol story began in 1942, when singer/songwriter Johnny Mercer, music store owner Glenn Wallichs, and executive movie producer B.G. "Buddy" DeSylva joined forces to create a new label to compete with the Big Three: Columbia, RCA Victor, and Decca. As Johnny Mercer put it in 1967, "We forged ahead with the undaunted enthusiasm of young men to whom nothing is impossible."

At first, with a wartime shortage of shellac and an industrywide musician's strike, the new venture looked hopeless— it was fortunate all three founders had day jobs to go back to. Mercer was one of the country's top composers, with four hits on the 1942 Hit Parade. DeSylva, who put

Newly renovated as part of the revitalization of Hollywood, Capitol Records Tower remains as vital today as it was upon its completion in 1956.

up the $10,000 seed money, was both a successful songwriter and an executive producer at Paramount Pictures. Wallichs was founder of the ahead-of-its-time Wallichs Music Store, located at the corner of Sunset and Vine. With DeSylva's show-biz savvy and talent contacts, Mercer's uncanny musical instincts and top songs, and Wallichs' ingenious ways of getting hits manufactured and distributed—in a time when distribution was controlled by the Big Three—Capitol, as the new label was named by Mercer's wife, Ginger, was founded by a very fortunate melding of talents. And the three founders never did get back to those day jobs.

With a prevailing mood of optimism, Capitol swiftly developed a roster that included Mercer, Nat King Cole, Peggy Lee, Benny Goodman, Les Paul and Mary Ford, and Kay Starr. In 1946, Capitol released the first Bozo the Clown album and promptly cornered the children's market for years to come. The firsts continued through the decade as Capitol, whose very survival depended on upsetting the status quo, became the first label to produce albums in all three speeds, the first to record on magnetic tape, the first to send DJs promotional copies of records, and the first to have world headquarters in Los Angeles, initiating the industry's growing emphasis on the West Coast. As a result, Capitol grew at an explosive rate. Sales in 1948 totaled nearly $18 million, compared to $195,000 just six years earlier. By the end of the 1940s, upstart Capitol had already been acknowledged as the industry trendsetter.

The Golden Fifties

The fifties for Capitol can be summed up with one word: golden. Between 1954 and 1958, annual sales more than tripled. In late 1955, Capitol had four out of five No. 1 hits. Les Paul and Mary Ford, Peggy Lee, Kay Starr, and Margaret Whiting topped the charts, along with new Capitol staples Tennessee Ernie Ford, Jackie Gleason, and Ray Anthony. Innovators in album cover design and in servicing records to retailers, Capitol now had the ability to attract world-class talent. In 1953, the company signed Frank Sinatra, who quickly became the label's signature artist, amassing nine Top 10 singles and 17 Top 10 albums (four gold) throughout the fifties, including *Come Dance with Me*, the Grammy 1959 Album of the Year. Sinatra, whose reascendance coincided with the birth of the long-playing record, made music of such strength and expressive power that the world stopped viewing popular singers as mere entertainers and began seeing them as artists.

Another Capitol artist began the decade on a personal note, with the birth of his daughter Natalie in February 1950. Soon after, Nat King Cole recorded "Unforgettable." Four decades later, Natalie Cole would overdub her part to turn this song into a unique Grammy-winning father-

daughter duet. In 1956, Cole landed his own TV series, the first major breakthrough for an African-American performer in the United States. In spite of 16 regional sponsors, the show never attracted a national sponsor, and Cole gave it up after 60 weeks. Still, music fans' love for Cole continued unabated. He compiled 14 Top 10 singles (two No. 1's) and five Top 10 albums before the decade was through.

A New Era

Capitol began the 1960s with trademark success from Cole, Sinatra, the Kingston Trio, Nancy Wilson, and Judy Garland's *Live from Carnegie Hall* album. Everything changed in late 1963, when Capitol released a single from four boys named John, Paul, George, and Ringo, known collectively as The Beatles. The single "I Want to Hold Your Hand" quickly hit No. 1. By April 1964, the Beatles owned the entire top five slots. By May, their singles had been number one for 14 straight weeks. Long considered to be the most influential

The extraordinary Capitol story began in 1942, when singer/songwriter Johnny Mercer (left), music store owner Glenn Wallichs, and executive movie producer B.G. "Buddy" DeSylva joined forces to create a new label.

group in the history of rock and roll, the Beatles released 16 gold albums and 19 gold singles in the 1960s. But more than that, the Beatles became role models, recasting America's social fabric, their ever changing music helping to define a decade of evolution, counterrevolution, assassination, and disillusionment.

Meanwhile, drawing on a creative well as deep as the nearby Pacific, Brian Wilson and the Beach Boys conceived musical innovations that would forever change the record-making process. The Beach Boys were the first group to make their own recording decisions, to write the majority of their material, to own their publishing rights, and to move out of the company's in-house recording studio. Fight-

In 1953, Capitol signed Frank Sinatra, who quickly became the label's signature artist, amassing nine Top 10 singles and 17 Top 10 albums (four gold) throughout the fifties. Other major stars for Capitol in the 1950s and 1960s were Judy Garland and Nat King Cole.

ing for these firsts took its toll on Wilson, who quit the music business in 1967, leaving behind what many of today's critics consider the most important pop music of our time, compiling an astounding 11 Top 10 albums and 13 Top 10 singles in a scant seven years on the label.

As the decade came to a close, Capitol saw success with artists as varied as Lou Rawls, the Lettermen, and Buck Owens, but it was five-time Grammy winner Glen Campbell (whose 35 pop/country crossover hits are matched only by Eddy Arnold, Elvis Presley, and Johnny Cash) who opened the door for singers like sometime partner Bobbie Gentry, a triple-Grammy winner in 1968 for her "Ode to Billy Joe." As sales topped the $100 million mark for the first time, Capitol celebrated its 25th anniversary in 1967 with an incred-ible 16 Grammys. "The best years are still ahead," the visionary Wallichs said at the anniversary party, his eye still firmly fixed on the future.

The Next Generation

One hundred days into the new decade, the Beatles, the biggest, most popular, and most prestigious act Capitol had ever had, called it quits. Luckily, Capitol's 1970

The Beach Boys compiled an astounding 11 Top 10 albums and 13 Top 10 singles in a scant seven years on the Capitol label (top left).

Long considered to be the most influential group in the history of rock and roll, the Beatles released 16 gold albums and 19 gold singles in the 1960s (bottom left).

Multiplatinum success stories for Capitol include Garth Brooks (top right) and Robbie Robertson (below). Bonnie Raitt's comeback hit, "Nick of Time," won three Grammys, including Album of the Year (bottom right).

roster included several future top sellers who would help offset the loss of the Fab Four: Bob Seger, the Steve Miller Band, Helen Reddy, Anne Murray, the Band, Linda Ronstadt, Merle Haggard, Natalie Cole, the Little River Band, Peabo Bryson, Grand Funk Railroad, and Pink Floyd, whose 1973 blockbuster, *The Dark Side of the Moon*, is the best-selling album in Capitol Records' history. By 1974, all four individual Beatles had become best-selling solo artists with their own No.1 hits. Surprisingly, the first to achieve this milestone was George Harrison, and the last was John Lennon.

The 1980s began with another tragic blow for the Capitol family, the death of John Lennon, whose talent and impact are still deeply felt today. On a more positive note, the multiplatinum success stories continued with Bob Seger and the Silver Bullet Band, Anne Murray, Juice Newton, Billy Squier, Duran Duran, and Tina Turner in the first half of the decade, while Heart, Poison, Iron Maiden, Great White, and M.C. Hammer were the big sellers in the second half.

Capitol in the 1990s

It is possible to pinpoint the exact date a recharged Capitol Records went into overdrive—February 21, 1990, when the 32nd annual Grammy Awards were presented. Bonnie Raitt's comeback hit, "Nick of

Time," won three Grammys at the event, including Album of the Year. Within six weeks, it was the best-selling album in the United States, and Raitt became, after 16 years in the business, an overnight, multiplatinum star. "Nick of Time" ushered in one of the most successful phases of Capitol's history, with Hammer bringing rap to unimagined heights, Megadeth continuing their still-going string of multi-platinum albums, and Garth Brooks becoming the best-selling solo recording artist of all time. Hammer, Raitt, and Brooks held the No. 1 spot on the pop album charts for a total of 32 weeks in 1990-1991. When *Billboard* published its Year in Music recap in December 1991, Capitol was the No. 2

label in pop album history, its highest year-end ranking since *Billboard* began keeping score in the early 1970s.

Capitol's legendary Blue Note jazz label is now home to Cassandra Wilson, Joe Lovano, Jacky Terrasson, and Charlie Hunter, some of the most critically lauded, musically adventurous, and genre-blurring artists working today. EMI Classics is home to renowned talents like Itzhak Perlman and Vanessa-Mae, while Angel Records has critical favorites like Bernadette Peters, Joan Baez, and the hugely selling Chant Series featuring the Benedictine Monks. The recently formed New Media division has created hollywoodandvine.com, Capitol's widely praised Web site.

This page, clockwise from top left: Marcy Playground, Jeb Loy Nichols, Everclear, John Hiatt, Rosanne Cash, Luscious Jackson, Supergrass, and (center) The Dandy Warhols

Opposite page, clockwise from top right: Meredith Brooks, Radiohead, Cassandra Wilson, Megadeth, Foo Fighters, Sean Lennon, and The Beastie Boys

Capitol's famed recording studios, the first ever built for high-fidelity recordings, are still in high demand, boasting some of the most acclaimed recordings being made today, including those by Chris Isaak, Missy Elliott, John Fogerty, and several of Capitol's own artists.

More than sales figures and platinum albums, Capitol has never forgotten the independent spirit with which the company was formed. With artists like Bonnie Raitt (active in many worthy organizations, including the Rhythm and Blues Foundation) and the Beastie Boys (whose Milarepa Fund supports nonviolence and founded the wildly successful and meaningful Tibetan Freedom Concert series), Capitol is a label that has always had a social conscience.

Capitol has carved out an identity as an artist-friendly label, where newcomers Sean Lennon, Bran Van 3000, and Marcy Playground mingle with established alternative artists Radiohead, Foo Fighters, Everclear, Luscious Jackson, and the Beastie Boys, while veterans Bonnie Raitt, Bob Seger, and Robbie Robertson continue to make the most vital and acclaimed music of their careers. Thanks to new leadership that embodies the independent, can-do spirit of the company's legendary founders, Capitol Records proudly enters a new millenium as a haven for artists—and executives—of vision.

PROVIDENCE HEALTH SYSTEM, LOS ANGELES SERVICE AREA

Nestled among the studios, film production companies, and suburbs that dominate the eastern San Fernando Valley are two facilities dedicated to providing quality health care with compassion: Providence Saint Joseph Medical Center and Providence Holy Cross Medical Center. The two community hospitals and their affiliates, which form Providence Health System's Los Angeles Service Area, collectively have close to 800 licensed beds and provide an array of health care services that run the gamut from outpatient surgery to trauma care.

Meeting Community Needs

When Providence Saint Joseph was established in Burbank in 1943, the San Fernando Valley was largely undeveloped, with some 300,000 residents living a quiet, rural existence north of the city of Los Angeles, just over the Santa Monica Mountains. But with World War II in full swing and the burgeoning defense industry producing more and more aircraft in the eastern valley, local leaders realized that the area desperately needed a hospital to serve the swelling population that had come to work in the defense industry. The Sisters of Providence in Seattle embraced the responsibility of establishing and running a hospital in the San Fernando Valley. On donated land, with federal grant money and the support of a handful of local physicians, the Sisters began work on Saint Joseph Hospital, a one-story, wooden building with 100 beds, on a lot filled with tumbleweeds and surrounded by ranches and farmland.

An immediate sign of the imminent population boom in the Valley was the 900 babies born in the hospital during its first year of operation. By the early 1950s, Burbank and the surrounding area had outgrown the tiny hospital. A number of celebrities, including Walt Disney and Bob and Dolores Hope, pitched in to raise money for the hospital's expansion.

Today, the eastern San Fernando Valley is virtually unrecognizable from the days of agriculture and aircraft. Aeronautics factories now house motion picture and television studios. Farms and orchards have been replaced by suburbs and businesses that serve the entertainment industry. To keep up with the population growth, Providence Saint Joseph now has 455 licensed beds, and its employees number more than 2,000. Its medical staff of 650 doctors represents family practice and internal medicine, as well as specialists and subspecialists in surgery, oncology, cardiology, emergency, and neonatal intensive care.

Holy Cross Medical Center, established in 1961 to the north in Mission Hills, provides health care to the San Fernando, Santa Clarita, and Simi valleys. It joined the Providence Health System in 1996 to establish a larger, stronger Catholic health system for the area. With 255 licensed beds, more than 1,300 employees, and a medical staff of 500-plus physicians representing nearly 40 specialties, Providence Holy Cross, as the hospital is now known, offers a full continuum of health services, ranging from

Clockwise from top:
Providence Saint Joseph Medical Center (pictured), Providence Holy Cross Medical Center, and their affiliates constitute Providence Health System, Los Angeles Service Area.

Sisters of Providence enjoy the garden area at the Providence Saint Joseph campus.

Walt Disney helps Sister Agnes, S.P., with breaking ground for the east wing of Saint Joseph Hospital in 1952.

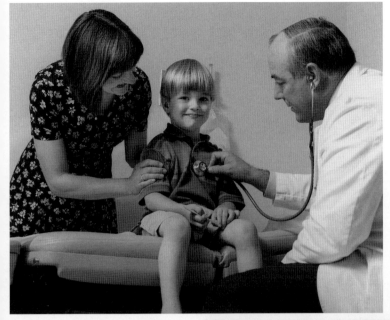

inpatient to outpatient to home health care. It has one of only two trauma centers in the San Fernando Valley.

One of Holy Cross' most compelling examples of service to the community was during the disastrous 1971 Sylmar earthquake, which registered 6.5 on the Richter scale. Within the first two hours of the quake, more than 250 emergency patients showed up. Patients were lying in corridors and any other place that was safe, where they could be evaluated and their wounds cleaned. The hospital's staff didn't think it could get worse, and then helicopters began bringing in more injured—intensive care patients who had been airlifted from a nearby hospital that was demolished by the quake. Although already overtaxed, Holy Cross accepted these patients and cared for them in its undamaged, single-story continuing care building until they could be moved. Holy Cross eventually had to be evacuated. Many of its services were soon resumed, but it was not until 1977, when a new building was completed, that it was able to return to its status as a full-service, acute care facility.

The Mission Continues

Providence Holy Cross and Providence Saint Joseph offer a full range of health services. The hospitals are known for their heart and cancer centers, as well as for their women's and children's services, which include a full range of maternity programs and prenatal education. Some of their special programs include the Parish Nurse Partnership, Senior Peer Counseling, Pets with Purpose, Latino Health Promoters, Pediatric After-Hours Referral Clinic, and in-house blood donor centers. Community education is key to the mission, and many

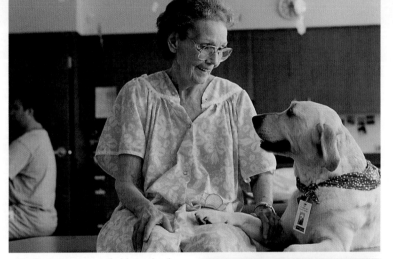

education programs are held, ranging from yoga to seminars on cancer and heart disease prevention.

In addition to its hospitals, Providence has several other facilities that allow the system to provide a continuum of health care to the community, including Providence Home Care and Hospice, Providence Saint Joseph Occupational Health Center, Providence St. Elizabeth Care Center, Providence Urgent Care Center, and Valley Radiation Oncology Center.

Quality, Compassionate Care

The Providence facilities provide proof that compassionate care and high-quality care are not mutually exclusive. Providence Saint Joseph is listed in the 100 Top Hospitals in the United States according to an HCIA, Inc. and Mercer, Inc. study, and Providence Holy Cross holds the Distinguished Achievement Citation, the highest honor that the Catholic Healthcare Association bestows.

"There's a strong feeling of compassion within our organization for the

vulnerable, the poor, and the elderly," says Michael J. Madden, CEO for Providence Health System's Los Angeles Service Area. "We live that mission." He describes the Providence Health Care System as a value-oriented system that focuses on the values of compassion, excellence, respect, justice, and stewardship.

"Those values are truly practiced throughout our organization," Madden adds. "We have excellent physicians and nursing care, and our surveys show very positive patient satisfaction ratings. We are proud that our facilities are so well respected in our communities."

Clockwise from top left:
Special services and programs offered by Providence Health System include the Pediatric After-Hours Referral Clinic.

(From left) Sister Colleen Settles (regional director, Mission Leadership) and Michael Madden (CEO, Providence Health System, Los Angeles Service Area), along with Connie Cruz, Reasie Flagg, and Deb Benada (from the Latino Health Promoters and Parish Nurse Partnership programs), accept the Catholic Healthcare Association's highest honor, the Distinguished Achievement Citation.

A Pets with Purpose volunteer visits a patient.

In 1998, a study by HCIA, Inc. and Mercer, Inc. listed Providence Saint Joseph in the 100 Top Hospitals in the United States.

PARK LABREA

What began as experimental urban living more than half a century ago has become a way of life for Park Labrea apartment residents. Both a park and a village, the futuristic apartment complex nestled within West Los Angeles features stately communal squares, long pedestrian esplanades, vast carpets of grassy lawns, and a forest of trees. Located in a beautiful, 176-acre park, this urban village is within walking distance of one

of the region's most important museum districts, popular shopping malls, and famous walkways. The gated community also offers easy accessibility to outstanding schools and extensive recreational activities. "The concept behind these apartments was to create a community within the larger community," says Greg Holihan, manager of the housing complex. "Since it was built, it has met all expectations."

Forward-Thinking Housing
When the original building plans for the apartment complex were drawn up, they described a community of 26 garden blocks. But it was decided to add eighteen 13-story towers to help meet the overwhelming demand for postwar housing—one-third of the community's original residents were returning World War II servicemen and -women. The garden apartments opened in 1944; the first tower was completed in 1951, and the remaining towers were completed in 1952.

Architects Gordon Kaufmann and J.E. Stanton developed an unusual design for

Park Labrea that eliminates a fault of many large buildings, where some windows look out onto unsightly air shafts or inside courts. An X-shaped plan, where the intersection of the lines forms a rectangular building core, eliminated that problem. The design ensures that every apartment has ample light and space, as well as outside views.

The garden blocks of the village are laid out using the superblock design of Paris, with open spaces shared by all residents. Each group of garden apartments also has its own private outdoor areas.

Park Labrea offers a rich array of floor plans, including one- to five-bedroom apartments, each with splendid views. Most of the two-story town homes, which

Park Labrea's towers were designed to provide extraordinary views from virtually every tower apartment. The geometric designs that grace the structures highlight the 1950s architecture.

Park Labrea has invested significant capital in new landscaping and on the bold stepped designs on the tower buildings. Many garden town home residents contribute their own efforts to the community's remarkably lush grounds.

feature one, two, or three bedrooms, include a private patio and face a spacious yard. The complex also offers corporate apartments, a popular concept in Hollywood because of the transient lifestyles of many writers, producers, and actors. The apartments also serve the booming technology industry, including many hardware and software companies that have moved to Southern California.

A Village within a City

The community's population is characterized by a diversity of lifestyles, professions, cultures, and interests. To accommodate this variety, Park Labrea offers a broad spectrum of amenities, activities, and special programs for residents. One of the best-kept secrets of the complex is its fitness opportunities. Park Labrea has an extensive system of exercise routes, a junior Olympic pool, a private club with tennis facilities, and two gym facilities.

There are also many local attractions within walking distance of the Park Labrea, including the George C. Page Museum of La Brea Discoveries, which houses prehistoric fossils discovered at the renowned La Brea Tar Pits; Los Angeles County Museum of Art; Petersen Automotive Museum; Carole & Barry Kaye Museum of Miniatures; and Farmers Market.

In addition, Park Labrea holds the annual Art at the Park celebration, and donations to the Park Labrea Family Art Fund provide access to the arts for families that might not otherwise be able to afford it. Adding to the community spirit that the complex has created, Park Labrea residents help raise funds for the local YMCA, and hold a partnership with the local police department.

A $7 Million Renovation

In 1995, Prime Park Labrea Holdings (PLB) acquired the property, and PLB Management took over the operation of the community. At that time, PLB Management allocated $7 million in landscape and general property renovation. The 18 high-rises were redone in a new paint scheme, accentuating the uniqueness of the neighborhood and the contemporary nature of the property. Today, as one approaches the Park Labrea complex, the towers' unmistakable signature colors stand as a monument to modern living.

The original granite facades from the tower double-door entries were also uncovered, after hiding for decades under layers of paint. At the same time, the lobby interiors, featuring marble facades, underwent renovation. An art deco motif now graces each lobby, creating an urbane

ambience and paying homage to the stylish era of Hollywood's heyday.

"PLB Management has brought the buildings up to date without threatening the structures' character," says Holihan. "The unique care the new owners have brought to the property is a recognition of the value of the experiment and the value of maintaining it." With its beautiful setting, spacious apartments, and abundance of activities and amenities, the experiment in urban living that resulted in today's Park Labrea apartments is sure to be successful well into the next millennium.

▶ PAT HOUSTON

Clockwise from top:
Park Labrea's annual Art at the Park celebration features original, hand-painted banners at street level and, in the Tallest Art Show in L.A., atop Park Labrea towers.

The Hollywood hills provide a dramatic backdrop for Art at the Park, a community-based arts celebration hosted by Park Labrea.

Park Labrea's swimming pool is the newest addition to fitness facilities that include a tennis club, two fitness centers, and exercise routes that trace the 176-acre property.

▶ ▼ PASCUAL BETTIO

Just after World War II, four young men took advantage of the ensuing construction boom and established the architectural firm of Daniel, Mann, Johnson, & Mendenhall (DMJM). Since then, Los Angeles-based DMJM has grown to become a highly respected player in the architectural and engineering fields worldwide, creating distinctive designs and structures that are as familiar to many as their own backyards. ▼ DMJM's projects run the gamut from office buildings to transportation systems to institutional facilities. They include the Vancouver SkyTrain; the Eastern Kentucky Correctional Complex; the maintenance hangar for *Air Force One* in Camp Springs, Maryland; the Central Valley Water Reclamation Facility in Salt Lake City; the Opel-Kreisel Building in Frankfurt, Germany; and the Taipei Mass Rapid Transit System in Taiwan. DMJM's aesthetic designs also include the elegant U.S. Botanic Garden Conservatory in Washington, D.C., and the new Elihu Harris State Office Building in Oakland.

Success in the Postwar Boom

The development of DMJM is, in many ways, a typical American success story. In 1946, architects Phil Daniel, Art Mann, and Ken Johnson joined forces with engineer Irv Mendenhall to establish a firm that would serve the new frontier of post-World War II California. They got their start by meeting the increased demand for schools, as the need for classrooms skyrocketed during the baby boom years. In the following decades, DMJM has continued to meet changing needs both at home and abroad, branching out beyond architecture into engineering, planning, program management, construction services, environmental services, and special services, a category that encompasses a broad range of facility modifications.

Today, DMJM maintains offices in 20 U.S. states, as well as Washington, D.C.; Puerto Rico; and nine foreign countries. In 1998, the firm was ranked as the nation's second-largest architecture/engineering firm, with annual billings in excess of $230 million. It has also been consistently ranked by the *Los Angeles Business Journal* as the architectural firm with the highest billings in Los Angeles County. DMJM currently employs a total of 1,620 people, including 500 in the Los Angeles corporate headquarters.

A Vast Array of Services

DMJM's team of specialists is adept at designing and building structures that are both appropriate to the specific needs of the firm's clients and reflective of the character of the clients and the building sites. Vital to this process is the integration of comprehensive services—what Senior Vice President Robert L. Newsom calls the "one-company philosophy."

"Every DMJM client—whether a small, private enterprise or a city or a county—receives local and regional expertise, with the instant ability to draw on the firm's additional resources and industry-leading experts around the world," explains Newsom. "So, with local sensitivity and international expertise, our one-company philosophy puts all DMJM resources at the fingertips of every client."

In addition to its well-known designs and creations, DMJM has managed an array of structural overhauls, including the seismic repair and earthquake retrofitting of buildings, bridges, and highways in California; the renovation of the Pentagon; and the reconstruction of bridges in Kuwait following the Gulf War. The firm is particularly creative when it comes to developing one-of-a-kind solutions. For example, DMJM helped develop the National Airport Pavement Test Machine, which can simulate and duplicate the landing force of

The architectural firm of Daniel, Mann, Johnson, & Mendenhall (DMJM), a highly respected player in the architectural and engineering fields worldwide, has created distinctive designs and structures all over the world. Pictured are two views of the Elihu Harris State Office Building in Oakland.

planes weighing up to 1.8 million pounds. The apparatus then collects data that is helpful in developing stronger concrete to withstand increasingly heavy aircraft that are powerful enough to crush existing runway pavement. "This is just one example of the many projects where DMJM has, if you'll pardon the pun, broken the ground with ingenuity," says Newsom.

DMJM attracts talented professionals who seek the creative freedom to explore and experiment, while delivering a quality product. "Though everyone here encourages and supports creativity and innovation, it all must serve the client's needs," Newsom explains. "Innovation without a solution-oriented, client-warranted focus is self-serving. At DMJM, we apply all of our creative energies to help streamline our processes and deliver innovative solutions to our clients around the world."

The firm's passion for problem solving is evident in its community involvement, as well. Today's DMJM continues a long-time commitment to the community, with a special interest in education. Firm members, for example, train a number of interns each year from area high schools, colleges, and universities. One of DMJM's newer initiatives involves helping install state-of-the-art computer learning and reading programs in kindergarten and first-grade classrooms. The program has met with great success, particularly in helping students whose native language is not English.

After 50 years of awards and billions of dollars in business, along with a passion for creating structures that are both functional and attractive, it is no surprise that DMJM has emerged as one of the country's preeminent architectural and engineering firms. The founders established their prac-

tice on two tenets: delivering nothing less than outstanding service to every client on every project and being in the right place at the right time. One look at such creations as the Staten Island Ferry Building and the San Francisco International Airport is evidence enough of DMJM's unfailing dedication to these ideals.

DMJM's team of specialists is adept at designing and building structures that are both appropriate to the specific needs of the firm's clients and reflective of the character of the clients and the building sites.

MAJESTIC REALTY CO.

Out of the optimism of the post-World War II era came a man with a vision of building a real estate empire. So in 1948, Edward P. Roski Sr. established Majestic Realty Co. in Los Angeles, which got its start by operating primarily as a brokerage company. By the end of the 1950s, the growing enterprise was purchasing land and constructing "build-to-suits" in Vernon and the City of Commerce. Today, Majestic is one of the largest privately held real estate firms in the United States. In 1998,

the City of Industry-based company received the Eddy Award for Excellence in Economic Development. Majestic's goal, according to President and Chief Operating Officer Edward P. Roski Jr., is to continue living up to the ideals embodied in that prestigious award.

A Real Estate Powerhouse

Majestic Realty has ranked as the number one commercial real estate developer in Los Angeles County for the past eight years. Along with its related companies—Majestic Management Co. and Commerce Construction Co.—Majestic provides full-service real estate development, offering in-house brokerage, design, engineering, construction, leasing, property management, and financial services. The firm's portfolio contains more than 32 million square feet of industrial, commercial, sports, entertainment, and retail structures. Essentially, Majestic deals in almost every kind of real estate, with the exception of residential.

With a staff of more than 100 employees, Majestic has worked to increase its development of industrial parks in cities like Atlanta, Dallas, Denver, Las Vegas, Phoenix, and Salt Lake City. According to Roski Jr., the company views all of its developments as long-term investments.

Majestic Realthy Co. founder and Chairman of the Board Edward P. Roski Sr. (seated), and President and Chief Operating Officer Edward P. Roski Jr.

Majestic provides full-service real estate development, offering in-house brokerage, design, engineering, construction, leasing, property management, and financial services.

"Majestic's goal is its continued expansion of industrial and retail development opportunities that will be revenue-positive, job-creating, eye-pleasing contributors to many growing, progressive communities throughout the United States," says Roski Jr. "We want to continue to do what we do best through hard work and dedication to our communities and this great country in which we live."

As a member of the founding family who boasts a long-term association with the business, Roski Jr. views Majestic's ongoing success from a unique vantage point. He joined the company's ranks in 1966 and took over as its chief operating officer in 1976. (Roski Sr. remains involved in the business as chairman of the board.) Roski Jr. says that throughout Majestic's half century in business, its greatest accomplishment has been the contribution it has made by providing more than 50,000 jobs, with more than $2 billion in annual wages. The company is proud of its significant contribution to various Southern California communities, including the City of Industry, Chino, the City of Commerce, La Mirada, Norwalk, Ontario, San Dimas, and Walnut, and to a number of other communities throughout the United States.

Staples Center

Majestic Realty's most recent accomplishment is taking place close to home, with the revitalization of downtown Los Angeles and the opening of the Staples Center sports complex. As the driving force behind the new facility, Majestic began development of the Staples Center the same way the company begins all of its deals: with a forward-looking vision and a prime piece of property that needs to be developed.

When Philip Anschutz, a Denver businessman and former owner of the Southern Pacific Railroad, teamed up with Roski Jr. as co-owner of the National Hockey League's Los Angeles Kings, the pair had one goal in common: to find a location that would best serve both the community and the professional sports teams involved. After months of negotiations with the City of Los Angeles, the land adjacent to the Los Angeles Convention Center was chosen to be the site of the Staples Center, the new home of the Los Angeles Kings, Lakers, and Clippers.

"The Staples Center is far more than just a building to house sporting events," says Roski Jr. "This monumental and unparalleled destination will host more than 280 events annually. Each year, millions of people will visit the Staples Center, which will help fuel an urban revitalization of hotel, retail, and dining venues never before experienced in downtown Los Angeles, creating a 24-hour environment similar to that of the great cities of the world."

DAVID L. CORNWELL

Majestic Realty has ranked as the number one commercial real estate developer in Los Angeles County for the past eight years.

A Winning Business Philosophy

Back in 1965, Roski Sr. said, "The prosperity of our great country is due in large part to the initiative, faith, vision, and dedication of its industrial leadership. Characteristically, Americans are the attributes of know-how and efficiency, which give momentum to initiative and which transform vision into accomplishment." More than three decades later, as Majestic prepares for a new century, the company's philosophy remains much the same. Its long-standing belief is that its future is limitless thanks to the vision, talent, drive, and resources of its employees and the companies with which it works.

When Roski Sr. was once asked about Majestic's current business philosophy, his response was simple: "Hard work." One look at the company's expansive portfolio is proof positive that the founder's answer remains a winning business philosophy today.

The firm's portfolio contains more than 32 million square feet of industrial, commercial, sports, entertainment, and retail structures. Pictured are the Atrium (middle), the Mattel building (bottom right), and the Aiwa building (bottom left).

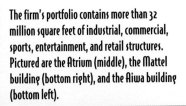

Dubbed "the world's most powerful consulting firm" by *Fortune* magazine, McKinsey & Company, Inc. is a well-known name, yet is still treated as a bit of a mystery by the popular press. McKinsey consultants grimace at media phrases like "the McKinsey mystique"—because although it is true they will not name or discuss their clients with outsiders, they are more forthcoming when asked what "the Firm" is all about. Widely regarded in the business community as the Rolls-Royce of its industry, McKinsey has built an impeccable reputation on discreet service to businesses running the gamut from energy to entertainment to health care.

It's about Trust

McKinsey & Company was founded in 1926 by a former University of Chicago accounting professor named James O. McKinsey, who had noted that when the top managers of large organizations wanted confidential advice, or just a well-informed but objective point of view from outside their own organizations, they had nowhere to turn. It was McKinsey's vision to create a consulting firm that would take what he termed "the top management perspective." He saw the need for a new kind of consultant who could look at companies from a CEO's viewpoint and thus be an effective partner to senior executives.

After McKinsey's death in the late 1930s, Marvin Bower, a graduate of both Harvard Law and Harvard Business schools, took over. Bower's vision was to professionalize management consulting, following the model of the top legal firms. He set out to shape McKinsey & Company into a professional services firm that would be as committed to its clients' financial health as a medical professional is committed to a patient's physical health. Bower articulated McKinsey & Company's guiding principles: to place client interests first; to accept only those assignments the firm is fully qualified to perform; and to maintain independence and objectivity, even if it means declining or withdrawing from an assignment.

Those principles have not changed over the decades. "We urge our clients to tell us at any time if they're not satisfied with the level of impact that we're achieving," says Charlie Schetter, managing director of McKinsey's Los Angeles office. "And by the same token, if we feel that our recommendations are not going to be acted on, if the client is not going to see impact on the basis of our work, then we will leave."

The combination of top management perspective and professionalism has been the foundation for McKinsey's success. Today, it employs 4,500 consultants in 76 offices in 40 countries. In the last three years, it has served more than three-quarters of *Fortune* magazine's top 25 most admired companies worldwide.

"Although McKinsey has grown and diversified to serve every sector of business and work in every corner of the globe, we still like to do business on a handshake basis," says Schetter. "At the core, it's all about earning your client's trust."

Another cornerstone of its trust-based relationships is McKinsey's insistence on working side by side with its clients. "When we take an assignment, we don't retreat to our offices to crunch numbers in splendid isolation," emphasizes Christiana Smith-Shi, coleader of McKinsey's retail practice. "We set up shop at the client's place, team up with some of their most talented managers, and problem solve together." This partnership generates better answers to business problems, transfers knowledge and skills to the clients, and builds support for implementing recommendations long before the final report is drafted.

McKinsey & Company has built an impeccable reputation on discreet service to businesses running the gamut from energy to entertainment to health care.

◄ PHILIP ALDERTON

◄ PHILIP ALDERTON

It's about People

McKinsey's mission statement has two parts. Its primary mission—to help clients make distinctive, lasting, and substantial improvements in their performance—requires McKinsey to succeed in the second part of its mission: to build a firm that is able to attract, develop, excite, and retain exceptional people. For many years, McKinsey recruited its new consultants only from the top 10 percent of graduates from a small handful of business schools. More recently, it has broadened its candidate pool in response to its continued growth and to increasing complexity in the business issues its clients face. Today, McKinsey recruits top graduates from outstanding doctoral programs in medicine, law, and the sciences, as well as from the leading business schools. "We found that this strengthens our ability to serve clients in sectors like health care provision and high technology that were once pretty much closed to management consultants," notes McKinsey partner Bernie Ferrari, who is a board-certified surgeon and an attorney, as well as a business school graduate.

"We also try to create an environment that enables all our people to grow farther and faster than they could anywhere else," Ferrari adds. It seems true that the experience McKinsey professionals gain from serving senior executives on their top agenda items would be hard to acquire elsewhere. Armed with this experience, alumni have gone on to lead some of the most successful companies in the world, including IBM, American Express, and Westinghouse.

"We generate a stream of alumni who are self-confident, well-rounded leaders," Schetter says. "That's why they end up in some extraordinary situations over time."

It's Global, but Local

McKinsey established its Los Angeles office in 1949, as Southern California began to take its place as one of the nation's most dynamic economies and the hub of its booming aerospace business. Fifty years later, McKinsey has worked with most of Los Angeles' leading institutions—either as counselor to the leaders of its largest businesses or as pro bono contributor to its major social and civic organizations.

McKinsey places great emphasis on its ability to draw from local and global resources for any given client situation. A typical McKinsey project may be led by someone who has in-depth familiarity with the local market, and supported by functional or sector experts flown in to provide specialized expertise.

"Whether we're opening a new office in Singapore or in Orange County, our goal is to staff it with a mix of experienced consultants from around the world and local professionals who understand the business environment and the needs of the community," explains Schetter. "We are part of the community partly because we build our offices with people from the community."

"We feel that we have attracted some of the most uniquely talented people in Los Angeles, and all of us—regardless of where on earth we started out—are enjoying the benefits of Southern California life," adds Tony Miller, the partner who coordinates McKinsey's pro bono activities in Los Angeles. "Therefore, we believe we have an obligation to give back to this community."

Accordingly, McKinsey is an active participant in many of the organizations that improve the quality of Los Angeles life. McKinsey provides teams of consultants to work on projects for the boards of

▶ PHILIP ALDERTON

directors of various nonprofit institutions, including the Los Angeles Philharmonic. In other cases, McKinsey has helped establish or provided analytical support for such organizations as the Los Angeles Business Advisors (LABA), a group of CEOs who work together to strengthen the local economy. A substantial portion of McKinsey's pro bono work focuses on helping the city's youth, whether through working with the Los Angeles Unified School District, the Boy Scouts, and 4-H, or through its own Adopt-A-School program.

The Adopt-A-School program, which encourages inner-city kids to continue their educations, illustrates McKinsey's hands-on approach to community service. McKinsey people work with a group of inner-city teenagers throughout their high school years, providing services like coaching in math and tours of local colleges. One of the main emphases of the program is helping these teenagers get accepted into summer college preparatory programs, including using the consultants' frequent flier mileage to provide transportation to out-of-state programs. "Last year, these kids had a 100 percent success rate on getting into college preparatory programs," Schetter comments. "We see that as an opportunity to have lasting impact."

McKinsey recruits top graduates from outstanding doctoral programs in medicine, law, and the sciences, as well as from the leading business schools (top).

The firm is an active participant in many of the organizations that improve the quality of Los Angeles life (bottom).

VIRCO MFG. CORPORATION

For nearly half a century, Virco Mfg. Corporation has produced a wide range of furniture for a diverse customer base. Led by President and CEO Robert A. Virtue, whose father, Julian A. Virtue, founded the Torrance-based company, Virco has become the largest manufacturer and supplier of educational furniture in the United States. With annual revenues that now exceed $250 million, Virco distributes its products to an expanding domestic and global market. ▼ Virco's history began in 1950, when

Julian Virtue purchased Slauson Aircraft. During World War II, Slauson had made carrying cases for ammunition and other equipment, but afterwards turned its attention to school furniture. Virtue renamed the company and soon began expanding its client base beyond Slauson's sole customer, the Los Angeles Unified School District. Within a matter of months, Virco had retained a second educational customer, the Torrance Unified School District.

An early eye toward diversification inspired Virtue to develop product lines, such as folding chairs and folding tables, that would reach additional markets. Later expansion included an array of furniture that is used in thousands of hotels, convention centers, auditoriums, churches, and office settings. As a result, Virco has achieved a record of steady growth, while maintaining its special interest in educational furniture.

Commitment to Southern California

Virco is committed to serving the needs of its customers in the midst of changing

times and circumstances—a commitment that has challenged the company in recent years. This was particularly evident in the turbulent economic times of the late 1980s and early 1990s, when many Southern California businesses were forced to downsize or relocate altogether. But, because of its strong roots in the area, Virco made every effort to stay. When the decision was made to transfer West Coast operations in 1994, Virco remained in the South Bay, leasing a 560,000-square-foot complex on Harper's Way in Torrance. The current facility has enabled Virco to consolidate its regional manufacturing plant and warehouse with its corporate headquarters, keeping all operations under one roof. In fact, to further confirm its commitment to

Southern California, Virco has relocated additional manufacturing operations from a *maquiladora* factory in Mexico to its new Torrance facility.

Virco's dedication to its hometown community is evident in its support of the local Adopt-a-School program. Students at South Torrance High School, Virco's Adopt-a-School partner, have benefited from a substantial donation of the company's Future Access™ computer furniture. Virco also provides area students with summer work through internship opportunities that give young people valuable work experience in a corporate environment.

In 1996, Virco expanded its relationship with the Adopt-a-School program as a whole. The company now works to

Virco's 560,000-square-foot complex, which includes its regional manufacturing plant, a warehouse, and corporate headquarters, is located on Harper's Way in Torrance.

Virco produces furniture that is used in hotels, schools, churches, and office settings. Clockwise from top: Vespers chair, Classic Series® chair desk, Mojave desking configuration

Virco's work with accomplished designers, including Charles Perry, Richard Holbrook, and Peter Glass, has resulted in still more innovative new products, such as the Plateau® table system and Virtuoso™ chairs.

coordinate the program's overall direction with the Torrance Area Chamber of Commerce. This broader role includes evaluating the needs of schools that aren't yet adopted, developing new fund-raising activities, and recruiting new business participants.

Furniture That Fits

Virco's focus on community interaction mirrors its approach to new product development. The company maintains a forward-looking, proactive attitude toward the introduction of dynamic new furniture. In addition to Future Access, other products that exemplify this attitude are the premium Core-a-Gator® line of lightweight folding tables and the newly released Mojave™ desking system for technology-based environments. Another new product, the Vespers™ seating system, was created in collaboration with award-winning designer Ron Kemnitzer expressly for churches and other places of worship. Virco's work

with accomplished designers, including Charles Perry, Richard Holbrook, and Peter Glass, has resulted in still more innovative new products, such as Virtuoso™ chairs and the Plateau® table system.

These new products complement a collection of long-standing Virco favorites, the foremost of which is the company's Classic Series® chairs and chair desks. Virco has sold more than 40 million of these popular units to customers across the nation and around the world.

Customer satisfaction is a cornerstone of Virco's success. By constantly monitor-

ing feedback from customers, and from its own management, sales force, and installation teams, the company works to continually provide the best possible service.

For nearly five decades, Virco has been an integral part of the local community, employing hundreds of Californians and helping to meet the furniture needs of an array of markets. Furniture That Fits is truly an apt slogan for this traditional, yet progressive company. Virco's dedication to product integrity and civic involvement make it a perfect fit in the dynamically diverse Los Angeles landscape.

Virco is the largest manufacturer and supplier of educational furniture in the United States and distributes its products both domestically and overseas.

ou're In Good Hands With Allstate® ranks among the best-known slogans in the history of American business. Starting with auto insurance, and today also offering home owners, renters, and life insurance, Allstate Insurance Company has been protecting Southern Californians for more than half a century. Allstate Insurance first came to Southern California through ads in the 1931 Sears catalog. The idea for the new product came from a discussion that General Robert E. Wood, president of Sears,

Roebuck & Company, had with a neighbor on the 7:28 commuter train to Chicago from Highland Park. The neighbor, an insurance broker, suggested that Sears sell auto insurance through its popular catalog, and borrow its name, Allstate, from the famous tires already sold in the catalog. From this beginning, Allstate has grown to be a leader in its field. Today, 950 agents serve Southern Californians, who hold more than 817,000 home owners policies, 549,000 auto policies, and 86,000 life policies.

In 1995, Allstate became an independent company. Its historic spin-off from Sears made it the largest publicly held personal lines insurance company, with nearly $25 billion in annual revenues. More than 15,000 agents in the United States and Canada provide sales and service for one of every eight homes and automobiles in the country.

A History of Innovation

To meet the diverse needs of its policyholders, Allstate tailors all of its services to the specific needs of the cities and communities where it does business. Allstate's history of innovation began in

1939, when the company launched the first auto insurance policies that tailored rates to the age, mileage, and use of the car. That same year, drivers using the burgeoning freeway system of Southern California relied on Allstate's new towing and emergency road services as a vital part of their insurance. In the 1950s, the company launched the first drive-in claim office,

and by 1959, had established one of the nation's first catastrophe plans.

Allstate's National Catastrophe Team has since set the standard for the industry. Allstate assures that whenever an area is hit by disaster, experts in catastrophe management will be on the scene within hours. Whether it's the 1993 Laguna Hills fire or the 1994 Northridge earthquake—for which Allstate processed more than 46,000 claims costing upward of $1.5 billion—the company has been on the scene to give its customers peace of mind. Allstate's state-of-the-art "cat mobiles"—satellite-equipped offices on wheels—help agents and claim personnel give devastated customers additional personal service.

Helping Hands of Allstate

The company's commitment to Southern California goes much deeper than providing insurance; Allstate truly partners with the communities it serves. This partnership dates back to the creation of The Allstate Foundation in 1952. Supporting and improving local neighborhoods, schools, and nonprofit organizations, the foundation now grants about $7 million each year to more than 1,400 programs targeting Allstate's four main focus areas: auto and highway safety, personal safety and security, neighborhood revitalization, and youth initiatives.

◄ BOB GICK

With nearly 1,000 sales agents in Southern California, Allstate Insurance Company is well poised to meet the insurance needs of the people in its communities (top).

All disasters are catastrophic. Whether the magnitude of destruction affects millions of people, or is one family's personal tragedy, Allstate promises to be there when its customers need help (bottom).

With its Neighborhood Partnership Program, Allstate took a leadership role in the Crenshaw neighborhood of Los Angeles in 1997 by committing $5.75 million to help that community address challenges such as recreation for youth, crime prevention, and fire safety. Much of that support meant that dilapidated housing could be converted into livable homes. And, to make sure the insurance needs of the individual residents were met, Allstate opened a sales and service office in the community. Allstate also holds $1.8 billion in municipal bonds in Los Angeles for housing, transportation, and public works projects, with an emphasis on funds to finance mortgages for residents with few resources.

Beginning in 1967, Helping Hands, a volunteer program run by and for Allstate employees, began targeting numerous social issues. In 1998, Allstate set the lead for other corporations by joining with the city's Volunteer Bureau to host the first Volunteer Festival. The Los Angeles City Council hailed the company that same year for joining the city in the Safe Home Los Angeles program, in which Allstate invested $2 million and helped with the creation of volunteer crisis response teams to assist the police and fire departments in improving public safety. Allstate also made a $25 million commitment to America's Promise—The Alliance for Youth™ to sup-

port programs throughout the country, including providing grants to four communities in Southern California.

Allstate has also received national attention for its community service. In 1995, the Points of Light Foundation gave the company its Award for Excellence in Corporate Community Service. The next year Allstate won the Exemplary Voluntary

Efforts Award from the U.S. Department of Labor, which is awarded to companies for innovative efforts to increase employment opportunities for minorities, women, individuals with disabilities, and covered verterans. The firm also received the 1997 Catalyst Award for launching initiatives to advance women in the workplace. In 1998, Allstate was named to *Fortune* magazine's list of the Best 50 Companies for Asians, Blacks, and Hispanics. That same year, *American Benefactor* magazine named Allstate as one of America's 25 Most Generous Companies.

After nearly 70 years, Allstate continues to focus on meeting the changing needs of its policyholders and of the communities in which the company does business. The trust between the "good hands people" and the customers they serve will continue to guide Allstate into the next millennium.

Clockwise from top left:
Customers can depend on the service Allstate claim representatives provide. Representatives spend a minimum of four months in specialized, hands-on training to give them the expertise needed to provide the best claim service in the industry.

Allstate agents and employees cook, paint, repair, teach, clean, feed, and garden when they volunteer their time and talent to local charities, organizations, and events through the Helping Hands volunteerism committees. More than 50 percent of agents and employees participate in hundreds of community-building projects annually.

Insurance is more than just a promise on a piece of paper to Allstate. To ensure the safety of children, agents and employees go beyond the promise by fingerprinting hundreds of little hands at local community events and making fire-safety presentations at local schools.

Litton Industries, Inc.

hile Litton Industries, Inc. may not be a household name, scarcely a household exists that has not been affected in some way by this technological giant. Litton began as a small electronics firm in 1953, and today, has more than 30,000 employees in 376 locations in 24 countries who develop and manufacture technology for land, sea, air, and outer space use. With annual sales of more than $4 billion, Litton serves commercial and military customers in more than 60 countries, and is traded on the New York Stock Exchange as LIT.

Far-Reaching Technologies

Understanding how Litton's technologies work is far less important than understanding how these technologies improve daily life. Litton's commercial navigation systems allow aircraft to fly anywhere in the world in any type of weather. The company's integrated bridge systems, which are installed in commercial and military ships, make those ships safer and more cost efficient by enabling them to navigate more precisely through treacherous—and sometimes crowded—sea channels. Its computer dispatch systems give police, fire, and emergency medical services the ability to do their jobs faster and more efficiently by reducing response times. Litton's information technology helps the National Weather Service more quickly and accurately forecast imminent bad weather so that citizens have time to take precautions. And Litton's threat warning systems protect airplanes, helicopters, and ships from missiles and enemy gunfire. In fact, during the Gulf War, more than 70 percent of aircraft flown by coalition forces used Litton's equipment for electronic warfare.

Litton is also a major supplier of components for avionics equipment and systems integration, and is a commercial and military supplier of aircraft, spacecraft, helicopters, ships, land vehicles, and missiles worldwide. In addition to its computer and electronics technologies, Litton, through its Ingalls Shipbuilding division in Pascagoula, Mississippi, designs and builds

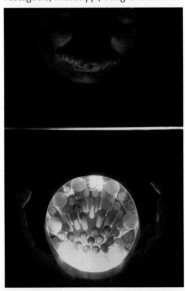

surface combatant ships for U.S. and international naval forces. In fact, Litton is the world's leading builder of large surface combatant ships for the U.S. Navy. It is one of two suppliers of Aegis guided missile destroyers, at more than $300 million each, and it is the sole manufacturer of amphibious assault ships, which are second in size only to aircraft carriers, at $1 billion each.

Litton's products and technologies have made the company an important supplier to the U.S. government. In 1998, 66 percent of Litton's sales were to the defense, civil service, and intelligence branches of the federal government. Most tactical military aircraft are equipped with Litton products. In short, virtually everything Litton produces is of significance to some facet of the U.S. government, whether it is the more tangible items, such as naval hardware, or the more technological products, including image-intensified night vision systems, data-handling systems, and communications systems.

"Our technology establishes our market leadership," says Arthur Bentley, Litton's manager of executive communications and corporate publications. "We've always considered technology our most important

Litton Industries supplies more than 75 percent of the world market for neodymium-doped yttrium aluminum garnet (Nd: YAG) crystals, which are grown at a Litton facility in North Carolina. Rods core-drilled from Nd:YAG crystal boules are at the heart of most of today's solid-state industrial laser systems (top).

Litton is the world leader in design and production of surface combatant ships, such as the Aegis guided-missile destroyer, which provides primary antiaircraft protection for the U.S. Navy (bottom).

From its own meteorological operations center, Weather Services International (WSI), a unit of Litton, supplies weather information to 50 percent of U.S. television stations and live reports to Fox News. Most major U.S. airlines contract with WSI for meteorological services.

competitive edge. We believe we provide outstanding technology and value in all our many activities.

"To cite just a few examples of technological leadership," Bentley continues, "our Sperry Marine unit was the first into production with ring laser guidance technology for ships and submarines. Our Ingalls Shipbuilding subsidiary originated modular construction techniques and developed a sophisticated three-dimensional, computer-aided design system. And early in the Vietnam War, Litton developed the first receiver systems to alert American aircraft to missile threats."

Far from the battlefield, Litton supplies industrial, computer, and medical industries with high-end computing and data storage technology. The company received a U.S. patent in 1998 for improvements in its sunlight-readable display technology. Information on a Litton sunlight-readable video screen is six to 10 times brighter than on a laptop computer screen, and

readily legible in the most intense sunlight. Litton currently serves the information systems needs of some 200 commercial customers, including Brooks Brothers, Star Markets, and Consolidated Edison, and has strategic alliances with a number of hardware, software, and information technology service companies, including Hewlett-Packard and Netscape.

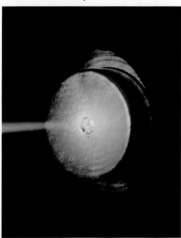

Fortified Hills of Success

According to Bentley, what sets Litton apart from its rivals is its ability to establish competitive positions in selected markets. "We consider these positions fortified hills that competitors have difficulty assailing," Bentley explains. "In many of our markets, we are either the leader or in second place."

Another point in Litton's favor is its broadly diversified business base, which shields the company from adversity in a single market. The company's revenue flows from a number of stable, reliable sources.

"It's fair to say that because of our position of leadership in many markets, we have a say in their course. That may be our most telling contribution of all," Bentley says.

With innovations running the gamut from amphibious assault ships to laser devices smaller than a postage stamp, Litton's products are a necessity in a variety of markets.

Clockwise from top:
A laser the size of a thumbnail represents a technological breakthrough for Litton. The military and commercial market potential is considered significant.

The company holds contracts for the integration of avionics aboard various kinds of military helicopters.

Litton is the leading integrator and provider of computer-aided dispatch systems for police, fire, and rescue services. Dispatchers working at consoles at this new center in Chicago, one of the largest of its kind in the United States, have at their fingertips all the electronic resources they need to direct almost immediate response to any emergency.

W hile Lockheed Martin has long been synonymous with the defense and aerospace industries in Los Angeles, the corporate giant also has a much more human, more personal aspect. Lockheed Martin IMS, a wholly owned subsidiary of Lockheed Martin Corp., is quite a different facet of the world's most well-known producer of aerospace technology. For more than two decades, Lockheed Martin IMS has focused on complex public policy issues, using its considerable

resources to build partnerships that help state and local governments in their delivery of human services and other civic activities.

With a Los Angeles office since the early 1980s and at least a dozen other locations in California, Lockheed Martin IMS is the fastest-growing company within Lockheed Martin Corp. It has eight business divisions, including Welfare Reform Services, Children and Family Services, Transportation Systems and Services, Municipal Services, Communications Industry Services, Information Resource Management, Criminal Justice Services, and Integrated Technology Solutions.

Through these divisions, Lockheed Martin IMS is able to form public/private partnerships with a variety of entities needing the expertise of an information management systems professional. What sets Lockheed Martin IMS apart from its competitors is the expertise of its staff. The

professionals hired to head the company's various operations and business units bring a wealth of experience in helping state and local governments address today's problems of trying to increase revenue, improve efficiency, and update technology.

A Wealth of Expertise

Lockheed Martin IMS delivers a broad range of municipal services to more than 100 clients in the United States, Europe, and Australia, helping them bring in nearly $500 million annually through programs designed to generate more revenue and recover backlogged debts that local governments were once forced to write off.

The Municipal Services provided by Lockheed Martin IMS include parking ticket processing, billing and collection for emergency medical services, and photo enforcement of red light and speeding infractions.

In another arena, the company uses its transaction processing capabilities to increase the collection and processing of child support payments. Currently, the company handles more than $2.5 billion annually— more than any other private sector firm— in helping deliver child support payments into the hands of needy families.

Lockheed Martin IMS expanded its services to include welfare-to-work programs in 1996, building a team of national leaders who operate work-related programs that help prepare welfare recipients to enter the workforce. The company already has placed more than 31,000 former welfare recipients in jobs, helping them rise from poverty. Lockheed's Welfare Services Program has been studied by the Harvard School of Business, which recognized its success in helping welfare recipients achieve self-sufficiency.

Lockheed Martin has spent the better part of the 20th century helping defend the nation's freedom and explore outer space. Now it is working to improve things at home by providing an array of services designed to help everyone from frustrated public managers to children in need of an absent parent's financial support.

As new social issues emerge and as old ones linger in 21st-century American society, the need for effective, systematic solutions will only grow. As these needs evolve, Lockheed Martin IMS will shape new approaches to help its partner organizations create a better world in which future generations can thrive and prosper.

Lockheed Martin IMS focuses on complex public policy issues, using its considerable resources to build partnerships that help state and local governments in their delivery of human services and other civic activities.

There is hardly a neighborhood in the United States that doesn't have the familiar CENTURY 21® For Sale signs posted in some of its yards. Indeed, the CENTURY 21 System has more name recognition than any other real estate sales organization in the business. For more than 25 years, CENTURY 21 professionals have worked to eliminate as much anxiety as possible from the home-buying and home-selling process, while maintaining the highest standards of service.

And their results are impressive. As the world's largest residential real estate sales organization, the CENTURY 21 System provides comprehensive training, management, administrative, and marketing support for CENTURY 21 professionals. The CENTURY 21 System has more than 110,000 professionals working in 6,300-plus offices in more than 25 countries.

In addition to its standard residential real estate services, the company offers custom marketing programs, including the CENTURY 21 Fine Homes and Estates℠ program, for those buying or selling a luxury home, and the CENTURY 21 Recreational Properties℠ program, which helps customers who are searching for a mountain, lake, or beachfront home.

A subsidiary of New Jersey-based Cendant Corporation since 1995, Century 21 Real Estate Corporation was established in Orange County in 1971. Its Santa Ana birthplace is now the location of the Franchise Service Center, which serves CENTURY 21 offices in 21 western states.

In addition to the services of its highly trained agents, CENTURY 21 offices offer an array of home-related products and services, including mortgage services, title insurance, home warranties, and home security systems through CENTURY 21 Connections℠. The CENTURY 21 System saves customers time and money, and provides informational services through the latest technology. Customers can be in touch with offices across the country.

through www.century21.com. Customers also can access information about neighborhoods, jobs, schools, the arts, recreation, and other opportunities in their target areas through CENTURY 21 Communities™ on America On-Line (AOL).

The company credits its success with a comprehensive advertising strategy that keeps its name and message constantly in the public's mind. CENTURY 21 is the first and only real estate company to develop an advertising and marketing program specifically for the Hispanic community nationwide.

Serving the Community

The CENTURY 21 System's dedication to the community is apparent in its work with the Easter Seal Society, for which it has raised more than $55 million in the past 17 years. The CENTURY 21 System is also a title sponsor for the Inner City Games in Los Angeles and Chicago during 1998 and 1999.

The company plans to focus on strengthening its presence in international markets in the 21st century. The CENTURY 21 System is dedicated to continuing its growth not only in the number of its offices, but, more important, in the quality and size of its offices around the world. Already the most recognized name in real estate, CENTURY 21 can truly move its clients "across town, across the country, or around the world."

Each office is independently owned and operated.

Clockwise from top:
The CENTURY 21 System has more name recognition than any other real estate sales organization in the business.

CENTURY 21 offices offer an array of home-related products and services, including mortgage services, title insurance, home warranties, and home security systems.

The CENTURY 21 System has more than 110,000 professionals working in 6,300-plus offices in more than 25 countries.

Mercury Air Group, Inc.

Mercury Air Group, Inc., a company dedicated to providing the most comprehensive air support services available, can trace its roots back to the days prior to World War II, when young volunteer pilots followed Colonel Clair Chenault to China to join the American Volunteer Group. These flying aces, in their Curtis P-40 airplanes painted with wide, toothy snarls, had a dream of helping the Chinese defend their country from Japan, and later became famous as the Flying Tigers. Admired for their many victories in the face of overwhelming odds, the Flying Tigers inspired a generation of future pilots.

After hanging up their goggles and flight jackets following World War II, three of those flyboys–Robert J. Raine, Thomas C. Haywood, and Robert P. Hedman–had a new dream. In 1956, with the goal of keeping U.S. airlines up and flying by meeting the growing need for aviation services, the three established Mercury Service in Los Angeles. The forerunner of Mercury Air Group, Mercury Service began with an investment of just $80,000, a handful of fuel trucks, and a single contract. Since then, Mercury Air Group has grown to offer a variety of services that provide support for such clients as *Air Force One* and the Blue Angels, and scores of slightly less-famous commercial, corporate, and private airborne clients.

In 1972, Seymour Kahn, who today serves as chairman of the board, left the electronics field on the East Coast and came to the West Coast to buy Mercury, fulfilling his dream of being a part of a service industry. At the time, the company was a refueling and ground handling company with annual revenues of under $2 million; by 1998, Kahn had built Mercury into a worldwide aviation services company, with annual revenues of more than $240 million. In 1997, *Fortune* magazine identified Mercury as one of America's Top 100 Fastest-Growing Companies, while *Forbes* magazine named it one of the country's Best Small Companies. Mercury Air Group has been traded on the American Stock Exchange since 1982 under the symbol MAX.

In 1998, Joseph Czyzyk, who has been with Mercury since 1984, was named president and chief executive officer. Between them, Kahn and Czyzyk have more than 50 years of leadership in the aviation industry.

The Mercury Family

Mercury Air Group comprises five divisions of aviation related services, all dedicated to the safe and efficient operation of the aviation industry. International Aviation Fuel Sales and Services provides fuel and fueling services to aircraft at major commercial airports around the globe. In fact, it is the largest such non-refiner provider at Los Angeles International Airport, the world's third-busiest airport. Mercury's alliances with petroleum refiners worldwide enable the company to purchase petroleum products at the best rates and provide jet fuel to its clients at reasonable prices.

Mercury Air Cargo, Inc., the company's cargo-handling division, is a three-fold operation. On behalf of its airline customers, the division handles everything from heavy cargo such as 50-ton generators to perishable goods, including flowers and baby chicks. Mercury Air Cargo also serves as a cargo space broker, acquiring air-cargo space in bulk so that it can provide worldwide air-cargo capacity to those with shipping needs. Similarly, it provides sales representation, as general cargo sales agents, for dozens of airlines worldwide.

Maytag Aircraft Corporation manages aviation fuel storage and provides transport, refueling, and maintenance at U.S. military bases and commercial airports around the world, in addition to air terminal, housing, and base maintenance and operations on numerous military and foreign airports on behalf of the U.S. government. Based in Colorado Springs, Maytag also provides weather observation and forecasting and air-traffic-control services for the FAA and local municipalities throughout the United States.

Mercury Air Centers operates 15 fixed base operations (FBOs) nationwide, providing full ground support services including refueling, hangar rentals, aircraft parking and tie down, as well as numerous pilot services. This division services the corporate jets of Fortune 500 executives, Air Force

Mercury Air Cargo's new cargo facility at Los Angeles International Airport operates 24 hours each day, handling shipments from domestic and international flights (top).

Mercury Air Centers supports Los Angeles air travel with fixed base operations at Los Angeles International Airport, Burbank International Airport, and Ontario International Airport, all in Los Angeles County, and 12 other locations nationwide (bottom).

© 1998 PATRICK KNISELY

© 1998 PATRICK KNISELY

One, and the private aircraft of the world's rich and famous.

RPA Airline Automation Services provides aviation information technology to more than 50 foreign and domestic airlines. RPA offers a variety of copyrighted software packages specific to the airline industry, including programs for purchase maintenance and inventory management, financial accounting, passenger and revenue accounting, flight operations accounting, and frequent-flyer management.

In addition to its superlative air services, Mercury Air Group supports a number of area schools and organizations, including Flight Path Learning Center, which educates young people about aviation in the hope of interesting them in the industry. Mercury also sponsors the Westchester Roundtable Forum for area residents and workers to meet and converse with speakers on a variety of political, educational, and civic topics.

The Mercury Team

Mercury Air Group is uniquely situated in the world of aviation services, with its five areas enabling it to provide valuable products and services to the aviation industry. Kahn credits the company's diversity as the reason for its strength. "The diversification of our activities within the aviation industry has been such that when one activity is down, the others are up, and they carry the company," he says. "It's been very instrumental in keeping us on target and strong. The company has always made money, even when the entire aviation industry has lost money."

Mercury Air Group's acquisition strategy is designed to help the company consistently upgrade its services. The company keeps a watchful eye on those businesses that will enhance its offerings. The company's purchase of RPA Airline Automation Services in 1998 was consistent with that goal.

"It took us 20 years to achieve $100 million in revenue," says Kahn. "When I met with our staff regarding that milestone, I said, 'I think we can double it in two years.' And we did. Our first $100 million was in 1994. In 1996, we hit $200 million. And last year we earned $240 million."

Kahn contributes this success to one thing: teamwork. At Mercury, teamwork and dedication are encouraged and rewarded. Mercury employees are supported by an agressive benefits program, and have ownership in the company through the employee stock purchase plan. Mercury also actively supports charities and organizations in the communities where its employees live and work.

Says Kahn, in summarizing the company's philosophy in his annual message to Mercury employees, "Our belief in teamwork is rooted in our historical ties to the legendary American Volunteer Group Flying Tigers in China before and during World War II. This same spirit of teamwork inspires our board of directors, contemporary management team, and employees today. In our core mission of service to the aviation industry today, we provide our customers with an exceptional level of service and in turn build lasting value for you, our shareholders.

"With the AVG Flying Tigers as our continuing inspiration, our best days are still ahead."

International Aviation Fuel Sales and Services includes the sale and delivery of fuel primarily to commercial airlines.

Turner Construction Company

I n 1964, Turner Construction Company came to Los Angeles to build Union Bank, the first high-rise office building to grace Bunker Hill. Since then, Turner has helped reshape the Los Angeles skyline by constructing some of the most well-known skyscrapers in town, including the Library Tower, the tallest building in the western United States. Turner also has put its years of expertise to work in Los Angeles by helping build educational institutions that will last for generations. It is a leader in constructing and rehabilitating entertainment venues such as Long

Beach Aquarium of the Pacific and Anaheim Stadium. And it has restored some of Los Angeles' most graceful landmark structures, including El Capitan Theater on Hollywood Boulevard and several other fanciful movie houses built in the early days of Hollywood.

Committed to Clients

Turner Construction Company was founded in 1902 by Henry C. Turner, a devout Quaker from Maryland who wanted to make a name for himself in the construction industry by building high-quality, enduring structures. Turner once explained his company's success by stating, "We are awarded most of our work based on reputation. Preservation of our reputation demands a commitment to quality, service, and operation within approved budgets and schedules. This is the foundation of our company."

Still infused with that commitment to quality, Turner Construction Company has grown into the nation's largest builder of commercial, industrial, health care, institutional, and government facilities. Those who have hired the company appreciate the commitment that Turner makes to its clients. Raymond A. Rodriguez, administrative consultant for the Los Angeles Unified School District, lauded the work the company has provided to date for the new Belmont Learning Complex adjacent to downtown Los Angeles: "Based on my 12 years managing school construction projects and my experience working with Turner Construction Company and their staff, it is without reservation or hesitation that I would recommend them . . . When it is all said and done, Turner is a highly competent, reliable, and ethical contractor who is very serious about getting the job done right."

Southern California's business elite trust Turner Construction Company to build their signature structures. The company has constructed such landmark towers as Arco Center, Arco Tower, Wells Fargo/ Crocker Center, and Southern California

Since arriving in Los Angeles in 1964, Turner Construction has been a key player in transforming the city skyline. Turner came to Los Angeles to build the first high-rise structure on Bunker Hill, Union Bank, shown in a 1969 photo of downtown (top).

Today, the Los Angeles skyline has nine towering landmarks built by Turner to date, which include (from left) Transpacific (Arco) Center, 333 South Hope, Arco Towers, Wells Fargo/Crocker Center, Library Tower, 801 Tower, and Southern California Gas Company Tower. These structures make up more than half of the Los Angeles skyline (bottom).

BIELENBERG

Turner's Los Angeles Special Projects Division is one of three operating groups of the Southern California region specializing in high-end interior improvements, building renovations, new construction, small buildings, and various high-tech, health care, and specialty projects. Projects range in size from $10,000 to $20 million, and are typically performed for corporate clients, major developers, and institutions. Interior improvement clients include Arthur Andersen & Co., Oppenheimer, Mattel, Rockwell, Disney, Warner Bros., and The Capital Group, to name a few.

Gas Company Tower. Turner Construction Company also helped create buildings at Southern California's most prestigious institutions of higher education, including USC, UCLA, California Institute of Technology, and Chapman University. It has built such Universal Studios attractions as WaterWorld and Jurassic Park-The Ride, as well as entertainment venues like the Long Beach Convention Center, Anaheim Convention Center, and California Speedway. Turner is also a well-known name in the health care industry. Ranked for the 12th consecutive year as the nation's leading health care builder by *Modern Healthcare* magazine, the company serves a client base in Southern California that includes Kaiser Pemanente, the County of Los Angeles, Glendale Medical Center, and Saint Joseph Medical Center in Burbank, to name a few.

Crowning Achievement

All of Turner Construction Company's projects are completed with one business philosophy in mind: "Seek originality, build character, and use new materials because quality is remembered long after price is forgotten."

Though each of the company's projects can be said to live up to that philosophy, Turner's crowning achievement has to be the Library Tower, perhaps the most recognizable building in downtown Los Angeles. The cylindrical steel structure rises 75 stories in the center of downtown and has occupied a special place in the hearts of residents since it was completed in 1989. Situated at the corner of Hope and Fifth streets, the high-rise straddles Bunker Hill's glitzy new office developments and the historic core of downtown Los Angeles. In addition, the project includes a series of staircases called the Bunker Hill Steps. Reminiscent of Rome's Spanish Steps, they are connected by winding terraces lined with a cascading fountain, and create an important link between Los Angeles' past and its future.

GARY KRUEGER

Turner's Special Projects Division has been involved with the historical renovation of seven Los Angeles landmark theaters to date. Turner provided historical renovation and restoration of the El Capitan Theater. The historic, 1926 theater is located in Hollywood.

In building Library Tower, Turner Construction Company accomplished one of the most significant construction feats of the 1980s—setting a building inside another building. It took years to plan the project and another 28 months to complete it. At the end of it, Turner had successfully converted 29,000 tons of steel, 375,000 square feet of Luna Pearl granite, 1.8 million square feet of metal decking, and 7,200 trusses into an elegant but rugged structure designed to absorb the shock of an earthquake registering 8.3 on the Richter scale.

Before construction began on Library Tower, the developers also agreed to aid in the renovation of Los Angeles' Central Library across the street from the building. The architectural jewel, built in 1926 and badly damaged in a 1986 fire, was in danger of demolition. Instead, the City was able to rehabilitate the building and replace the books, thanks in large part to the Library Tower project.

Turner was also very successful in the development of a mentor-protégé program for the second-tier minority subcontractors during the construction of Library Tower. Turner is proactive in its efforts to include minority firms, regardless of size, in most of its projects.

Commitment to Communities

Los Angeles is one of 42 communities nationwide where Turner maintains operations. In each community, the company operates as a local contractor, working closely with local owners, architects, subcontractors, and municipal agencies. Charles W. Koch, Turner's vice president and operations manager, believes that employees take great pride in their work when they are building in their own communities. "It is very exciting because there is something they can point to and say, 'I helped build that.'"

Turner Construction Company's commitment to quality and service is rivaled only by its commitment to the community. The company devotes its resources and expertise to training new generations of construction workers and managers, and to working closely with the area's women- and minority-owned subcontractors.

"We truly believe it's our duty to give back to the community," says Koch. "And it makes good business sense because as the economy grows, we need more quality subcontractors and we need to make sure they are there. To accomplish that goal, Turner Construction Company created a Minority/Woman Business enterprise program, through which the company gives financial support and maintains regular contact with all the minority business associations in Los Angeles. Turner subcontracts approximately 25 percent of its business to minority- and women-owned construction firms based in Los Angeles.

In cooperation with the minority business associations in Los Angeles, Turner Construction Company sponsors a seven-

The tallest building west of the Mississippi is Library Tower, rising 75 stories, in the heart of Los Angeles (left). The project includes the Bunker Hill Steps (right), which are reminiscent of Rome's Spanish Steps, and create an important link between Los Angeles' past and future through a series of winding terraces and cascading fountains.

week, 14-course seminar on construction management. Also, through its partnership with the INROADS program, it trains minority youths in Los Angeles each summer. The students return each summer until they complete college, and several have been hired by Turner Construction Company at the end of their training.

The company also began a program called Youth Force 2000 to introduce young people to careers in construction. The program is designed to ensure that the younger generation is aware of the rewarding job opportunities that exist in construction and is given the chance to explore them. Nationwide, nearly 40 percent of Turner's employees are involved in the Youth Force 2000 efforts.

Turner Construction Company's efforts at promoting minority business participation and youth training have been lauded by other professional organizations over the years. For example, Turner Construction Company was recognized for three consecutive years by the Black Business Association of Los Angeles for demonstrating the highest level of responsiveness to minority business enterprises of any major contractor in the construction industry. Turner Construction has also been honored five times by the National Association of Minority Contractors as the Majority Corporation of the Year—given to the com-

pany that has shown the most interest and best results in utilizing minority- and women-owned business enterprises throughout the country.

In addition, Turner Construction Company has volunteered its time and expertise to help several community service organizations—including Operation Hope, Community Build, YMCA, and Drew Economic Development Corporation—complete their construction projects.

Looking Ahead to the Millennium

Turner Construction has grown from a small contractor that stressed quality, integrity, and excellence to an international

contracting giant that is responsible for creating some of the most remarkable structures in the world. Still, nearly 100 years later, the company recognizes the significant challenges that face construction companies in today's fast-paced business climate.

"As Los Angeles approaches the millennium, Turner Construction is ready to work within the diverse Los Angeles community to build a bright and prosperous future," says William Cody, general manager of the Los Angeles office. "Turner is the premier builder in Southern California and is committed to serving our clients."

CHARLES LENOIR, LENOIR PHOTOGRAPHY

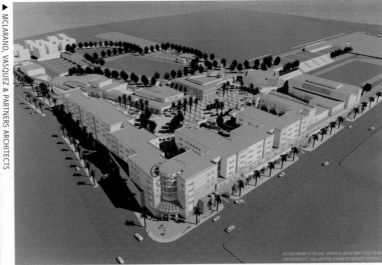

MCLARAND, VASQUEZ & PARTNERS ARCHITECTS

APPLAUSE, INC.

or more than 30 years, Applause, Inc. has been tugging on the heartstrings of America, triggering fond memories by creating products that bring out the child in everyone. With plush and figural gifts that recapture the magical moments of youth pop culture–such as Mickey Mouse, Bugs Bunny, Snoopy, Kermit the Frog, and Raggedy Ann and Andy–the company's clapping-hands logo says it all: Everyone loves to get Applause. ☟ Applause isn't just about plush toys and plastic figurines, though. It's also about

memories for every occasion: mugs and plates, key chains and picture frames, and a plethora of gift items that make appealing window displays for the company's nearly 50,000 retail clients. Rather than supplying the mass market, Applause items are found in places like specialty gift stores, card shops, video stores, bookstores, specialty infant shops, and comic book stores.

"We understand small-town America and independent business owners," explains Jonathan R. Mather, president and CEO of the company.

The Essence of Applause

Applause measures its success by the number of retailers that want more of its products. The company has a seamless capability of providing seasonal, tourist, and everyday items in many different recognizable product lines: Mickey Unlimited and Mickey for Kids, Pooh 100 Acre Collection, Looney Tunes, Sesame Street, Pea-

nuts, Muppets, Lucasfilm's Star Wars Classic Collectors Series, Nickelodeon's Rugrats, Raggedy Ann and Andy, and Applause's own Dakin Brand of plush and infant merchandise. In addition, Applause has licenses for many of Disney's animated film properties such as *Simba's Pride* and *Mulan*, and *A Bug's Life* from Pixar.

"We take the essence of who the character is, whether it's Bugs Bunny, Mickey Mouse, or Elmo, and put that into a three-dimensional gift so that there is an emotional connection," says Mather from his Woodland Hills office, amid a crowd of plush toys of all sizes. "Our salespeople love to sell our products because what we sell brings a positive, welcome mood to everyone."

The company's other distribution channels are through custom premiums among consumer packaged-goods companies, quick service restaurants, and retail chains. Applause has also established strategic alliances with several major food-related chains including Taco Bell, KFC, Kellogg's, General Mills, Pillsbury, and ConAgra's Kid's Cuisine Division.

The recognizable hands of the Applause trademark have extended internationally as well, holding an extensive network of foreign distributors in 55 countries throughout Europe, the Middle East, the Far East, Australia, Mexico, and Central and South America.

Little Blue Hands Worth a Billion

Applause's success story began with the arrival of little blue men, but the company's history started with two New Jersey brothers' desire to make and sell items that would bring warm, fuzzy feelings to people's hearts. In the early 1960s, Wallace and Russ Berrie manufactured and sold drugstore novelty items on the East Coast. By 1966, the two brothers had split their business: Wallace would go west, Russ would stay in the east.

The Wallace Berrie Company flourished during the early 1970s, but it grew into a giant shortly after acquiring worldwide rights to little blue caricatures about three-stacked-apples tall. The little-known characters were the Smurfs–a product line that ultimately became a leader in the licensing industry, selling more than $1 billion in merchandise.

© 1998 JIM HENSON PRODUCTIONS, INC.

In 1982, Berrie acquired the Applause Company from Knickerbocker Toys. and inherited a number of classic licenses such as Disney, Sesame Street, and Raggedy Ann and Andy. When Berrie left the company in 1986, it adopted the Applause name and expanded its portfolio of both classic and entertainment properties. Nine years later, Applause grew even larger after purchasing Dakin, Inc., one of the oldest branded designers, importers, and distributors of quality plush products and accessory items.

Today, the company has about 600 employees, one-third of whom are on-the-road salespeople, taking the Applause product to independent shops around the country. At the Woodland Hills headquarters, another 250 employees comprise the creative, operational, and managerial staff; the remainder are based at Applause's distribution center in the centrally located city of Carson, south of Los Angeles. Outside of the United States, Applause has operations in Hong Kong, Korea, and China.

"We are a company that is growth focused, that is built on a team of creative people," Mather says. "We will continue to build on our strengths, focusing on innovation and creating new trend products for the future."

Hands That Help

The Applause philosophy is built around the idea that the future is about children. The brand's enormous emotional appeal springs from its concentration on ideas and products that children relate to. "We make products that are so three-dimensionally perfect that they are valuable as a gift or as a collectible," Mather says.

With its Dakin Brand, Applause has been able to develop products that serve as educational tools for parents and teach-

ers. For example, many of the plush toys under the Dakin name aim not only to entertain, but to put children in touch with nature and natural history. Everything from lions to insects to dinosaurs is part of the Dakin line.

It is natural for a company that brings joy to kids of all ages to give to the disadvantaged as well. Applause has developed a plush bear line—Bears For A Cause—whose proceeds will be donated to the

Susan G. Komen Breast Cancer Foundation. Each year, Applause will develop a new bear that will benefit a different foundation. The company also provides toys to various Los Angeles and national children's charities, including the Ronald McDonald House, City of Hope, and Children's Hospice of Los Angeles, among others.

As Mather says, "Helping others ties into what we do, who we are, and what we believe."

Clockwise from top:
In addition to having licenses for many of Disney's animated film properties and strategic alliances with several major food-related chains, Applause produces its own Dakin Brand of plush and infant merchandise.

Applause is a major player in the children's meal premium arena. In 1997, Applause designed and produced the highly acclaimed Taco Bell Star Wars toys, many of which are now collector items.

The success of the Smurfs in the early 1980s launched Applause into becoming one of the foremost gift companies

or more than 30 years, Romac International has provided talent and consultation to progressive companies requiring permanent placement, contract, and temporary staffing. Through its recent merger with Source Services Corporation, Romac–also known as the KnowledgeForce Resource–has strengthened itself as the leader in recruiting and placing the nation's top professionals in the information technology (IT), accounting and finance, and engineering industries. ⚜ Romac has successfully guided the careers of professionals

nationwide. At the same time, executives responsible for hiring at the nation's top firms have looked to the Romac team to help them find experienced people with the right skills and credentials.

"Our associates are professionals with extensive experience from the disciplines that we serve," says Paul L. Ratajczak, regional vice president of Romac's Source Consulting division. "So we are better able to understand and position our candidates because we have been there ourselves."

Reaching Career Goals

Romac prides itself on taking a long-term, relationship-building approach to client service for the two groups of customers it serves: client companies and job candidates. The key to the company's business success is the personal service given by every Romac International professional. To provide this service, Ratajczak says, the company identifies and retains the highest-quality people, and then trains them.

"Our philosophy is to provide our client companies and job candidates the best customer service possible," Ratajczak says. "Customer intimacy and developing long-term relationships is a theme we adhere to in order to satisfy each of their needs."

Romac has been recognized as a leader in compensation issues and career development in the information technology, accounting and finance, and engineering industries. Professionals in these industries have relied on the firm for the most current industry trends and the latest career strategies.

In addition, in the Romac culture, an environment is created for each person to attain his or her goals and to develop professionally. Also, adds Ratajczak, contracted consultants are provided with a group health insurance package, 401(k) plans, stock options, and technical training to enhance their skills. "This ensures that our consultants grow with the company," he says.

The strength of the KnowledgeForce network is such that when a consultant is placed, he or she is not a technical island. If the Romac consultant runs into a problem, the firm has an expert somewhere across the country that he or she can contact for assistance. All of the company's professionals work together through a state-of-the-art, computerized network.

Michael Ellis, a business unit manager from the Gardena office, says, "When a client company brings in one of our professionals, it actually brings in all of Romac. The company's consultants feel that they have the power of a multinational corporation behind them."

The company maintains an exclusive database—that was augmented with the merger—of more than 1 million skilled professionals nationwide, so client companies have instant access to people best suited for specific openings and consulting projects. Clients range from Fortune 100

Romac International prides itself on taking a long-term, relationship-building approach to client service for the two groups of customers it serves: client companies and job candidates. (top).

Romac has had a presence in Southern California since 1966 and has offices strategically located throughout the region: Sherman Oaks, Century City, Gardena (pictured), Irvine, and San Diego (bottom).

companies to entrepreneurial start-ups in a broad spectrum of industries: entertainment, areospace, financial services, banking, software development, medical, and utilities, to name a few.

A Future of Growth

The staffing industry has grown rapidly in recent years, as companies have utilized temporary employees to reduce personnel costs, while also meeting specialized or fluctuating staffing requirements. According to a study by Dataquest, total U.S. IT services expenditures were an estimated $64 billion in 1997 and are expected to reach $97 billion by 2000, representing a compounded annual growth rate of almost 15 percent. Bureau of Labor employment statistics corroborate the strong demand picture, with the computer and data processing services sector far and away the employment growth leader over the past five years.

"Romac has been growing with a 50 percent growth rate over the last three years," says Ratajczak. "Combined now, we are about a three-quarters-of-a-billion-dollar company in 1998, and will reach $1 billion in 1999."

Romac's Source Services division—which consists of Source Consulting, Source EDP, Source Finance, and Accountant Source Temps—has had a presence in Southern California since 1966 and has offices strategically located throughout the region: Sherman Oaks, Century City, Gardena, Irvine, and San Diego. The firm has approximately 120 associates and about 500 consultants working at client sites locally. Romac has more than 1,000 associates internationally and more than 6,000 consultants worldwide.

Ratajczak points out that several of Romac's top performers are based in Southern California. "Our overall goal is to become number one in every market

in which we operate," he says. "We are strong in the information technology consulting practice, and are expecting strong growth in the finance and accounting temp area." In 1998, the *Los Angeles Business Journal* ranked Source Services number one in contingency job-search placement and number nine in consulting. "What sets us apart is that our associates come from the industries they represent," Ratajczak explains. "We have CPAs placing accountants, and technology professionals working with IT consultants and managers. It makes a huge difference when we all speak the same language."

On the eve of the new century, Romac is poised to take on the challenges of the ever changing global marketplace. The company will continue to provide flexible and permanent staffing by creating strategic alliances between the nation's top professionals and the industries that need their skills for years to come.

The staffing industry has grown rapidly in recent years, as companies have utilized temporary employees to reduce personnel costs, while also meeting specialized or fluctuating staffing requirements.

One of 71 community college districts in California, the Los Angeles Community College District (LACCD) is the largest community college system in the state and in the nation, boasting more than 98,000 students. LACCD's nine colleges—collectively known as Los Angeles Community Colleges—are fully accredited by the Western Association of Schools and Colleges. Each stands ready to partner with business, industry, education, and governmental agencies in the development of

custom-made programs designed to educate and train the workforce of the 21st century. For this and many other reasons, LACCD is truly where Los Angeles learns.

In addition, LACCD is part of a state-wide system that is the largest provider of a college education in the world. Throughout California, there are 107 community college campuses serving 1.7 million students. An affordable avenue to higher education, LACCD functions as a bridge to a four-year degree for more than 30 percent of its student population. Transfer programs in such classes as English, mathematics, science, the social sciences, foreign languages, and the humanities are accepted at many leading universities with which the district partners, including UCLA, Pepperdine, and USC.

With nearly 340 occupational specialties and approximately 200 academic programs (ranging in length from one semester to two years), LACCD thoroughly prepares students to enter the workplace. In addition to providing hands-on experience in the classroom, many training programs provide for internships in the field. Each school also adapts and develops courses according to the needs of businesses that rely on that school as an important source for their labor pools.

Unique in its ethnic makeup—reflecting the 35 municipalities and 11 school districts

With nearly 340 occupational specialties and approximately 200 academic programs, the nine institutions of the Los Angeles Community Colleges thoroughly prepare students to enter the workplace.

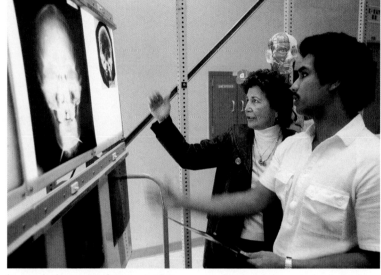

it serves in the Los Angeles area—LACCD is also noted for its multilingual student assistance centers, Extended Opportunity Program and Services opportunities, disabled student services, and foreign student programs.

Board of Trustees

In 1929, there were 35 junior colleges in California. Over the next decade, enrollment doubled as the importance of community colleges increased nationwide. Today, Los Angeles Community College District is a premier educational system, with a direct link to its electorate through a publicly elected board of trustees.

Serving as the governing body of LACCD, the board of trustees is independent of the city and the county of Los Angeles. The board members are elected at large for terms of four years. Elections are held every two years, with three members being chosen at one election and four members at the other. A student member is elected annually. The college district includes approximately 882 square miles—nearly double the area of the city of Los Angeles.

East Los Angeles College

East Los Angeles College (ELAC) was chartered by the Los Angeles City Board of Education on June 7, 1945, and opened its doors the following September in a wing of Garfield High School. Curricula in the early days centered around agriculture, business, health, civics and welfare, home-making, fine arts, industry, and cultural heritage. The college soon outgrew its quarters at the high school, and by 1947, moved to an 83-acre spot on Brooklyn Avenue that was being used for grazing cattle and growing barley. As the college's enrollment continued to grow, the school built new classrooms, administrative quarters, a permanent library, a planetarium, gyms, a theater, a swimming pool complex, and an art gallery.

A strong community awareness has always been a key characteristic of the founding and development of the college.

Students enjoy a painting exhibit in an art gallery at one of LACCD's nine colleges.

Today, with an enrollment of more than 15,000 students, ELAC continues to meet the community's needs by training in new occupations and responding to evolving technologies, specializing in media arts with departments in theater arts, photography, speech communications, journalism, art, architecture, and computer science.

Los Angeles City College

When Los Angeles City College (LACC) opened on the eve of the Great Depression, there wasn't much else for young, out-of-work people to do except go to college. As a result, LACC moved into a ready-made, former UCLA campus and opened its classroom doors at a location in the heart of the city where oil derricks, broadcasting studios, and aircraft plants had sprung up among the orange groves.

Today, LACC serves more than 20,000 students, offering educational programs in more than 80 different areas. In addition to such career majors as business, accounting, computer science, office administration, electronics technology, and child development, LACC offers the popular Cinema-Television Academy and Professional Theater Training Program.

The college's new Media Arts Academy provides training in video game design, illustration, and production; video and film tilting, including graphics, signage, and packaging for print and electronic media; typography and composition for CD-ROM and Web pages; and animation. In addition, LACC offers training in four health career fields: dental technology, dietetic technician, human services, and radiological technology. Additional career training programs include law and legal assistance, family and consumer studies, and transportation/travel/tourism.

Los Angeles Harbor College

Los Angeles Harbor College has been serving the communities in the area of the Port of Los Angeles for more than four decades. Just four miles from San Pedro and 17 miles south of downtown Los Angeles, Harbor College is an 85-acre campus bordered by a park and golf course.

Students can choose from dozens of major areas of study in both the academic and occupational realms. Among the academic programs are architecture, art, business, English and communications, music, nursing, science, theater, and technology. Certificate programs, which can lead to an associate's degree, are offered in most departments. In addition, the college's Project for Adult College Education (PACE) program, through which working adults can earn a degree, is considered a pioneering effort in the western United States.

Los Angeles Mission College

Nestled in the foothills of the San Gabriel mountains in the city of Sylmar, Los Angeles Mission College (LAMC) has created a

multidimensional learning environment through its educational development programs and services. Since the college opened in 1975, a comprehensive program of student services and activities, including extensive counseling and guidance services, has developed. The college maintained operations out of storefront facilities in and around the city of San Fernando until moving in 1991 to its permanent, Spanish-mission-style campus in Sylmar.

LAMC's M2.LRN program of multimedia studies provides a multidisciplinary approach that focuses on portfolio development in a project-based learning environment. The program is divided into five blocks: foundation, which provides essential art skills and the philosophy of art; interactive media design, which emphasizes creating a completely interactive virtual environment through video and animation; advanced presentation graphics, where students are challenged to reach the next level of sophistication through in-depth study of art production techniques; video production, which works in the

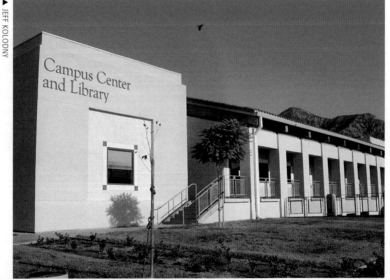

▶ JEFF KOLODNY

Clockwise from top:
Mission College opened its beautiful
Spanish-mission-style campus in 1991.

Students majoring in science utilize a science lab for experiments.

Hazardous Materials Technology is one of the many specialty programs offered by Los Angeles Community Colleges.

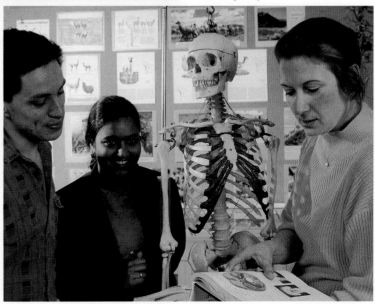

digital domain, where students learn to create video for television; and the animation block, where drawing and computer animation meet.

Los Angeles Pierce College

Originally called the Clarence W. Pierce School of Agriculture of the Los Angeles City Schools, Pierce College has come a long way from being an agricultural junior college. Founded in 1947 on 420 acres of land in the West San Fernando Valley, Pierce College has grown in line with its surrounding communities, which have changed from rural to suburban.

Based in the city of Woodland Hills, Pierce College is in the process of developing the Institute for New Media, a program that combines existing curricula with state-of-the-art education and training in all new media fields. Programs are offered in animation, graphic design, digital imaging, electronic music, game development, instructional media design and management, interactive educational software design, journalism, photography, special effects, and theater arts.

Los Angeles Southwest College

Southwest College, founded in 1967 on 71 acres of land in south-central Los Angeles, serves nearly 5,000 inner-city students. The college recently built the three-story, $7 million Technical Education Center, complete with state-of-the-art equipment. In addition, construction is under way for a physical education complex and lecture lab.

The college has recently broken ground for the Fine Arts and Community Center, which will provide a unique opportunity for college staff and business-industry planners to create a facility that is directly responsive to the training needs of the entertainment industry. Rather than house new programs within current facilities, this new complex will respond to the future needs of the community.

Los Angeles Trade-Technical College

The Los Angeles Trade-Technical College evolved from a trade school for Los Angeles' labor force in the mid-1920s. Named the Frank Wiggins Trade School—after a former secretary of the Los Angeles Chamber of Commerce—the college trained nearly 50,000 persons during the war years. In the following years, it provided postwar training to veterans, and added necessary academic courses required for associate in arts and sciences degrees. After moving to its permanent location of 25 acres off

Clockwise from top left:
Hands-on instruction is an important part of printing technology classes.

Fashion Design is one of the many programs offered through the Los Angeles Community Colleges.

Engineering students demonstrate a robotic project for their class.

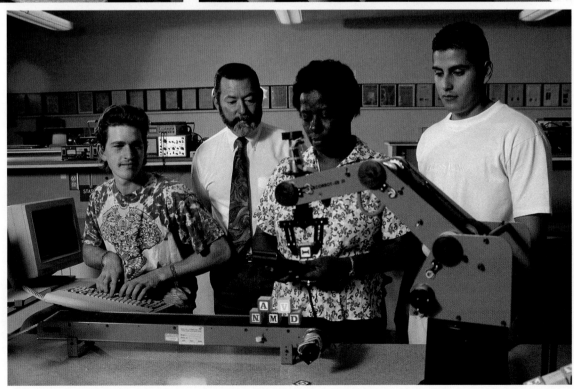

Washington Boulevard in downtown, the school was renamed Trade-Technical College to better reflect the broadening of its course offerings.

Today, Trade-Tech provides highly trained workers for a variety of specialized industries. In visual communications, the college instructs students in illustration, design, and production using computer-generated images. The Fashion Center offers the programs that prepare graduates for careers in wardrobing and costume design. The architectural technology department provides hands-on training with AutoCAD and GIS technology employed in three-dimensional simulation of buildings, sets, and designs for theater and film production. In the construction trades, the college offers degrees and certificates in electrical technology, carpentry, plumbing and refrigeration, and air-conditioning.

Los Angeles Valley College

Over the years, as the demographics of the San Fernando Valley have changed, so have the demographics of the Los Angeles Valley College. Today, the Valley College student body, averaging 17,000 per semester, is reflective of California's entire ethnic spectrum. The 50-year-old college, located in the city of Van Nuys, offers more than 50 majors that are transferable to four-year colleges.

Serving the Valley's entertainment industry through its media and communication arts programs, the college specializes in art, cinema, television, radio, journalism, theater, engineering, business, music, computer science, and electronics. Its media arts curriculum includes writing for the media, media history/criticism/literacy, performance for the media, visual imaging and design for the media, audio imaging and sound for the media, and media-related computer applications.

West Los Angeles College

Located on the west side of Los Angeles, and serving the area comprised of the DreamWorks Studio, Sony, and 20th Century Fox, West Los Angeles College is uniquely positioned to train the new media workforce of the next century.

To prepare students for employment in the animation and multimedia industries, the college offers training for a range of new media positions, including animator, visual development artist, storyboard artist, layout artist, cleanup artist, effects animator, CGI animator, background painter, graphic designer, Web designer, interactive designer, CD-ROM games designer, and presentation designer.

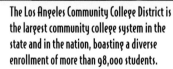

The Los Angeles Community College District is the largest community college system in the state and in the nation, boasting a diverse enrollment of more than 98,000 students.

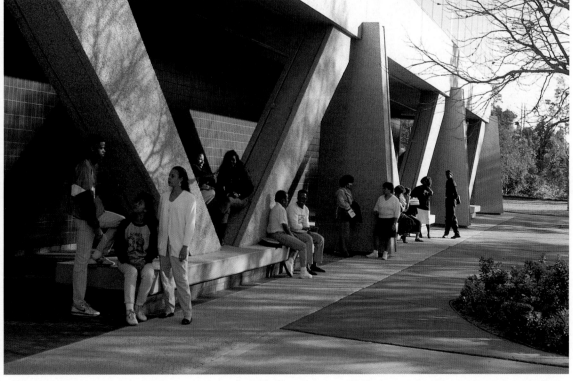

GEORGE D. BJURMAN & ASSOCIATES

George D. Bjurman & Associates may not be a household name, but companies and governmental agencies across the country often turn to the firm for sound advice on investments and quality money management. Founded in 1970 by George D. Bjurman, the company has made a name for itself by successfully managing the investment portfolios and pension and profit-sharing plans of large companies, government agencies, and foundations across the nation.

When Bjurman opened shop in Century City, he had decades of experience managing pension funds for several large Los Angeles-based firms, including Occidental Life Insurance Co. and TransAmerica Counselors Inc. Bjurman's son, G. Andrew Bjurman, joined the firm at its inception as a founding vice president and became president of the company in 1978. Andrew Bjurman and Chief Investment Officer O. Thomas Barry, along with several senior associates, have overseen the growth of the company, which currently handles approximately $2 billion in assets.

Professional Service in a Family Atmosphere

The heads of George D. Bjurman & Associates have worked hard to maintain a close-knit, family atmosphere at the company's headquarters. Part of maintaining that feeling has involved ensuring that the company grows at a manageable pace. After 28 years of business, the firm now

has 27 employees, each with a large and comfortable workspace from which to enjoy a spectacular view of the apartment towers that line the sky just beyond the greens and fairways of the Los Angeles Country Club.

The comfort of the physical surroundings mirrors the corporate culture at George D. Bjurman & Associates. Employees freely share information and ideas, and the firm prides itself on being open to suggestions from all its employees, no matter what their position or how long their tenure. By offering financial assistance for education in the field of finance, the company encourages all of its employees to pursue the highest levels of education. "That is one of the best things about working here," says Senior Coordinator Zena Cronyn. "It is a very supportive atmosphere, and we really work together as a team."

George D. Bjurman & Associates is involved in the Los Angeles community, providing yearly charitable donations to benefit hospitals and homeless shelters.

The firm is also a member of the Los Angeles Chamber of Commerce. Employees have participated in local food drives, as well as 5K runs to benefit cancer and AIDS research. Finally, George D. Bjurman & Associates has an office recycling program that provides additional services to the Los Angeles community.

Better Decisions through a Team Approach

Teamwork describes how all decisions are reached at the company. While many investment companies allow one manager to oversee a portfolio of equity or fixed-income investments, George D. Bjurman & Associates has always relied on a team of investment decision makers to pick the stocks and bonds that make up a portfolio.

The company also relies on a sophisticated computer program developed by Barry. The software was designed to sift through information on thousands of publicly traded companies in order to pick out the companies George D.

Founded in Los Angeles in 1970 by George D. Bjurman, George D. Bjurman & Associates has made a name for itself by successfully managing the investment portfolios and pension and profit-sharing plans of large companies, government agencies, and foundations across the nation.

O. Thomas Barry III, chief investment officer
(left), and G. Andrew Bjurman, president and CEO

Bjurman & Associates ultimately deems to be potentially good investments. The program flags any companies with above-average growth prospects because the firm believes that in the long term, it is corporate earnings that will drive a company's stock price.

George D. Bjurman & Associates also looks for companies with capable management teams and competitive positions within their respective industries. Once the computer has made its selections, the firm's investment policy committee considers other factors—such as the economy and the growth of certain sectors of the economy—before deciding how to invest its clients' money. As a team, the investment committee conducts periodic reviews of its portfolios and fine-tunes its investment decisions in an effort to maximize gains.

In the mid-1990s, the company decided it was time to expand its operations by allowing individuals to invest in portfolios of stocks that had previously only been available to institutional clients. On March 31, 1997, Bjurman successfully launched a mutual fund.

With a consistent investment philosophy, George D. Bjurman & Associates attempts to ensure a secure future for the clients who entrust the firm with their financial resources.

Neil G. Cumming, senior vice president

Many of the emotions that pushed early Americans on their historic march westward to explore and discover the nation's vast resources can be conjured up with a single word: oil. The companies that came together to create ARCO, the seventh-largest oil company in the nation, helped lead the way in early oil exploration in North America. Based in Los Angeles, ARCO still reaches out to discover and explore untapped resources in lands around the world.

ARCO's roots date back to one of the country's earliest industrial pioneers, Philadelphia's Atlantic Petroleum Storage Company, founded by Charles Lockhart in 1866. Sold to John D. Rockefeller's Standard Oil Trust in 1874, the company was left on its own in 1911, when the Trust was dissolved by the federal courts. Atlantic soon made significant discoveries of crude oil in the Southwest and, during the next few decades, went on to acquire a fleet of oil tankers, build a network of pipelines, and establish a system of service stations. Atlantic purchased Hondo Oil & Gas Company in 1963, and merged with Richfield Oil Corporation in 1966 to form the Atlantic Richfield Company. In 1969, Atlantic completed another merger, this time with Sinclair Oil Company, founded by Harry F. Sinclair in 1916.

In 1968, when ARCO and its partner, Exxon, made the biggest oil strike in the Western Hemisphere on the north shore of Alaska, the company's orientation became permanently focused on the West.

By expanding its refining facilities and marketing on the West Coast, ARCO faced the challenge of sending 13 million gallons of oil through the trans-Alaska pipeline. The company moved its headquarters to a new, permanent home in Los Angeles in 1972.

Today, ARCO has gross revenues of more than $19.2 billion and assets totaling $25.7 billion. Its holdings extend from urban Long Beach and the Alaskan wilderness to remote operations in China and Venezuela. The ARCO name is familiar in the United Kingdom and Indonesia, where the company has found some of the largest gas fields in the world.

Leading the Way

New techniques for tapping hidden reserves have become ARCO's hallmark. Advanced drilling techniques began to get industry attention in the 1940s, when ARCO discovered and patented the process of using high-pressure gas to displace crude oil. This discovery made it possible to recover up to 60 percent of oil in the field, compared to previous yields that averaged 20 to 40 percent. Today, massive churning drills have given way to designer drills that have much greater range underground, vastly extending the world's oil supply. With a new technology called coiled tubing, which allows drills to reach out horizontally, ARCO can recover more oil from fewer wells, dramatically decreasing the impact on the environment. At Prudhoe Bay in Alaska, ARCO has saved more than $300 million over 10 years with coiled tubing technology.

ARCO's proven leadership in finding and recovering even the most recalcitrant gas and oil resources has taken its employees around the world. A joint venture with Lukoil—one of Russia's largest oil companies—gave ARCO entry to the Caspian Sea's vast reserves. The company discovered China's Yacheng natural gas field in 1983 and constructed the world's second-longest subsea pipeline. Ties with nations in the Middle East date from the 1980s,

Based in Los Angeles, ARCO is a leading retailer of gasoline on the West Coast, with more than 1,500 branded retail outlets in California, Oregon, Washington, Arizona, and Nevada.

and in 1982, ARCO made Dubai's first on-shore rich-gas discovery. ARCO's work extends into South America, North Africa, Europe, and the Near East.

Bringing Efficiency to the Gas Pump

The company's success is due in part to its mammoth and highly complex refineries in Los Angeles and Cherry Point, Washington. The sophisticated technologies in use at these refineries allow ARCO to market gasoline that meets the demanding requirements of Californians and other motorists in the United States and Canada.

Finding and recovering the world's fuel supplies is exciting and profitable for the company. But consumers tend to be more familiar with the innovations ARCO has made closer to home. The company produced the first emission-controlled gasoline in the nation—EC-1—and continues to reduce the pollutants from all of its products. ARCO is committed to cleaning up Southern California's smoggy skies.

Californians also are used to convenience. ARCO eliminated its credit card in 1982 and passed the savings onto its customers. It became the first in the industry to install PayQuick™ Island Cashiers in its gas stations. Busy customers can use a bank debit card or insert $5, $10, or $20 bills into the automatic cashier to pay for gas; fill up their tanks; and then drive off, receipt in hand, without wasting a minute. Beginning in 1980, gas customers could also do some quick shopping at ARCO's global network of gas station fran-

chises, which combine quality food with convenience store items.

Lending a Helping Hand

With operations that span the globe and projects that affect millions of people, ARCO's social commitment embraces the belief that the free-market philosophy cannot thrive on profits alone—it requires healthy, educated, prospering people. In Los Angeles, ARCO pledged $10 million to help build Disney Hall, the ultramodern, 2,380-seat concert hall that is destined to be a symbol of the 21st century. ARCO's

giving edged over the $33 million mark in the mid-1990s, and extends everywhere that ARCO goes. The company has never lost sight of the people it serves throughout the world.

Nearly a century and a half after its founding, ARCO's key goals have never changed: superior execution and a relentless pursuit of new opportunities in the global marketplace. Coupled with an environmental sensitivity and a concern for the community, ARCO's tradition of excellence and leadership in the industry is sure to continue for many years to come.

P

ublic Storage, Inc. is the largest owner and operator of self-service storage facilities in the United States. President Harvey Lenkin says the company's slogan—The First Choice—is appropriate on two counts: "We're the first choice among consumers who need storage, and we're the first choice among investors who want to invest in mini-warehouses." Public Storage must be doing something right, because research analysts at three major investment concerns all named the company as their top real

estate investment trust (REIT) pick for 1998. Public Storage has more than 1,100 facilities in 37 states, representing about 65 million square feet of rentable space. With assets of more than $3 billion, the company earns in excess of $250 million annually. One of the 10 largest REITs in the country, its securities are traded on the New York Stock Exchange.

Exemplary Service

An innovator in the self-service storage industry, Public Storage established a national telephone reservation system, which is similar to those used by airlines, hotels, and car rental agencies. Operators in the call center receive phone calls from consumers across the country who have storage problems, and attempt to meet the callers' needs. "This service has enabled us to produce operating results significantly superior to those of our competitors," says Lenkin.

A stroll through the call center, which is located at the company's corporate head-

Public Storage is the most recognized name in the self-storage industry (top).

Public Storage's facilities represent state-of-the-art design, with climate controlled spaces, retail outlets, and truck rental operations (bottom).

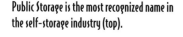

quarters in Glendale, reveals an impressive operation, bustling with more than 200 operators working in shifts and fielding calls from all over the United States. A row of clocks on the wall provides the time in locations from New York City to Hawaii. An electronic board stationed in their

midst flashes the number of calls coming in and the number being answered, followed by the call answering percentage. "We try to stay at around 92 percent of calls," says Lenkin, as the board flashes 94 percent.

Across the hall are training facilities for those who staff the call center. Corporate headquarters also houses a separate training center for employees who manage storage facilities, including a mock storage facility and a moving supply store.

History of a Winner

Public Storage was established and incorporated in 1972 as a private company by Wayne Hughes and Ken Volk (now deceased). In 1980, it sponsored the public offering of a new corporation, Storage Equities, Inc.— a public real estate investment trust owning a number of warehouses. Public Storage acted as the adviser and property manager of the public company, and all of Storage Equities' properties operated under the name of Public Storage. In 1995, the two merged and took the name of Public Storage, Inc., becoming a self-advised, self-managed real estate investment trust.

The company's original purpose is still its primary purpose: to own and operate self-service storage facilities. While Public Storage also provides truck rental services and retail outlets, Lenkin describes these as conveniences, not as significant

The company's properties are located in major metropolitan areas of the United States.

moneymaking arms of the company. But convenience counts in a competitive market, and additional conveniences—such as allowing customers to pay with credit cards and complete rental applications through the company's Web site—enable Public Storage to emerge as an attractive option for both businesses and individuals who are in the market for self-service storage space.

Public Storage stands out from the competition in other ways, too. "We are certainly bigger than anybody else in the business, by multiples," says Lenkin. "The quality of our locations, the depth and seniority of our management, the innovative ideas that we have brought to the

storage business over time—all of these things give us a significant edge over our competitors."

A Strategy for Growth

Public Storage operates primarily in major U.S. cities having metropolitan statistical areas with a population of 1 million or more. The company currently is not building or buying facilities in markets where it does not already have a presence. Those markets are unlikely to help it maintain its occupancy rate of more than 90 percent. "The innovative and prudent attitude of management with respect to growing our company without the use of debt is a very major investment consideration," Lenkin notes.

Lenkin credits the company's founder—current Chairman of the Board and Chief Executive Officer Wayne Hughes—with the success of Public Storage. "Wayne Hughes is a brilliant and innovative person, whose leadership in this organization since 1972 has been the driving force behind the growth and success of this company," Lenkin says.

The growth of self-service storage facilities is propelled by events that occur in all people's lives: birth, marriage, divorce, death, and the success or decline of a business. And Public Storage, Inc. meets those growing storage needs with its familiar purple-and-orange facilities that offer clean, competitively priced self-service storage space from coast to coast.

A full line of moving and storage supplies offers convenience for self-storage customers (left).

Truck rental operations encompass the majority of markets in which Public Storage does business (right).

TUTOR-SALIBA CORPORATION

A major force in the California construction industry and one of the nation's largest building and civil works contractors, Tutor-Saliba Corporation is among the nation's top 50 contractors, according to the *Engineering News-Record*, the national authority on construction business. In 1997, Tutor-Saliba boasted nearly 1,800 employees, earning $584.4 million in construction revenue in the United States and $65.3 million internationally. A leader in transportation and heavy civil works projects, the corporation has worked on everything from major city convention centers to airports to underground transportation.

And in Los Angeles alone, Tutor-Saliba is responsible for building the majority of the Los Angeles Metro Rail Subway System, constructing the Los Angeles Hyperion C117 Full Secondary Wastewater Treatment Facility, building the Tom Bradley International Terminal at Los Angeles International Airport, and completing the seismic repair of the Los Angeles Memorial Coliseum.

Making Its Mark

Founded by Ron Tutor in 1972, Tutor-Saliba has made a name for itself by completing projects on time, within budget, and at high levels of quality. As a result, it has become one of the industry's largest construction organizations, and has developed a reputation for quality performance in the areas of heavy, civil, and building construction.

The firm's experience in large, complex, cut-and-cover stations and tunnels is

Founded by Ron Tutor in 1972, Tutor-Saliba has made a name for itself by completing projects on time, within budget, and at high levels of quality.

unparalleled on the West Coast. Tutor-Saliba has completed more than $600 million of construction and currently has an additional $230 million in work ongoing for the Los Angeles County Metropolitan Transportation Authority (MTA), representing 26,000 linear feet of tunnels and 12 cut-and-cover stations.

Tutor-Saliba has worked on countless projects throughout California, including the San Diego Convention Center; Oakland/Alameda Coliseum; Bay Area Rapid Transit's (BART) Concord/Martinez Trackway; San Francisco Metro turnback, tracks, and tunnels; San Francisco Moscone Convention Center; San Francisco International Airport terminals; Redwood National Park Freeway; and San Fernando Valley-Ventura Freeway.

In addition, the corporation currently holds more than $800 million in contracts in various stages of development at the San Francisco International Airport. Recently, Tutor-Saliba broke ground on its $525 million contract for the BART Colma Extension to the airport, an eight-mile line section on a design/build basis.

For several decades, Tutor-Saliba Corporation has made its mark on the California landscape. Such attention to quality will ensure the corporation a place at the top of the industry for many decades to come.

The firm's experience in large, complex, cut-and-cover stations and tunnels is unparalleled on the West Coast. Tutor-Saliba currently has $230 million in work ongoing for the Los Angeles County Metropolitan Transportation Authority (MTA), representing 26,000 linear feet of tunnels and 12 cut-and-cover stations.

MARRIOTT INTERNATIONAL

The world-renown Marriott International has roots that trace back to 1927, when J. Willard Marriott opened a root beer stand in Washington, D.C. Soon after, Marriott added food to the menu and the first Hot Shoppe was founded. The business prospered, and there were seven Hot Shoppes in the nation's capital by 1932. ▼ In the years that followed, Marriott continued to expand the Hot Shoppes, which featured family-style dining at bargain prices. In 1937, Marriott added in-flight catering and food

service management, and in 1953, he first offered company stock to the public. Four years later, Marriott opened his first hotel, near what is now Ronald Reagan Washington National Airport, which was followed quickly by facilities in Philadelphia and Dallas.

In the 45 years since its public debut, Marriott has grown into a multibillion-dollar-a-year company that owns 1,500 hotels across the world. Under the current leadership of Marriott's son, J.W. Marriott Jr., the company expects to manage 2,000 hotels by 2000.

Built on 14 acres adjacent to Los Angeles International Airport, the 1,020-bed Los Angeles Airport Marriott opened in July 1973. And true to the aggressive spirit of the company's founder, the $52 million hotel—the 31st hotel built in the Marriott chain—was the costliest project the company had undertaken to date.

With more than 46,000 square feet of event space, the hotel also features several restaurants, a pool, a health club, and a business center. The hotel's amenities have made it a favorite location for many of Los Angeles' important local and national political events, and the hotel of choice for many of the fans attending the 1994 World Cup, several Super Bowls, and the 1984 Olympics.

A Hotel for Every Season

Whether travelers want to hit the beach, stay in town, see clients, or visit Los Angeles' many landmarks, Marriott International can accommodate them all. The company's hotels in Los Angeles are as varied as the city itself. The Marina Beach Marriott boasts spectacular waterfront views of the Pacific coastline and Marina del Rey. The Los Angeles Marriott Downtown—the newest of Marriott's Los Angeles-area hotels—is located in the heart of the central

Clockwise from top left:
The Marina Beach Marriott boasts spectacular waterfront views of the Pacific coastline and Marina del Rey.

Other Marriott hotels in the Los Angeles area are located in Manhattan Beach, Woodland Hills, Long Beach, and Torrance (pictured).

Built on 14 acres adjacent to Los Angeles International Airport, the 1,020-bed Los Angeles Airport Marriott opened in July 1973.

454

The Los Angeles Marriott Downtown—the newest of Marriott's Los Angeles-area hotels—is located in the heart of the central business district.

business district. Other Marriott hotels in the Los Angeles area are located in Manhattan Beach, Woodland Hills, Long Beach, and Torrance.

Marriott has grown and added services to meet the needs of today's travelers. To that end, it has expanded the number of its full-service hotels, and opened several Courtyard by Marriott and Residence Inn locations in Los Angeles, which give vacation and business travelers several lodging options with the same high quality that Marriott International is known for.

Courtyard by Marriott, designed by the business traveler for the business traveler, is a moderately priced hotel product. The hotels are built around beautifully landscaped courtyards, have few meeting rooms, and are typically situated in a suburban environment.

Residence Inns by Marriott are hotels that cater to business travelers who are relocating to Los Angeles, or are in town for special projects and need a place to stay for an extended period. Residence Inns have the look of a town house with a full range of conveniences, such as kitchens, fireplaces, dining areas, and living rooms.

A Name That Means Comfort
Visitors who stay at any Marriott Hotel, Courtyard, or Residence Inn may participate in Marriott's Reward Program, a concept pioneered by Marriott. Similar to the programs offered by airlines, Marriott customers accumulate points during their visits that are good toward future stays at any Marriott product.

J. Willard Marriott died in 1985 at the age of 84, but his values and innovative spirit remain at the core of the company. Throughout its history, the company has grown rapidly, but it has never compromised the top service that has made it a leader in the hospitality industry. As it continues its aggressive expansion in the United States and abroad, Marriott will continue to seek ways to make travel more convenient and comfortable for its clients.

Residence Inns have the look of a town house with a full range of conveniences, such as kitchens, fireplaces, dining areas, and living rooms (left).

Courtyard by Marriott, designed by the business traveler for the business traveler, is a moderately priced hotel built around a beautifully landscaped courtyard (right).

THE SEINIGER ADVERTISING GROUP

Creating fresh, innovative, and unique advertisements that get results has been the hallmark of The Seiniger Advertising Group for 25 years. Growing from a one-man operation in 1973 to an 80-person team today, Tony Seiniger's advertising agency provides strategic marketing and advertising to the motion picture industry and the entertainment world at large. With a strict eye for detail, Seiniger personally gives his stamp of approval on each and every piece of

advertising that his agency creates. "By not accepting mediocrity, by not accepting what has been done before, Tony Seiniger stands out among his peers," says Stephen L. Hayman, chief operating officer for The Seiniger Advertising Group. "Everybody hits some singles and some doubles, and even home runs. But on a consistent basis, the quality of our creative work is what makes the difference."

Housed in a spacious building on Wilshire Boulevard in Beverly Hills, The Seiniger Advertising Group is conveniently located about 20 minutes' driving time from each of the major television and motion picture studios throughout metropolitan Los Angeles. Virtually all production is done in-house. The hand-picked group of people who make up Seiniger's award-winning creative team produce work from conception to the finished piece.

Award-Winning Creative Team

Seiniger believes that his business is no better than the people who work for it. As a creative director, Seiniger is very selective when he seeks individuals to hire. In add-

ing to the team of creative talent, Seiniger and Hayman look for people who understand how to tap into emotions effectively, because, as Hayman says, entertainment advertising is "selling something that is artistic and emotional."

For a quarter century, Seiniger Advertising has shaped the advertising and design direction of motion pictures in the United States. Because of the advertising

group's reputation as a leader in the field, it attracts highly competitive artists from the advertising world. A major part of The Seiniger Advertising Group's business is cutting trailers—in-theater previews for forthcoming movie releases—that must be produced quickly while maintaining Seiniger's high standards for quality. That's why the agency has become vertically integrated, which allows for quality control at every stage of the creative process.

The creative team of writers, art directors, graphic artists, and producers work with state-of-the-art computers, video editing, and photo manipulation equipment. They have access to the company's own sound recording studio and in-house music and photo libraries. This enables the production staff, when necessary, to create advertisements from existing pieces of art.

As a result, The Seiniger Advertising Group has amassed a roomful of awards from the advertising industry, including more than 30 special Key Art Awards from the entertainment industry, dozens of Clio Awards (the equivalent to an Oscar from

"By not accepting mediocrity, by not accepting what has been done before, Tony Seiniger stands out among his peers," says Stephen L. Hayman, chief operating officer for Seiniger Advertising.

Founded by Tony Seiniger, The Seiniger Advertising Group has shaped the advertising and design direction of motion pictures for a quarter century in the United States.

the Academy of Motion Picture Arts & Sciences), and numerous prizes from New York and Los Angeles advertising clubs.

The Making of an Image Maker

Seiniger moved to Southern California in the early seventies to work as the in-house marketing manager for MGM studios. When the Hollywood studio closed its marketing offices, Seiniger started his own agency—and MGM became Seiniger's first client.

For nearly a decade, Seiniger made posters and print ads for MGM, then little by little started to branch out to other studios around Hollywood. By the early 1980s, Seiniger had expanded his products to include audiovisuals and the creating and editing of trailers, television commercials, and radio spots.

In a few short years, Seiniger's company was doing full campaigns for motion pictures. In the 1990s, he expanded into a variety of entertainment fields, starting with sports, by introducing the National Football League, the National Hockey League, and Major League Baseball for Fox-TV Sports. The Seiniger Group also entered into consumer advertising, where it created offbeat soft drink television spots for Coca-Cola.

The ad agency is also in charge of marketing for such high-profile entertainment institutions as Ringling Bros. and Barnum & Bailey Circus, and recently helped introduce a new casino-hotel in Las Vegas. In keeping with the times, Seiniger added a technology division to

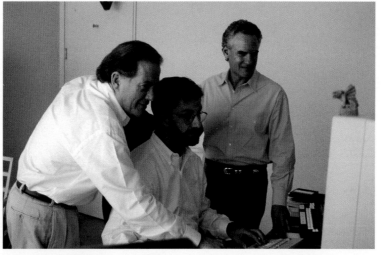

The creative team of writers, art directors, graphic artists, and producers work with state-of-the-art computers, video editing, and photo manipulation equipment, and have access to the company's own sound recording studio and in-house music and photo libraries.

his company, and has increased ad production for small-screen clients through the Seiniger Television/Home Video Advertising division.

Still, promoting the latest blockbuster or independent film remains the Seiniger Group's specialty. Today, the Seiniger Group handles 50 motion pictures a year, and from *One Flew Over the Cuckoo's Nest* to *The Fugitive*, Seiniger's fingerprints are all over the film industry's Oscars. In June 1998, Tony Seiniger was honored with the *Hollywood Reporter's* Key Art Lifetime Achievement Award. Seiniger is only the seventh person to receive this very prestigious award in the motion picture advertising business.

An Image Builder

During the last two decades, The Seiniger Advertising Group has been in the forefront of agencies whose creative abilities stretch across print, film, television, and radio to provide a unified identity to product marketing. This means when Seiniger works on a campaign, whether it's for a movie or a hotel, the agency puts together an integrated look and feel for that campaign.

The Seiniger Advertising Group aims at reaching the consumer with a particular image or perception in mind of whatever product is being marketed. The agency then seeks to promote a brand awareness that identifies consumers' interests so that it will ultimately become the consumer's first choice when making a purchase decision.

"The end result for everything that we do is that we are building images," says Hayman. And it is the agency's success in creating these lasting images that ensures that The Seiniger Advertising Group will also leave a lasting image in the creative field of advertising.

The ad agency is also in charge of marketing for such high-profile entertainment institutions as Ringling Bros. and Barnum & Bailey Circus, and recently helped introduce a new casino/hotel in Las Vegas.

KTI (Kinetics Technology International) Corporation is a recognized leader in providing innovative technology, proven design procedures, and high-quality standards in the refining, petrochemical, and mineral industries. ⚒ KTI takes a hands-on approach to offering process technology, project control, construction management, training, and operations support to its clients. The company provides single-source responsibility for installation or revamping of process plants and

for gas processing facilities, refining and petrochemical projects, combustion applications, and the production of ethylene, synthesis gas, hydrogen, and ammonia. By specializing in high-temperature reactions of hydrocarbons, KTI has become an acknowledged leader in olefin and synthesis gas production. KTI has designed more than 180 synthesis gas plants all over the world using steam reforming. It is the leading supplier of reforming furnaces, having supplied all firing configurations, including the largest reformers in the world for the production of methanol synthesis gas and hydrogen.

Executing projects on every continent is the company's specialty. KTI provides cost effective, turnkey facilities that meet client requirements for schedule, efficiency, reliability, and safety. The company is proud of its track record of assisting operating companies to achieve environmental compliance in the most cost-effective manner. KTI has implemented more NOx abatement programs than any other contractor.

Since establishing operations in the metropolitan Los Angeles area in 1974, KTI

has enjoyed sustained growth, and today has annual revenues in excess of $300 million. With approximately 700 employees, the company—based in San Dimas, just northeast of Los Angeles—has expanded with offices in Houston and in Concord, California.

During the past 25 years, KTI has supplied the process industries with tech-

nology, process plants, and fired heaters. The San Dimas office specializes in hydrogen, ammonia, ethylene, (nearly 25 percent of the world's ethylene is produced in KTI-designed pyrolysis furnaces) and other refining processes. KTI also offers the trademarked Dorr-Oliver FluoSolids® system technology, which supplies equipment and engineered systems for liquid-solids separation and thermal processing that serves the chemical, environmental, and minerals markets. Dorr-Oliver® FluoSolids Systems is the world's most experienced supplier of fluid bed technology. Almost 1000 FluoSolids® reactors have been supplied for a wide variety of applications, including incineration, roasting, mineral and catalyst calcining, reduction, and drying.

KTI's Houston-based KTI Fish has 50 years of experience in gas processing, gas transmission and storage, fertilizer, chemical/petrochemical, and refining industries. KTI's Fired Heater Division offers reliable, cost-effective furnaces of every size and configuration to the entire process industry.

By serving a highly specialized industry with single-source responsibility—from site assessment and engineering through procurement and construction—KTI has won loyal accounts throughout the world. Whether identifying, refurbishing, and relocating a world-scale ammonia complex or utilizing financing from the Export-Import Bank of the United States for an overseas project, KTI will remain on the cutting edge for decades to come.

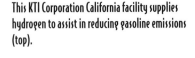

This KTI Corporation California facility supplies hydrogen to assist in reducing gasoline emissions (top).

This KTI hydrogen plant in California is involved in the reduction of sulfur emissions (bottom).

A wholesaler that distributes both domestic and imported beverages, Westside Distributors has delivered primarily Anheuser-Busch, Pabst Brewing Co., and Barton Beers products to the Greater Los Angeles area for more than two decades. Its clients, numbering just under 600, include the Los Angeles Memorial Coliseum, Great Western Forum, and Hollywood Park, in addition to a number of restaurants and lounges, mass merchandisers, supermarkets, and other outlets. From the time it began operating in 1974,

WESTSIDE DISTRIBUTORS

A wholesaler that distributes both domestic and imported beverages, Westside Distributors has delivered primarily Anheuser-Busch, Pabst Brewing Co., and Barton Beers products to the Greater Los Angeles area for more than two decades. Its clients, numbering just under 600, include the Los Angeles Memorial Coliseum, Great Western Forum, and Hollywood Park, in addition to a number of restaurants and lounges, mass merchandisers, supermarkets, and other outlets. From the time it began operating in 1974, Westside Distributors quickly rose to be among the top 10 percent of Anheuser-Busch wholesalers nationwide, according to *Black Enterprise* magazine's list of the top 100 black businesses. But, like most of the businesses that operate within the South Los Angeles communities, Westside Distributors suffered devastating setbacks as a result of the civil unrest that affected most of the central city area in 1992. After the riots, the company slipped from the top rankings. But today, in spite of the setbacks, it continues to be one of the area's most viable businesses.

A Story of Survival

Westside Distributors' story is one of survival. The typical ups and downs of business are enough to keep the average entrepreneur awake at night. But president and owner Ed Lara led his business through one of Los Angeles' most troubling times, the 1992 riots that leveled parts of the city, including a good deal of his distribution territory.

The company had enjoyed a period of growth and prosperity in the 1980s and early 1990s, and had just expanded its facilities to accommodate its growing snack food division when the unexpected happened. The 1992 riots did not physically damage Westside's facility, but many of its client businesses were either damaged or destroyed.

"It was difficult, but we were able to take steps to keep the business open and viable during that time," says Lara. "That first year, we lost around $12 million off of our sales projections." It took good strategies and planning to survive the losses sustained from the outbreak. "One thing the riots taught me is that at all times you have to maintain a good contingency plan," he adds. "That's important because we had extended ourselves as a result of our growth, and we couldn't have foreseen anything like the riots happening."

A Model Corporation

Westside has been located on Southern Avenue in South Gate since 1983, when it outgrew its old location on Crenshaw Boulevard in South Los Angeles and the

Ed Lara, president and CEO of Westside Distributors

company moved into its present, 100,000-square-foot facility. The South Gate site includes 70,000 square feet of storage and facilities for maintaining the company's fleet of trucks, tractors, trailers, vans, and cars.

At the helm is Lara, who has more than 30 years of experience in the beer industry. He was elected chairman of Anheuser-Busch's wholesaler advisory panel in 1983, assuming responsibility for the interests of more than 950 independent Anheuser-Busch wholesalers across the United States. Lara served as president of the California Beer Wholesaler's Association (now the California Beer and Beverage Distributor's Association) in 1983 and 1984.

In the past quarter of a century, Lara has built Westside into a model corporate and community citizen, instilling in his 85 employees the importance of investing in the community.

Pride in Product and Service

While the rebuilding and repair of its former client base is incomplete, the company continues to work its way back up. New trends in public taste—primarily the growth of light beers and the import segment of the malt beverage industry—have helped strengthen Westside's sales. Through it all, Westside Distributors has governed itself by its slogan: Pride Makes the Difference.

"Pride for us means Personal Responsibility In Daily Efforts to give the best customer service," says Lara. "Our most important assets are our people, the Westside family."

Troop Steuber Pasich Reddick & Tobey, LLP is among the largest and fastest-growing business law firms in California. The firm has an outstanding reputation for technical excellence and exceptional responsiveness, as well as for creating and implementing innovative solutions to complex transactions and business disputes. ▼ Founded in 1975 by an entrepreneurial team of four attorneys, Troop's practice has grown to 156 lawyers offering expertise in 22 areas of business

law. The firm's exceptional growth propelled a relocation in 1998 from its long-standing home in Westwood to its new, 137,500-square-foot quarters in Century City.

Driven by Clients' Needs

The key to Troop's success is pursuing a highly focused practice development strategy, concentrating on defined areas of business law that specifically address the needs of the firm's dynamic clientele: fast-tracking new ventures, high-growth middle-market companies, and leading privately held and publicly traded companies. The firm serves Fortune 500 companies with its niche expertise in insurance coverage, entertainment finance and litigation, and specialty finance law.

Troop evaluates the quality of services rendered in terms of the contribution made to supporting client growth and meeting client objectives. Partners continually review their portfolio of offered services, and hone their expertise to address changing complex legal issues. They maintain close, ongoing dialogue with clients to learn and respond to client preferences for the delivery of needed services.

Paramount importance is placed on human resource development and management. The firm is well regarded for the academic credentials and highly focused expertise of its lawyers. Many Troop attorneys have graduated at or near the top of their classes from the nation's leading law schools and were members of Law Review and/or Order of the Coif. To ensure the highest-quality representation and work product, the firm supports an extensive continuing education program for its attorney staff.

The firm also invests heavily in support staff development and information technology to keep the entire organization efficiently in step with the latest changes in legal and corporate practices. Professionalism and teamwork are enhanced by having all members of the firm housed in one centralized location. The common workplace facilitates efficient, close interaction among all attorneys and support staff members, critical in managing complex transactions and disputes.

Transactional Expertise

Long regarded as having one of the leading business transaction law practices in Southern California, the firm's Business Department represents clients ranging from start-up companies to large, multinational corporations. The department's Corporate and Securities practice designs creative approaches to capitalize or re-capitalize ventures and established companies in diverse market settings during all stages of their development.

Corporate and Securities attorneys are skilled in structuring, negotiating, and documenting virtually every form of corporate finance transaction. Recently, the firm's Corporate and Securities attorneys successfully represented a major media corporation in a milestone acquisition merger valued at more than $1.9 billion. These attorneys also represent clients in a wide variety of international transactions, including financing, licensing, and joint ventures.

Over the years, the Business Department has expanded its expertise into a wider range of practice areas, including Financial Services, Specialty Finance, Intellectual Property, Technology, Bankruptcy and Insolvency, and Tax, Estate, Probate, and Compensation Planning.

The firm has one of the most respected entertainment transaction law practices in the United States. The Entertainment Department represents many of the major entertainment production and distribution companies in Hollywood. Entertainment Department attorneys also represent numerous independent production companies and other institutional entertainment and media entities.

Troop's Real Estate Department represents many domestic and foreign institutional and noninstitutional developers and

Troop Steuber Pasich Reddick & Tobey, LLP, founded in 1975 , now has 156 lawyers housed in its new offices in Century City.

investors in connection with transactions involving all major project types, including residential (tract and condominium), commercial office, retail, medical office, strip center, raw land, agricultural, mini-warehouse, and hospitality.

Dispute Resolution Expertise

The firm has one of the most effective dispute resolution practices in Southern California, having successfully represented clients in a variety of complex litigation and arbitration matters before courts, administrative agencies, and arbitration panels. Client-specified objectives determine how each matter is handled by Litigation Department attorneys. They aggressively pursue negotiation and settlement approaches whenever such options meet client-specified goals, optimize recovery, and effectively contain litigation costs.

The Litigation Department's vast experience in the courtroom offers clients a distinct advantage when their cases come to trial in any California or federal venue. These attorneys handle contested issues in insurance coverage, labor and employment, environmental harm, intellectual property, product liability, securities, toxic torts, and white-collar crime, as well as general business disputes.

With Hollywood as one of Los Angeles' major centers of commercial activity, Troop's Entertainment Litigation practice concentrates on representing institutional entertainment companies across a full range of arbitration and litigation matters, through trial and appeal, in both state and federal courts. Entertainment Litigation attorneys provide preventive counseling and representation in disputes concerning motion picture and television program finance, development, production, domestic and international

distribution, intellectual property (copyrights, trademarks, idea submission and misappropriation, and licensing), mergers and acquisitions, tax, employment and labor, risk management, and insurance coverage.

Going into the next millennium, Troop Steuber Pasich Reddick & Tobey, LLP will continue to tailor its portfolio of services and pool of expertise to maximize the firm's key value proposition—business law counseling and representation to support client growth and strategic development needs.

The firm pursues a highly focused practice development strategy, concentrating on defined areas of business law that specifically address the needs of its dynamic clientele: fast-tracking new ventures, high-growth middle-market companies, and leading privately held and publicly traded companies.

1976 - 1998

1976 Katell Properties
1977 Bugle Boy Industries, Inc.
1978 Compensation Resource Group, Inc.
1980 University of Phoenix
1981 National Coatings Corporation
1981 Party Planners West, Inc.
1982 Southwest Airlines Co.
1983 Hilton Los Angeles Airport
1983 Watson Pharmaceuticals, Inc.
1984 The Sheridan Group
1986 Amptron International, Inc.
1986 Ernst & Young LLP, Entrepreneur Of The Year Program
1987 Kingston Technology Company
1987 ViewSonic Corporation
1988 Koo Koo Roo, Inc.
1988 Nelson Shelton & Associates
1988 Northern Trust Bank of California
1989 Bragman Nyman Cafarelli, Inc.
1990 Baker & Hostetler LLP, Counsellors at Law
1990 McKesson Water Products Company
1990 Nestlé USA
1990 Relaxor
1991 Aref & Associates
1991 92.3 The Beat
1995 Raytheon
1996 Washington Mutual
1997 The Boeing Company
1997 The Getty Center
1998 MediaOne

Gerald L. "Jerry" Katell, president and founder of Katell Properties, a Los Angeles-based commercial real estate development company, is one of the city's business leaders at the forefront of a new era of economic vitality in the Greater Los Angeles area.  More than three decades ago, the native New Yorker felt opportunity beckoning in the West and decided it would be the place to create his future. California appeared not only wide open, but also opportunity rich. Katell sensed a dynamic

environment that would foster innovation and reward the forward-thinking entrepreneur. Upon receiving his B.S. in civil engineering from the Massachusetts Institute of Technology in 1962, Katell moved west, earning his MBA at the Graduate School of Business at Stanford University in 1964.

Today, privately held Katell Properties maintains a 100 percent-leased portfolio of more than 1 million square feet, and is credited with developing more than 5 million square feet since the company was founded more than 22 years ago. During this time, the company has provided office and manufacturing facilities to such long-

established firms as Allstate, Great Western Bank, Teradyne, GMAC, and Toyota. With the entrepreneurial spirit that drove Katell to the West and to the development business, Katell Properties has built facilities for pioneering firms such as Amgen, J.D. Power & Associates, 3D Systems, and NetCom Systems.

Currently in development is Warner Ridge, a mixed-use office and multifamily residential project encompassing nearly 700,000 square feet of office space and 125 multifamily housing units. It is planned as the San Fernando Valley's first mixed-use office project since 1991.

Creating a Development Niche

Katell credits his company's success to a conscious decision he made to specialize in the late 1970s. He saw a great opportunity in that Southern California, while it had great urban centers, was spread over a very wide area. He observed that most executives and employees lived in the suburbs, and that a need existed to develop office and industrial park facilities nearby.

Having identified this development niche, Katell spent more than two decades perfecting his brand of beautifully landscaped, campus-style business parks. His emphasis was on providing value, functionality, and attractiveness. All projects encompassed designs that provided efficient space for fast-growing entrepreneurial companies and created enriching work environments that appealed to employees.

Among the successfully completed campus-style projects bearing Katell Properties' development trademark are Oaks Business Park, Agoura Hills Business Park, Northridge Business Park, Park Place and Promontory in Fox Hills Business Park, Valencia Technology Park, Irvine East Business Center, and Continental Grand Plaza in El Segundo.

In addition to its specialized focus, Katell Properties' longevity can be credited to a strategy that balances risk taking, such as building 75 percent of its projects on speculation with conservatively structured financing. Katell says a developer must be somewhat of a futurist, trying to build the right product at the right time to satisfy the growth requirements of tenants. The time cycle to bring products to market requires predicting demand three to five years in advance.

This aggressive risk taking is tempered by a conservative approach to both project selection and financing. Katell has avoided building projects just because ebullient economic conditions enable deals to get done. He has also avoided over-leveraging, which leaves little margin for error when a down cycle depresses rents or creates vacancies.

More than an individual success story, Katell is considered an innovator whose projects are viewed as catalysts for economic activity in the marketplace. In the late 1970s, he pioneered the conversion of more than 2,000 apartments to condominiums. In one

Katell Properties maintains a 100 percent-leased portfolio of more than 1 million square feet, and is credited with developing more than 5 million square feet since the company was founded more than 22 years ago. Among the successfully completed campus-style projects bearing Katell Properties' development trademark are Agoura Hills Business Park (below) and Northridge Business Park (right).

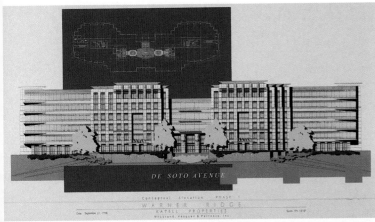

high-rise project in San Francisco, Katell transformed self-described "perpetual renters" into home owners, thereby enhancing the community's financial complexion. This project was viewed as so successful that its mechanics were made into law and served as the prototype for subsequent conversions.

In the late 1970s, Katell created the now widely used concept of a participating long-term ground lease for what became the 1 million-square-foot Northridge Business Park. This 75-year lease provided the landowner, Catellus Development Corporation, with a fixed base rent and participation in future increased rents from tenants.

A Leader in the Community

Katell enjoys an enviable reputation as an innovator and business leader, having been listed consistently in the *Los Angeles Business Journal*'s 50 Most Powerful People in the Commercial Real Estate Field. His philosophy, simply stated, is that "reputation counts for everything. Government officials need to know that you will get the deal done and honor your commitments. Lenders must

be assured that you will fulfill your obligations. Good broker relationships must be maintained to ensure that there will be flow, and these relationships are based entirely on trust."

Recently, Katell became a member of the board of directors for Los Angeles' BEST (Better Educated Students for Tomorrow)

program. This inner-city, after-school program provides a safe and productive alternative to being home alone or out on the streets after school in some of the city's more troubled neighborhoods.

Many of Katell's philanthropic efforts are focused on education for disadvantaged children and arts-related programs. Additionally, he has been involved with fundraising efforts for the Los Angeles Music Center and the Norris Community Theatre, and serves on the board of the building committee for the planned, Frank Gehry-designed Walt Disney Concert Hall.

For the future, Katell views the Los Angeles area much as he did more than three decades ago: attractive for its potential for opportunity and growth. The combination offers entrepreneurial freedom and access to the Pacific Rim, making Los Angeles a continuing, vibrant economic environment for the 21st century.

Currently in development is Warner Ridge, a mixed-use office and multifamily residential project encompassing nearly 700,000 square feet of office space and 125 multifamily housing units.

Valencia Technology Park (above) and Continental Grand Plaza in El Segundo (left) were developed by Katell Properties.

Bugle Boy Industries, Inc.

A leader in fashion that reflects the changing trends in American lifestyles, Bugle Boy has become a household name across the country in just two decades. One of the largest privately held apparel companies in the United States, Bugle Boy has positioned itself to become the brand name of choice for the world. ▼ Dr. William C.W. Mow, who founded the company in 1977, expects this goal to become a reality within 10 years. "It's a tall statement, but we are on our way to accomplishing our

vision," says Mow, the company's chairman and chief executive officer.

Providing stylish and comfortable clothing at a moderate price has been the key to the company's success. Bugle Boy—a name Mow says represents eternal youth—began as a manufacturer of young men's clothing, and now produces and markets extensive lines of sportswear and denim clothing for men, women, young men, boys, and children. In 1986, the company began to license its popular brand name to companies in the United States and abroad, and that same year began distribution to foreign markets. Bugle Boy now sells in Canada, Latin America, the Caribbean, and the Far East.

From the beginning, Bugle Boy pioneered such popular fashion items as the parachute pant and the cargo pant for young men. In 1984, the company launched its boys division, and has since evolved to include fashion for the whole family. The Bugle Boy product line now includes sportswear, jeans wear, footwear, underwear, outerwear, loungewear, uniforms, socks and hosiery, belts, ophthalmic eyewear, watches, hats, and infant and toddler wear.

Today, Bugle Boy's Simi Valley headquarters houses about 400 employees. The company's sales personnel and planners work closely with wholesale customers to determine product mix, plan sales volumes, and confirm delivery needs.

Bugle Boy sells its merchandise nationwide through department stores, family stores, specialty stores, and its own retail outlets. Bugle Boy products are currently manufactured in more than 40 foreign countries, and the company has more than 4,600 employees worldwide. All production, whether domestic or imported, is shipped from Bugle Boy's distribution facilities located in Southern California and Atlanta.

Strategic Marketing

A hallmark of Bugle Boy has been its creation of extremely savvy marketing strategies, in order to remain a leader in a crowded marketplace. On television airwaves during the late 1980s, a sexy model in a fast car asked the question: "Excuse me, are those Bugle Boy jeans you're wearing?" It was the start of Bugle Boy's first, widely copied, and now legendary television advertising campaign.

Bugle Boy followed the success of its television campaign with substantial outdoor advertising, the first in the apparel industry to do so. These days, Bugle Boy has continued to lead the industry with family-oriented campaigns and through extensive in-store promotion of its brand name. Continuing to explore the latest in communications and advertising, Bugle Boy launched a Web site on the Internet (www.bugleboy.com) in 1996. The popular site features a Bugle Boy Virtual Store™, a game arcade, and immediate access to product information.

"We are very creative as a company," Mow says from his company's headquarters in northwest Los Angeles County. "We don't make the covers of fashion magazines, but we stay in a position where we interpret the cutting edge of fashion for Middle America."

An American Success Story

The success story of Bugle Boy—a $550 million company—is the story of Mow, a self-made man who immigrated to the United States as a member of a diplomat's family in 1949, settling in Washington, D.C. Three years later, his mother moved the family to Great Neck, New York, and, to support her five sons through school, opened a restaurant. It was at his mother's Yangtse River Cafe that Mow first devel-

Dr. William C.W. Mow, who founded Bugle Boy Industries, Inc. in 1977, has positioned the company to become the brand name of choice for the world (top).

In the early 1990s, Bugle Boy turned its attention to clothing the whole family (bottom).

Bugle Boy operates its own retail outlet stores, which today provide stability and a revenue stream for the company.

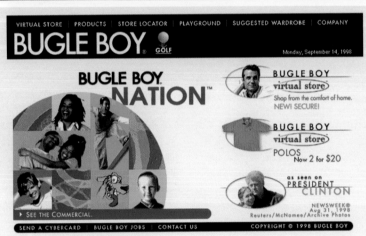

oped an understanding of marketplace requirements and business initiatives.

Faith in the importance of an education and an interest in advanced technology drove him to work toward a doctorate in electrical engineering. In 1969, after earning his doctoral degree in 1967 from Purdue University in Indiana, Mow founded Macrodata, a groundbreaking computer control diagnostic equipment company for large-scale integrated circuits and chips. By 1976, he had sold his interest in that company to form Dragon International, an importer of apparel and the precursor to Bugle Boy.

Through Bugle Boy Industries, Mow saw that he could reach a broad market by manufacturing young men's clothing, and by following fashion trends and expanding upon them. An early advocate of global sourcing, Mow established a worldwide infrastructure for production that now operates in 25 countries, assuring optimum value and affordable prices for Bugle Boy's customers. Mow also set up a management and operations team capable of supporting the company's dynamic growth.

A History of Rapid Growth

In 1980, Bugle Boy's annual sales were nearing $4 million. By 1987, sales had skyrocketed to nearly $190 million, thanks

Bugle Boy launched a Web site on the Internet in 1996 that features a Bugle Boy Virtual Store, a game arcade, and immediate access to product information.

Mow began by manufacturing young men's clothing, reaching a broad market by following fashion trends and expanding upon them.

to the launching of the denim division, as well as the now famous television ads. Soon after, Bugle Boy shifted its focus from young men's casual clothing to moderately priced apparel lines for men, women, and children. Mow also began opening his own retail outlet stores, which today provide stability and a revenue stream for Bugle Boy.

In the 1990s, Bugle Boy's annual sales had topped $500 million, as Mow introduced further innovations. Besides expanding its lines of merchandise and initiating new products such as wrinkle-free garments, the company installed state-of-the-art inventory and retail management systems to track the selling results of products, and spent $15 million on a new, automated distribution computer system in a large warehouse in Atlanta. To help its retailers, Bugle Boy instituted Partner Managed Inventory, an automatic replenishment system that is driven by consumer

Bugle Boy followed the success of its television campaign with substantial outdoor advertising, the first in the apparel industry to do so.

demand. In addition, Bugle Boy's central computer links its designers in New York and Simi Valley with design support teams in China and Hong Kong, manufacturers in various overseas countries, and customers in the United States, thus cutting off weeks of production time.

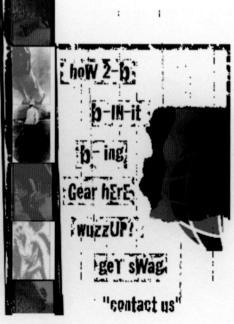

Continuing to innovate and to introduce new products—1998 saw the launch of the Bugle Boy Signature™ Golf Series—Mow predicts that by the early 2000s, the company will be doing $1 billion a year in business. As a part of the company's plan for growth, Mow has his sights set on his former homeland. His dream for the next decade is to establish as many as 1,000 Bugle Boy stores in China's giant retail market.

As a high-profile citizen, Mow has taken a leadership role in the local community. He was recently inducted into the World Trade Hall of Fame as an outstanding business leader who has made a historic contribution to the global economy. Mow also serves on the board of trustees of several engineering universities, and has become instrumental in breaching the gap between universities in China and the United States, specifically concentrating on management of technology (MOT) and MBA programs that will eventually bring to society the unique talents necessary for the next millennium.

"Bugle Boy is fortunate to be part of Los Angeles," says Mow. "It is without a doubt the gateway to business in the next millennium."

S ince beginning service in 1971 with three planes out of Dallas, Southwest Airlines Co. has grown to become one of the country's most admired airlines. The Fortune 500 company operates out of 52 cities in 26 states and is the fifth-largest U.S. airline, based on the number of domestic customers carried. With more than 2,300 flights each day and more than 25,000 employees nationwide, Southwest is the only major short-haul, low-fare, high-frequency, point-to-point carrier in the United States.

Fortune magazine named Southwest Airlines "the best company to work for in America" in its January 1998 issue, while *Condé Nast Traveler* recognized it as the world's safest airline. *Money* magazine ranked the airline number one in its first rating of major U.S. carriers, and in the magazine's survey of more than 1,000 fliers, Southwest was rated first in safety, price, on-time performance, baggage handling, and customer service. In addition, Southwest was named number one for the third year in a row in the National Airline Quality Rating conducted by researchers at the University of Nebraska at Omaha Aviation Institute and the W. Frank Barton School of Business at Wichita State University.

A Fun-Loving Airline

Time flies when you're having fun, or so the saying goes, and having fun while you fly is what Chief Executive Officer Herb Kelleher set out to do when he and Rollin W. King founded the "Love Airline." The first thing Southwest did was to outfit its flight attendants in orange hot pants, lace-up go-go boots, and wide, hip-slung belts. These flight attendants set the tradition for the airline's trademark Positively Outrageous Service.

Along with having fun, Southwest initiated many industry firsts. Southwest was the first major airline to offer electronic ticketing; first to develop a Web page (www.southwest.com); among the first to accept ticketing over the Internet;

and the first to offer employees profit sharing.

Southwest continues to pioneer a unique corporate culture in the industry, garnering the distinction of being one of the top 10 companies to work for in the United States, according to the Robert Levering, Michael Katz, and Milton Moskowitz book *The 100 Best Companies to Work for in America*. Southwest—an 84 percent unionized company—has come to be seen as an icon of employee motivation and customer service.

Spreading the Love

Los Angeles, a Southwest market since 1982, began with eight daily nonstop flights to El Paso and Phoenix. Service has grown to today's level of 117 daily flights and eight gates. Southwest is the largest carrier in California and is Boeing's largest 737 cus-

tomer worldwide. In 1995, the airline unveiled the California One, a plane designed to honor the company's customers and its 2,700 employees in the Golden State.

Many of the company's nearly 500 employees working in Los Angeles invest their time in community programs such as Project Take-Off Tutoring, an educational outreach program created by Heart of Los Angeles Youth (HOLA). The Ronald McDonald House program, cornerstone of the Ronald McDonald Children's Charities, is the airline's primary corporate charity. The company annually sponsors the Southwest Airlines LUV Classic golf tourney, with proceeds of more than $1.7 million over the last 10 years going to the McDonald's children's houses.

It is this desire of each employee to do his or her best—at work or in the community—that gives Southwest its competitive edge: the Southwest spirit.

Since beginning service in 1971 with three planes, Southwest Airlines Co. has grown to become one of the country's most admired airlines. With more than 2,300 flights each day and more than 25,000 employees nationwide, Southwest is the only major short-haul, low-fare, high-frequency, point-to-point carrier in the United States.

Herb Kelleher is an unconventional CEO of an unconventional airline. He chain-smokes, dresses in costume, drinks Wild Turkey bourbon, and created a sensation in Dallas when he arm-wrestled the chairman of an aviation company over a legal issue (left).

One of Southwest's customer service agents displays the airline's legendary POS—Positively Outrageous Service (right).

Compensation Resource Group, Inc.

Beginning with the turbulent economic climate of the 1970s and then the exploding financial market of the 1980s, William L. MacDonald knew that executive compensation was—and would continue to be—the driving force in attracting and retaining talented professionals. To that end, he created Compensation Resource Group, Inc. (CRG), a firm dedicated entirely to the conceptualization and administration of executive compensation and benefit programs. Recognizing the rising trend for large

Clockwise from top:
William L. MacDonald, president and CEO, Compensation Resource Group, Inc.

To meet clients' needs, CRG operates two divisions: Executive Benefit Practice and Executive Compensation Practice.

Specialists in the design and implementation of nonqualified benefit plans work with executive compensation specialists to ensure an effective mesh of benefit programs.

public and private companies to compete in the hiring and retaining of senior level management, MacDonald founded CRG in 1978, when he was 29 years old. The concept behind his firm became so attractive to large financial institutions that MacDonald sold the business to Merrill Lynch in 1982. MacDonald became founder and executive director of that firm's Executive Compensation Division, but five years later, he and two associates purchased the division back from Merrill Lynch, reorganizing it under its original name.

At that time, MacDonald says he couldn't have imagined that his company would grow into the nation's leader in the design, funding, implementation, and administration of executive compensation and benefit programs for Fortune 1,000 and large public and private corporations.

MacDonald owns controlling stock interest in the firm, and many of CRG's senior staff are also stockholders. A recognized authority in his field, MacDonald has written numerous articles on executive compensation and benefits, and frequently lectures on the subject to trade and professional groups.

Today, with headquarters in Pasadena, the firm has expanded with 11 regional

offices in Atlanta, Boston, Chicago, Cleveland, Dallas, Denver, New York, Phoenix, San Francisco, Silicon Valley, and Seattle. The current staff at CRG numbers about 150, more than half of whom are professionals. Approximately two-thirds have postgraduate degrees or professional designations. CRG also retains a very strong board of directors and advisory board that help guide and support the company's continuous growth and success.

Benefit and Compensation Specialists

To meet clients' needs, CRG operates two divisions: Executive Benefit Practice and Executive Compensation Practice. Specialists in the design and implementation of nonqualified benefit plans work with executive compensation specialists to ensure an effective mesh of benefit programs.

CRG's Executive Benefit Practice focuses on the design, funding, and administration of nonqualified executive benefit plans. Typically, CRG reviews and evaluates a company's existing benefit structure and suggests methods to deliver executive benefits more effectively. CRG's staff of CPAs and benefit professionals examine a

CRG process consulting

CRG flexible

CRG™ your partner

http://www.crgworld

CRG™ innovative

company's current benefits under varying financial assumptions. At the same time, CRG professionals make cost projections of current funding methods to evaluate cost efficiency and analyze funding alternatives. Consultants take into consideration present value cost, cash flow constraints, earnings-per-share requirements, stockholder disclosure sensitivity, and analysis of tax implications. In the analysis, CRG consultants also compare existing programs to those offered by competitors and other companies, and recommend improvements to existing benefits programs.

CRG's Executive Compensation Practice provides compensation consulting services for clients on a fee basis. The consulting approach typically includes in-depth fact-finding to understand a client's organization, culture, and business strategy. After analyzing the business strategy and its performance, consultants determine the factors that drive the creation of value for shareholders. They also make a competitive assessment of existing pay practices, and an analysis of tax accounting and cost considerations. These analyses are combined to develop a statement of total compensation strategy that covers all key aspects of a compensation program design.

The firm makes specific recommendations for changes in existing programs based on the compensation strategy developed. CRG then assists in all aspects of program implementation. The result is a total compensation program that is strategically, economically, and culturally sound.

Serving the Community

CRG's executives and personnel are committed to the Los Angeles community and take pride in being involved in various local organizations. MacDonald currently serves on many organizational boards: the National Association of Corporate Directors (NACD), Los Angeles Area Chamber of Commerce, California Chamber of Commerce, Hugh O'Brian Youth Foundation (HOBY), Pepperdine University George L. Graziadio School of Business and Management Board of Visitors, Loyola Law School Board of Visitors, and Imperial Bank. He is also the chairman of the board of the San Gabriel Valley Council of the Boy Scouts of America, where he received the Distinguished Citizen's Award. MacDonald is an active member of the Young Presidents' Organization (YPO) and is an associate member of the American Society of Pension Actuaries.

For the past 15 years, CRG has been a sponsor of the John R. Wooden Award, which recognizes outstanding high school athletes and enables underprivileged inner-city children to attend summer basketball camp. CRG is a supporter of HOBY, which seeks to develop leadership skills in high school students throughout the world. The company's executives and personnel also extend support to the Covenant House of Los Angeles, Boys and Girls Clubs of Los Angeles, Red Cross, Tournament of Roses, Junior League of Pasadena, Pasadena Historical Society, California Heritage Museum, Pasadena Playhouse, Pasadena Symphony, University of Southern California, Pasadena Junior College, University of La Verne, and UCLA Alumni Association.

As an industry leader, CRG has a client base that includes many Fortune 1,000 and large public and private corporation. CRG was one of the first firms to address the complexities these organizations face in attracting and retaining talented executives and directors. Through MacDonald's leadership, Compensation Resource Group will continue to help companies keep their talented executives while investing in the communities CRG serves into the next century.

CRG has a client base that includes many Fortune 1,000 and large public and private corporations.

UNIVERSITY OF PHOENIX

or more than two decades, University of Phoenix has been meeting the needs of working adults with remarkable results. The undisputed quality of University of Phoenix programs, the expertise of its faculty, and the success of its students and graduates have given the university a well-deserved reputation for educational excellence. In only 20 years, University of Phoenix has grown to become one of the largest private universities in the United States. ⅏ While it offers degrees in

counseling and nursing, University of Phoenix is primarily a business school, with both undergraduate- and graduate-level courses in accounting, marketing, information systems, business administration, and management. Since all University of Phoenix students also hold full-time jobs, they enroll in one course at a time and attend class one night a week. Classes are taught by professors who must possess a Ph.D. or a master's degree at a minimum, and must be currently engaged as a practitioner in his or her area of instruction.

Although University of Phoenix is large, its orientation is highly specialized, with individual attention the norm rather

than the exception. The university purposely keeps its learning groups small, with classes averaging just 20 students each. Students are required to work in study groups of three to five members during the run of each course to discuss assignments and work on projects. The effect is improved learning of the course material, as well as a reflection of a real-life work environment. So while students are learning procedures and techniques, they are also learning to think critically, to collaborate, to communicate, and to lead today's workforce. The concepts and problems that are taught in the university are those that the business sector deals with on a daily basis.

Taking the University to Students

University of Phoenix campuses are different from those of most traditional universities. There are no dormitories, no clusters of buildings around sprawling lawns, and no sports stadiums. Early on, the founders of the university realized a central campus would force students to drive long distances to attend classes. To make class sites more convenient for students, the university was given its decentralized nature—rather than having students come to the university, the university goes to them. University of Phoenix opens classrooms wherever there is a demand from students. Classes are held in office buildings and hotel conference rooms. In Southern California

University of Phoenix has 22 locations in Southern California alone, from Fountain Valley to Santa Barbara to San Bernardino to Lancaster.

alone, students can take classes at any one of 22 locations, from Fountain Valley to Santa Barbara, and from San Bernardino to Lancaster.

University officials recognize that many students have to travel extensively for their jobs and others are transferred unexpectedly in the middle of a semester. To enable students to complete their studies, University of Phoenix designed two programs to allow them to continue their studies should such an event occur. The first allows students to interact with other class members and faculty through computer conferencing. The second, an independent course of study, gives students the freedom to pursue their studies at their own pace.

Although many of University of Phoenix's concepts were considered unusual at the time they were instituted, they have blazed a trail that traditional universities have followed in recent years. Many now offer night programs for professionals, as well as extension courses for professional development. Several universities have also begun decentralizing their campuses, add-

ing branches to make it more convenient for a greater number of people to attend classes.

Despite tremendous growth in the nearly quarter century since its founding, University of Phoenix officials believe the

school has not yet reached its full potential. As the demand for better-educated workers grows, university officials plan to expand course offerings and campus sites in order to meet the needs of both students and businesses across the United States.

Classes are taught by professors who must possess a Ph.D. or a master's degree at a minimum, and must be currently engaged as a practitioner in his or her area of instruction.

For more than two decades, University of Phoenix has been meeting the needs of working adults with remarkable results. The undisputed quality of University of Phoenix programs, the expertise of its faculty, and the success of its students and graduates have given the university a well-deserved reputation for educational excellence.

National Coatings Corporation

National Coatings Corporation is a leading manufacturer of durable, energy-efficient, and environmentally friendly acrylic roofing systems that each year are used on some 20 million square feet of commercial roof projects valued at $50 million. Leveraging off a major presence in the huge California commercial facility market, National Coatings supplies building owners and contractors both nationally and overseas. In 1981, Rick Sexauer founded National Coatings to manufacture high-performance AcryShield™ acrylic coatings, which are applied over sprayed polyurethane foam (SPF) roofing systems. Prompted by his sales experience with a major Southern California paint company, Sexauer focused on providing dedicated service and superior weatherproofing products based on new, all-acrylic chemistry technology. From these roots as a small entrepreneurial manufacturer, National Coatings expanded its market focus well beyond SPF roofing, and now has Fortune 500 clients in entertainment, electronics manufacturing, telecommunications, heavy industry, major retailing, and hospitality. Recent customers include MCI WorldCom, Hewlett Packard, Universal Studios, Disneyland, Caesar's Palace, Vons Supermarkets, and the University of California. National Coatings maintains its corporate headquarters and first advanced coatings production plant in Camarillo, northwest of Los Angeles.

Committed to Total Roofing System Solutions

The hallmark of National Coatings continues to be a commitment to offering building owners and facility managers a total service that combines technical expertise with proven waterproofing technology. Their service includes initial roof inspection and analysis, detailed system specification, installation using professional preapproved applicators, post-job inspection, and warranty coverage. Ensuring total customer satisfaction also means using the latest software tools for roof energy analysis and total life-cycle costing. National Coatings' "systems approach" covers complete re-roofing offerings such as the Duraplus™ Roofing System (offered in partnership with the inventor of Plexiglas®, Rohm and Haas Company), AcryShield SPF Roofing Systems, and reinforced acrylic membranes called AcryPly™ Roofing Systems, along with AcryShield Restoration Systems that extend the leak-free lives of many commercial roof types such as Built-Up, Modified Bitumen, EPDM, Hypalon®, PVC, and Metal. Throughout, National Coatings maintains a unique focus on avoiding costly roof tear-offs and unnecessary landfill waste by employing its proven, all-acrylic waterproofing technology and by partnering only with applicators who demonstrate excellent workmanship and meet demanding business standards.

Leaders in Energy Efficiency and the Environment

With years of experience dealing with climate extremes in the western states and the persistent air quality challenges faced in Southern California, National Coatings is leading the way on Cool Roofing. Federal and state EPAs, air quality officials, and utility companies all agree that installing reflective, high-performance roofing systems can mean huge direct energy savings through reduced air-conditioning needs and improved air quality in "urban heat islands" like Los Angeles, Atlanta, and Dallas, where lower city temperatures can greatly reduce photochemical reactions that cause smog and respiratory illness. Not only has National Coatings collaborated with leading researchers on Cool Roofing at Lawrence Berkeley National Laboratory, it is a founding manufacturer member of the Cool Roof Rating Council, a consultant to and Charter Partner with the EPA ENERGY STAR® Roof Products Program, and an active participant in a key Cool Communities pilot program in Sacramento, California. Chris Harris, vice president at National Coatings, comments, "Studies on Los Angeles show that if 15 percent of roofs were reflective, peak temperatures might drop by 6°F, and smog levels would be cut the equivalent of permanently taking 3 to 5 million cars off Los Angeles freeways. We also know that nearly 10 percent of rapidly shrinking landfill space has been taken up by tornoff roofing materials. National Coatings, with experience and focus on durable and renewable reflective acrylic

National Coatings, headquartered in Camarillo, northwest of Los Angeles, is a company dedicated to sustainable roofing that will last the life of a commercial building (right).

This Robinsons-May department store was surfaced with an AcryShield™ Restoration System over its original Hypalon® single-ply roof. Its new Cool Roof will resist harsh desert conditions to preserve a leak-free roof life and reduce costs (below).

Companies like Hewlett Packard (above) and MCI World Com (left) have installed millions of square feet of AcryShield™ SPF Roofing Systems to provide seamless and fully adhered waterproofing, along with extra insulation. SPF Roofing is highly adaptable to both new construction and re-roofing.

roofing systems, has taken and will continue taking a leading role in Cool Roofing that offers superior waterproofing, saves money, improves air quality, and conserves our environment."

Looking Forward to Sustainable Architecture

National Coatings knows that traditional roofing practices involving short, leak-free lives and premature tear-offs should be a thing of the past. The company is dedicated to developing and marketing roofing system and wall coating solutions that can last a building's lifetime, and plans to double

sales over the next few years. Their Cool Roof Systems are critical to achieving this goal and to providing building professionals with alternative systems that are renewable and sustainable. Harris confidently adds, "For two decades, National Coatings has demonstrated long-term performance of innovative, all-acrylic roofing technology. We expect continued, robust growth, due to our excellent track record providing building owners with renewable roofing systems and cost-effective ways to extend useful roof life using our advanced cool roofing."

Sexauer, president of National Coatings, reflects upon his company's

achievements and prospects: "In an industry often criticized for substandard products and installations, National Coatings strives to always offer total value and maintain the highest integrity. I am proud of our business results. But I am most proud of our people, both for their professionalism and for their commitment to the community and organizations like World Vision. And I am confident we have sound strategies in place to continue satisfying our customers with long-term building solutions, while growing our business and doing more for the world around us."

AcryShield™ Restoration Systems and AcryShield SPF Roofing Systems protect Caesar's Palace along The Strip in Las Vegas.

Los Angeles, the city of dreams, can proclaim many notable event successes in its history. It is the only city in the United States that has hosted two modern-day Olympics, it was selected to host the first Super Bowl game, and it is the hub of the global entertainment industry. Throughout the years, the Los Angeles event industry has grown tremendously, and the way Los Angeles' events are produced has been emulated throughout the world. A long-established leader in the business of corporate event production is Party Planners West, Inc. (PPW).

For many years, business leaders in the sports, entertainment, fashion, automotive, high-tech, and finance industries have turned to Party Planners West, Inc., a full-service event production company. PPW has managed a variety of events from high-level business presentations to extraordinary galas. Clients seek out the company's expertise and its unique ability to create events that reflect individual corporate personalities.

"We consider ourselves a strategic marketing company that uses live events to help companies realize their marketing goals," says Patricia K. Ryan, president and founder of the company. "These are not parties the way we are used to thinking of parties. They are marketing events that are carefully structured to engage or entrance either consumers, employees, or potential investors. Press attention and value for the dollars spent are key objectives of our clientele."

Defining an Industry

PPW was originally founded in 1981 by Ryan, who left the hotel industry when she recognized the need for event coordination expertise as clients ventured out of traditional venues. Since then, she has guided the company from a one-person firm to its current status as an internationally recognized, full-service special events company. Production, design, location, technical, creative services, project management, and several other departments have been added to keep up with clients' growing demands.

Today, PPW operates out of a 53,000-square-foot production compound in Marina del Rey, where more than 50 full-time employees conceptualize, design, and execute the production of live events. Its staff has been educated by the most demanding clients, and has become a

Royce Hall at the UCLA campus was transformed by PPW for the premiere of *Independence Day*.

Tented events, this one an elegant gala, are a specialty of PPW.

resource to companies and organizations that demand quality and creativity.

PPW has been recognized as a member of *Inc.* magazine's Top 500, is currently one of the 15 largest woman-owned businesses in Los Angeles County, and is included on *Working Woman* magazine's America's Top 500 Women-Owned Businesses list.

Technology, Ryan says, has become the catalyst that has helped PPW to grow. State-of-the-art communications equipment has allowed the company to manage events simultaneously throughout the United States and around the world. PPW uses technology much in the same way as its clients do, allowing the technology to interface to meet the demanding expectations of large-scale events, regardless of where the event is planned or executed.

Diverse Clientele

A large variety of companies who seek to build their corporate identity, their brand, and their exposure, and who understand the value of the live event, call upon PPW to help them maximize their impact. Studios that require assistance producing movie premieres, film promotional tours, and video release events all turn to PPW. Disney, Fox, MGM, Sony, and DreamWorks all utilize events to market their movies and related products.

PPW experienced its first major growth period during the 1984 Olympic Games in Los Angeles. Partly as a result, festivities surrounding sports have become the company's forte. The National Football League, Major League Baseball, MLB Properties, Australian Football League, CBS Sports, and a variety of sports sponsors have all called upon PPW to produce memorable sports-related events. It was Ryan's long-term relationship with the National Football League that led it to appoint her as executive producer of the NFL Experience at its inception in 1992, and as the producer of the NFL Super Bowl Tailgate Party.

Nonprofit groups have begun to utilize the same marketing techniques as corporations, and PPW's memory-making expertise has benefited such organizations as the Los Angeles Music Center, AIDS Project Los Angeles, Children's Institute International, Children's Diabetes Foundation, and City of Hope. Key cultural institutions nationwide have also utilized its services, including the Smithsonian Institution and, most recently, the newly opened J. Paul Getty Museum.

Although Party Planners West is located in Los Angeles, 60 percent of its business takes place outside California. PPW has taken its broad expertise worldwide, including Ireland, Mexico, Canada, Taiwan, and Europe with the Australian Football League, NFL International, the Olympics for CBS, and an array of other clients. Film studios have also utilized its international expertise from New Zealand to South Korea to South America.

"PPW has developed the organizational skills and systems that are not bound by geographical or cultural boundaries," says Ryan. "The skills that apply to events are based on an understanding of the psychology of the people being entertained, their likes and dislikes. Our understanding of the basic component parts of entertaining is not encompassed within geographic or cultural boundaries. Whether your tent is on a hilltop in Norway or a parking lot in UCLA's campus, the comfort of tables, the points of service, or how quickly it takes to load a motor coach are universal components of entertaining."

PPW measures the success of an event with one criterion: the quality of the guest experience. Says Ryan, "The first question we ask a client in the initial planning stages of an event is 'What do you want your guests to remember the day after your event?' The answer to this question is the most important element we must remember in planning; and, after the event, the real reward is to know that the guests walked away with this intended guest experience."

Clockwise from top:
Dramatic lighting and technology create a contemporary feel for this film premiere.

The NFL Experience, produced by PPW, is the largest annual sports festival worldwide and has entertained more than 1 million football fans since its inception.

The scene may look like New York City, but it's Los Angeles—where PPW transforms film studios in Hollywood to create spectacular events.

HILTON LOS ANGELES AIRPORT

Serving one of the busiest airports in the world, the Hilton Los Angeles Airport has become one of the world's largest airport hotels and conference centers. The hotel has maintained a tradition of pride for excellence in service under the banner of one of the most recognized names in the hospitality industry: Hilton. ⚘ Since 1983, the nearly 1,250 rooms of the Hilton Los Angeles Airport have been a beacon to business and leisure travelers worldwide. With a 600-person staff providing

award-winning products and services, the hotel became even more competitive after a $22 million renovation in the mid-1990s.

Conveniently located five minutes away from the airport along Century Boulevard, the hotel and conference center is ideal as a Southern California lodging destination. The Hilton is half a mile away from the nearest freeway, four miles from the beach, seven miles from Beverly Hills, and 14 miles from downtown Los Angeles.

Southern California-Style Hospitality

Reflecting the comfortable elegance that characterizes the Southern California lifestyle, the hotel's 1,234 rooms and suites are configured in varied styles to fit the needs of individuals, families, business travelers, and groups of all sizes. The hotel offers a 24-hour complimentary airport shuttle service every 10 minutes, car rental, sight-seeing desk, 24-hour fully automated business center, same-day laundry and dry-cleaning facilities, audiovisual services, and an ATM. In addition, all rooms are equipped with voice mail, data port connections, irons and ironing boards, hair dryers, coffeemakers with complimentary coffee, and newspaper delivery.

For the ultimate in hospitality, the Hilton offers the elegant Towers concierge accommodations: three entire floors of suites and rooms with large work desks have been devoted to premium guest rooms, with separate registration and an exclusive lounge featuring complimentary continen-

tal breakfast, honor bar, and hors d'oeuvres each evening.

Each one of the hotel's deluxe 114 lanai rooms opens onto a lavish garden terrace or the poolside recreation deck. The beautifully landscaped gardens are also an escape for conference-weary guests seeking a coffee break.

Helping to ensure that hotel guests receive the same quality service throughout the Hilton chain, the company's time-saving registration service—which includes zip-in check-in, zip-in checkout, and video checkout—and HHonors frequent traveler benefits keep the Airport Hilton on top of the times.

Hospitality Innovators

As a gateway to the world, the Hilton Los Angeles Airport looked east—to the Far East—for ways of improving its ability to please guests. What hotel managers found was *feng shui*, the Chinese art of geomancy, which is an ancient form of interior and exterior design. The Hilton Los Angeles Airport is the only hotel in Los Angeles that has undergone this exercise.

Feng shui literally translates to "wind and water," suggesting balance. When a *feng shui* master saw that the hotel lobby's escalator crossed like an X, it was the most obvious structure to alter. (A cross means "unwelcome" in ancient Chinese

The Hilton Los Angeles Airport maintains a tradition of pride for excellence in service under the banner of one of the most recognized names in the hospitality industry: Hilton (left).

A prime advantage for Hilton Los Angeles Airport guests is its health club. With state-of-the-art exercise equipment, aerobics classes, and racquetball courts, the hotel's 25,000-square-foot, 24-hour Fitness Center is the largest within a hotel in Los Angeles. The hotel also has an outdoor swimming pool with four whirlpool spas (right).

art, a symbol of difficulty.) The escalator was removed from the lobby and was replaced with a stately staircase, which more closely resembles the character *ji* or "luck." The new lobby, enveloped by exquisite marble, is now an awe-inspiring symbol of welcome, says General Manager Dennis A. Clarke.

Guest rooms, offices, and eating areas underwent similar changes to improve the hotel's inner climate. By applying a *feng shui* master's advice on how to make guests feel more welcome to their temporary place of residence, it is said the hotel has reached harmony—which is believed to increase wealth.

Impeccable Service and Amenities

The Hilton Los Angeles Airport boasts more than 55,000 square feet of state-of-the-art banquet, meeting, and exhibit space. The Pacific Conference Center offers 34 separate meeting rooms out-fitted to accommodate groups of all sizes on one floor. The hotel's extravagant ballroom can hold 1,300 people theater style and 860 people banquet style. A meetings and conventions specialist is available every day.

Meeting planners can earn thousands of Hilton HHonors bonus points or airline miles for choosing participating Hilton, Conrad International, and Vista Hotels worldwide. Each time an event is held that includes a minimum of 10 or more occupied guest rooms per night, the planner can earn Hilton HHonors bonus points good toward free nights or earn miles with any participating airline partner programs.

Another advantage for Hilton Los Angeles Airport guests is its health club. With an outdoor swimming pool and four whirlpool spas, state-of-the-art exercise equipment, aerobics classes, and racquetball courts, the hotel's 25,000-square-foot, 24-hour Fitness Center is the largest within a hotel in Los Angeles.

The hotel caters to sophisticated palates by serving fresh, delectable cuisine. Café L.A. offers breakfast, lunch, dinner, and Sunday brunch. Guests seeking romantic dining can find it at Andiamo, which features northern Italian specialties. An old-fashioned deli is open 24 hours, and the hotel's multimedia sports bar caters to the sports fan.

Behind the scenes, the Hilton's staff generates a pride that has become critical to the hotel's success. Employees are hired based on their enthusiasm and dedication to maintaining the hotel's preeminence in the industry. Volunteerism is encouraged in the surrounding vicinity, and a structured community environment for employees has fostered top-quality service providers.

"What sets us apart form the competition is our services and the people who provide them," says Clarke. "So when customers come to the Los Angeles area, this hotel is the hotel of choice."

Reflecting the comfortable elegance that characterizes the Southern California lifestyle, the 1,234 rooms and suites are configured in varied styles to fit the needs of individuals, families, business travelers, and groups of all sizes (left).

All rooms are equipped with voice mail, data port connections, irons and ironing boards, hair dryers, coffeemakers with complimentary coffee, and newspaper delivery (right).

Bistro (left) offers an old-fashioned deli that is open 24 hours a day, and a multimedia Sports Bar that caters to sports fans. The Café offers breakfast, lunch, dinner, and Sunday Brunch. Guests seeking romantic dining can find it at Andiamo (right), which features Northern Italian specialties.

Watson Pharmaceuticals, Inc.

In an industry where companies often find themselves lost in the pack, Watson Pharmaceuticals, Inc. has become a leader by building its financial strength with technology-driven enterprises, strong market shares, broad product lines, and sophisticated manufacturing capabilities. Watson made a name for itself in generic, or off-patent, drugs in the late 1980s and early 1990s, but now the company draws half of its revenue from branded, or proprietary, pharmaceuticals. ▼ A Corona-based manufacturer of a comprehensive array of pharmaceutical

products, Watson was founded in 1984 by Dr. Allen Chao, who currently serves as chairman and CEO. As a manufacturer of generic products—an industry today valued at nearly $8 billion annually in the United States—Watson quickly established an enviable reputation for quality and service, and became a model for success in the eyes of Wall Street observers. In February 1993, the company went public at a price of $12 a share, splitting 2-for-1 in late 1997 for a split-adjusted price of $6 a share, and eventually soaring to an impressive high of $57 a share.

In the years since, Watson has boosted earnings growth by an average of 31 percent annually. Its return on equity, a measure of how well a company uses shareholder invested capital, reached 21 percent in 1997. And since 1993, when Watson went public, revenues have grown more than fivefold.

Chao believes that flexibility has been the key ingredient to the company's phenomenal success. "We are quick to respond to developing new product oppor-

tunities," he says. "As the market changes, we know that we must react very quickly."

A Persistent Leader

The genesis of Watson Pharmaceuticals came from one man's determination to make it in America by delivering quality pharmaceutical products and services at the best prices.

When Chao's Chinese parents sent him to the United States to pursue pharmacy studies in 1968, they never intended for him to stay. Instead, they hoped he would earn an American degree and return to China to run the family's pharmaceuticals manufacturing business. But after Chao received a master's degree in pharmaceutics from West Virginia University and a Ph.D. in industrial and physical pharmacy from Purdue University, he was well on his way to building a career in the United States. As a result, Chao's parents sold their manufacturing business and moved to California to retire.

Upon graduation, Chao accepted a job at G.D. Searle Laboratories, a midsize pharmaceutical company, where he worked in several departments, immersing himself in the many steps of drug development and production. In 1979, at the age of 34, Chao was named Searle's director of pharmaceutical technologies. Heeding his mother's advice to give up corporate life, Chao began laying the groundwork for a new course in his career, with the goal of

Allen Chao, Ph.D., chairman, president, and chief executive officer, Watson Pharmaceuticals, Inc.

Watson Pharmaceuticals, Inc. has become a leader by building its financial strength with technology-driven enterprises, strong market shares, broad product lines, and sophisticated manufacturing capabilities.

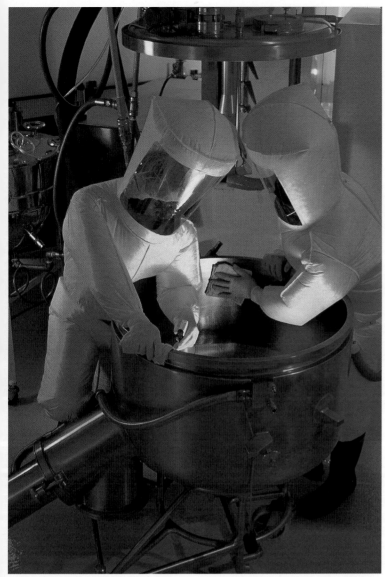

▶ RENE SHERET

business community. With the support of family, friends, and local investors, Chao raised the start-up capital to launch his pharmaceutical firm.

Propulsive Growth

From the beginning, Chao's intimate understanding of the drug manufacturing process gave him an edge, as one of the few chief executives in the industry with the personal know-how to develop his own products. Chao avoided high-volume drugs, like Valium, where competition is generally stiff. Instead, he concentrated on generic versions of difficult-to-copy medicines. Throughout most of its history, the company's philosophy has been to target niche, complex, off-patent products. As a result of this approach, Watson has enjoyed a steadily increasing financial momentum.

Beginning with the company's first generic product approval in 1985, Watson has offered real savings to patients throughout the United States with a variety of drug needs: Now, pharmacists can select any one of more than 90 off-patent products in approximately 200 dosage strengths to fill prescription needs. As the generic drug industry has consolidated in recent years, Watson has further strengthened its position by acquiring smaller generic drug makers, while also producing its own steady stream of off-patent products.

In 1996, the company expanded from its one-dimensional focus on generic drugs, which have relatively short product lives and low gross profit margins, into the realm of branded drugs, which have longer life cycles and steadier returns. "By the early '90s, we had established a strong company," says Chao. "To sustain that growth rate, we added branded pharmaceuticals, which required a different organization in sales and marketing, product

Watson quickly established an enviable reputation for quality and service, and became a model for success in the eyes of Wall Street observers.

someday establishing and operating his own proprietary drug company.

While still employed at Searle, Chao began taking business courses at Northwestern University. By 1983, he had left the company to start Watson—a name that is a tribute to Chao's mother, whose maiden name is Hwa. In a concession to the English language, "Hwa's son" became Watson.

At the time, Chao needed nearly $2 million to get his first lab up and running, and to win approval from the FDA to begin manufacturing drugs. Mainstream venture capital groups wouldn't fund the endeavor, nor would the banks he approached. Refusing to let rejection curb his drive, Chao relocated to Orange County, where he and his family had ties with the Taiwanese

Watson made a name for itself in generic, or off-patent, drugs in the late 1980s and early 1990s, but now the company draws half of its revenue from branded, or proprietary, pharmaceuticals.

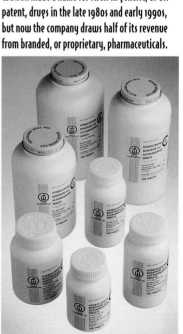

development, manufacturing, and regulatory affairs."

Within a year of broadening its focus, Watson had achieved record results. Revenues increased 35 percent to $338 million in 1997, marking the company's fifth consecutive year of earnings growth. Watson stock performed so well, in fact, that the company declared a 2-for-1 stock split in October 1997. During that same year, Watson acquired a number of complementary companies and products that further diversified its revenue base.

The acquisition of Oclassen Pharmaceuticals Inc., for instance, helped Watson expand into the $2 billion branded dermatology market. At the same time, Watson bought the marketing rights for seven generic contraceptive brands. With these product purchases, combined with those developed internally, the company's sales force grew to 300, up from just 20 the previous year.

For Watson's California workforce of just under 800—combined with its out-of-state employee base of another 600—Chao's entrepreneurial spirit has fostered a cooperative environment in which all 1,400 employees are encouraged to contribute their talents toward the company's ongoing success. "As Watson gets bigger, I can't make all the decisions," Chao says. "Our management team makes their own decisions. Our current structure empowers the managers, who, in turn, help the company grow."

Watson's remarkable growth potential prompted *SmartMoney* magazine to list the company among the best six investments for 1997. Calling Chao's plans bold and ambitious, *SmartMoney* quoted analysts who praised Watson for "going places where other companies can't follow." Analysts also predicted that the company's earnings will compound at 25 percent annually through 2002.

Complementing its well-established success in the generic market, Watson's newer proprietary pharmaceutical strategy, Chao says, is designed to ensure long-term growth by identifying product opportunities within specific therapeutic areas and by making the investments necessary to capitalize on those opportunities. A number of acquisitions made during 1997 have already expanded the breadth and scope of the company's offerings, thereby reducing its vulnerability to changes in the competitive, regulatory, and technological environments for any single product.

Chao's entrepreneurial spirit has fostered a co-operative environment in which all employees are encouraged to contribute their talents toward the company's ongoing success.

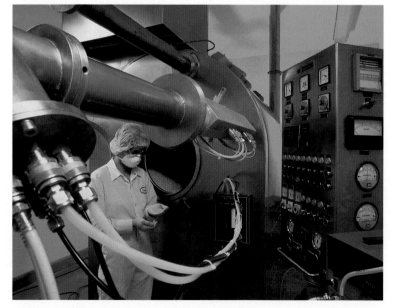

Specialty Drug Markets

Watson currently markets its proprietary products through four divisions: Dermatological, Women's Health, Neuro/Psychiatric, and Primary Care. The company entered the dermatology market through its purchase of Oclassen, which specializes in prescription products for the treatment and prevention of skin disease. As the overall dermatology market continues to grow at about 10 percent a year, Watson has directed its efforts at the largest segment—prescription acne therapies. To aid in the treatment of condyloma, a genital wart that ranks as the fastest-growing sexually transmitted viral disease, Watson markets Condylox. Additionally, the company's Cordran and Cormax products are marketed to treat inflammatory skin conditions, which comprise the second-largest prescription drug category in dermatology.

Building on its expertise in developing and manufacturing hormonal oral contraceptives, Watson created the Women's Health division with three in-house branded products. In 1997, the company expanded its offerings by acquiring four oral contraceptive products from Searle: Genora, Trivora, Levora, and Nor QD. In late 1998, it further complemented the oral contraceptive product line with three additional Searle product acquisitions: Tri-Norinyl, Norinyl, and Brevicon.

Watson's branded products in the neurology market include Eldepryl for Parkinson's disease. In the area of psychiatry, the company has reintroduced Loxitane for the treatment of schizophrenia and psychotic disorders.

Through its Primary Care division, which accounts for Watson's largest sales force, the company promotes products to more than 20,000 primary care physicians nationwide. Watson launched this division in 1997 with the FDA approval of Microzide to treat hypertension. The main products distributed through the Primary Care division include Norco, which is used for pain management, and Dilacor XR, another hypertension therapy.

Each of the company's branded product divisions focuses on offering drugs to satisfy the needs of physicians who specialize in the diagnosis and treatment of specific medical conditions. Watson operates with the assumption that this focused marketing approach will enable it to develop highly knowledgeable and dedicated sales representatives, while fostering close professional relationships with physicians.

Although branded products now represent more than 50 percent of Watson's gross profit, generic pharmaceuticals will continue to play a key role in the future growth of the company, Chao says. To that end, Watson maintains an aggressive product development program designed to introduce new off-patent products on a regular basis. In 1997 alone, the company launched 10 off-patent drugs. This, in addition to the products acquired in 1998, has expanded its portfolio to 93 products in 200 dosage strengths.

Looking Ahead

As it embraces the future, Watson will continue to seek and evaluate opportunities to acquire businesses, technologies, and products to strengthen its presence in today's fast-changing pharmaceutical industry. To sustain its accelerated growth into the next century, the company will continue its strategy of diversification from a specialty generic drug manufacturer into a fully integrated generic and branded pharmaceutical company.

Watson has already become a major supplier to chain drugstores, distributors, wholesalers, and managed care organizations throughout the United States, delivering products that are in great demand by physicians and patients alike. Through the use of state-of-the-art production machinery, as well as its significant investment in personnel and facilities, Watson has been able to manufacture the finest-quality products, control overhead costs, and remain competitive.

"In the future," says Chao, "we plan to retain the entrepreneurial spirit, discipline, and practices that have resulted in Watson's consistent financial performance."

Watson maintains an aggressive product development program designed to introduce new off-patent products on a regular basis.

THE SHERIDAN GROUP

I n a city where esthetics take second place only to the weather, The Sheridan Group has built a reputation as a full-service furniture dealer with a keen eye for details and the highest standard of customer service. Furnishing the offices of an impressive client list composed primarily of Fortune 500 companies, the firm has a hands-on approach to delivering its service. "The main element that makes us different among others in this industry is that we stress service," says Dannine Sheridan, founder and principal of the

firm. "We are not a sales organization. Once we bring in a project, we want to ensure the client is really happy."

Being proactive and anticipating problems are the key ingredients to the company's successful projects, which include furniture specification, purchasing, delivery, and installation.

New Beginnings

In 1984, Sheridan—who graduated with a degree in fine arts from the University of Southern California—launched a two-person furniture distribution operation. Three years later, the business was bought by PHH, a corporation traded on the New York Stock Exchange. But by 1990, Sheridan had bought the firm back. The bold move paid off. Sheridan saw sales skyrocket from $10 million in 1994 to $18 million in 1997. During this growth, the firm's employees increased from 18 to 30.

Sheridan has put together a team of professionals who create innovative, high-quality office environments that integrate the important elements of form and function. The staff utilizes a project-oriented approach to service, where they become an extension of their clients' design teams.

"I attribute our success to the people that are here," says Sheridan from her West Los Angeles office. She opened the new office in Santa Fe Springs to best suit the staff's needs—which meant being

closer to home for the working mothers on the team.

The Sheridan Approach

In the early stages of each project, whether large or small, account executives work to prepare budgets, study inventory, evaluate and refurbish existing furniture, and determine what outside specialists need to be contracted for specific jobs. The Sheridan Group's CADD department does drawings of various workstations on in-house computer systems, which are then reviewed by the client.

"We ensure that nothing slips through the cracks," Sheridan says. "It's those last details that we are remembered by."

Over the years, Sheridan has worked with large corporate institutions such as Capital Group Inc., Herbalife International, and the Getty Center, filling office spaces of more than 100,000 square feet with combinations of desks, tables, cabinets, dividers, chairs, and other furnishings. After finishing its largest account to date—the Metropolitan Transit Authority's 700,000-square-foot, newly built high-rise in downtown Los Angeles—the group tapped into the entertainment industry. By providing its signature service to such firms as Sony Pictures International, Dreamworks, and Saban Entertainment, The Sheridan Group is poised to further expand its operations, ensuring its continued success well into the next century.

The Sheridan Group has built a reputation as a full-service furniture dealer with a keen eye for details and the highest standard of customer service. In the early stages of each project, whether large or small, account executives work to prepare budgets, study inventory, evaluate and refurbish existing furniture, and determine what outside specialists need to be contracted for specific jobs.

NTA, INC.

I t's not about the money—it's about how you treat your employees. This is the message that Fountain Valley's Kingston Technology Company strives to convey as it conducts its business of providing critical memory to computer makers and users around the globe. ⚓ In an age when state-of-the-art technology rules supreme, Kingston emerges as the "nice guy" in the highly competitive computer industry. The company has proven that having gross annual sales of more than $1 billion is not incompatible with

treating its employees well. In fact, from the firm's start back in 1987, founders John Tu and David Sun have promoted the idea that Kingston's strength lies in its employees and that people, not products, are its greatest asset. In keeping with that philosophy, Tu and Sun encourage a family-style work environment. Rather than cloistering themselves in plush corner suites, for example, they work in cubicles alongside Kingston's other dedicated employees.

The company's nice-guy approach has helped make it the world's largest independent manufacturer of memory enhancement products for PCs, notebooks, servers, workstations, printers, and electronic devices. Kingston Technology went from a small start-up venture to $800 million in annual sales in just seven years; by 1996, its revenues totaled $1.3 billion. From its origins as a manufacturer of a SIMM, or single in-line memory module, Kingston now maintains offices and manufacturing sites worldwide devoted to developing and manufacturing nearly 5,000 products for global distribution.

The company's rapid success has not gone unnoticed by industry watchers. In 1998, *Fortune* magazine ranked Kingston Technology second in its list of the 100 best companies to work for in the country. And in 1992, *Inc.* magazine ranked Kingston number one in its list of America's top 500 fastest-growing companies.

DAVIS BARBER

Webmaster Tim Westland has worked diligently to bring fun and cyberspace to Kingston Technology Company.

Computing without Limits

Kingston Technology works to make sure that when a new computer system is released, the company is prepared to offer the memory necessary to support it. And Kingston prides itself on providing memory for older systems when even the PC makers cannot supply memory.

Memory—in addition to being one of the primary enabling technologies for computer system and software performance, and constituting more than 20 percent of the retail value of a typical PC—is the most rapidly growing segment of the overall semiconductor market. In fact, the company's slogan, Computing Without Limits, could actually be recast as "growth without limits," for Kingston shows no signs of slowing down. Not even its 80 percent acquisition by Japan's SOFTBANK Corp. in 1996 has diminished the style that Tu and Sun have cultivated over the previous decade. Rather, the founders see the partnering of the two companies as a mutually beneficial arrangement.

With its phenomenal success in a highly competitive field, Kingston Technology Company is vivid proof that nice guys don't finish last.

Husband-and-wife team Minh Nguyen and Tawny Tran exercise their talents in shipping and international sales, respectively (left).

Rosanne Carrillo has been involved with sales for Kingston from the moment the company moved out of one of the founder's garages and into a real office space (right).

DAVIS BARBER

Amptron International, Inc.

When President and CEO Leon Hsiao established Amptron International, Inc.—a manufacturer of personal computer motherboards—in 1986, his aim was to put service and support before making the sale. The result? In slightly more than a decade, he sold more than 5 million motherboards, and today, Amptron is a $40 million design and manufacturing company. In 1997, the *Los Angeles Business Journal* ranked it 24th in its list of the 100 fastest-growing private companies in Southern California.

Amptron's annual revenues have increased from $800,000 in 1986 to $45 million in 1998, as its staff has grown from three employees to 80. At 110,000 square feet, the company's new headquarters is five times the size of its previous structure. Amptron is located in City of Industry, the center of computer manufacturing and distribution for Southern California. The company currently sells its products through domestic and global market distributors and resellers.

In 1998, Amptron expanded its product line to include a variety of high-quality monitors and other computer components, which are available through value-added resellers, system manufacturers, and wholesale direct mail companies. In its introductory year, Amptron shipped about 70,000 sets of monitors.

Best Value and Service

Amptron's motto—Best Value and Service—expresses an idea that permeates everything the company does. Hsiao credits Amptron's competitiveness and strength with this approach, and says that it is what sets the company apart from the competition. "Amptron's guiding philosophy has always been 'to provide the best service and the best products at the most competitive price,' " says Hsiao. "The entire organization is set up in such a way that providing service and solutions is our primary goal, contrary to the traditional product-oriented approach that is typical in the generic computer component industry. This is what really sets us apart from the competition. Using leading overseas manufacturing facilities is another key factor for our success."

Amptron's manufacturing sites have long been known for stringent quality control standards—all Amptron motherboards are ISO-9002 certified, and its monitors are ISO-9001 certified. Amptron's winning policy includes providing immediate service at the customer's request, and offering direct customer access to the company's engineering department. Amptron's Web site also complements the company's services by providing a no-frills, practical, user-friendly, and content-rich tool for customers.

Amptron designs its products based on what the customers and the market want in the most current technology, compared to products that are designed solely based on technical merit commonly available. The company has a professional

Amptron International is located in City of Industry, the center of computer manufacturing and distribution for Southern California.

Founded in 1986 by President and CEO Leon Hsiao, today Amprtron is one of the fastest growing companies in Southern California.

In 1998, Amptron expanded its product line to include a variety of high-quality monitors and other computer components.

management team made up of highly experienced and educated personnel, with sales executives who are well trained in the personal computer industry. Their primary goal is not simply to sell the products, but also to provide technology information, solutions, and insightful product analysis.

"Amptron has been growing steadily because we are doing the right things," says Hsiao. "We are helping our customers make profits. They will remember us as a reliable service and solution provider." Hsiao feels that through its dedication to value and service, Amptron has introduced a new way of doing business into the personal computer industry.

The company's commitment extends beyond the customer to the employee, as Amptron strives to maintain a work environment in which its employees can thrive. "We feel that people want to do a good job, a creative job, and if provided the proper environment, they will do so," says Hsiao.

Amptron is the first in the generic motherboard and monitor industry to transform itself from a product-oriented manufacturer to a service- and solution-providing organization. To further enhance Amptron's leading position in the industry, the company plans to introduce new product lines, including high-speed 48X CD-ROM drives and advanced 8X DVD-ROM drives, while providing the best ratio of price to performance in personal computer systems.

Amptron's manufacturing sites have long been known for stringent quality control standards—all Amptron motherboards are ISO-9002 certified, and its monitors are ISO-9001 certified.

Hsiao predicts that eventually the high-end market in the personal computer industry will be reduced to about a dozen firms, as the fast pace of technological advancements eliminates those companies that are unprepared to handle rapid change.

Formerly a senior engineer in semiconductors with Texas Instruments, Hsiao has seen enough changes in the computer industry over the last 20 years to know that his company is well positioned to continue its successful growth in this competitive market.

Ernst & Young LLP provides assurance and advisory business services, tax services, and consulting for domestic and global clients. The firm has 30,000 people in 87 U.S. cities and, in 1986, established an ambitious annual program to honor entrepreneurial spirit around the globe—the Entrepreneur Of The Year® program. Through the Entrepreneur Of The Year Institute, created to celebrate the accomplishments of the world's outstanding entrepreneurs and to make the general public more

aware of the benefits they provide to society, the institute's program has helped provide a forum for entrepreneurs to express their views; be a source of information; facilitate networking and idea sharing; help educate members; promote entrepreneurship; and commemorate the achievements of successful businesspeople.

Now in its 12th year, the Entrepreneur Of The Year program has succeeded as spectacularly at that goal as many of its award recipients have at theirs. Each June, outstanding entrepreneurs are chosen at 47 regional conferences throughout the United States and in another 80 locations around the world. Locally, there are

roughly 100 nominees in the Greater Los Angeles region. In 1998, there were 28 finalists, and nine award recipients chosen at a gala banquet sponsored locally by J&H Marsh & McLennan; The Citibank Private Bank; Wedbush Morgan Securities; Riordan & McKenzie; Paul, Hastings Janofsky & Walker; and Capital Resources Consulting.

A Prestigious Award

A panel of distinguished independent judges—fellow entrepreneurs and prominent leaders from academia and business—selects the finalists and award recipients. Industry categories vary each year, but can include business services, communications, entertainment, financial services, life sciences, real estate/construction, and technology, among others.

Each finalist represents a company with significant established values, as measured by its substantial economic benefits to the local economy. Recent Los Angeles-area award recipients include Bernard Howroyd, founder of AppleOne Employment Services; Joe Kaplan, founder of Superior Bankcard Service; Debra S. Esparza, director of the USC Business Expansion Network; Richard Ziman of Arden Realty; Jim Ellison of Sierra Concepts Corporation; Edward Gavaldon of Peerless Systems; Li-Pei Wu of GBC Bancorp; and Carlos DeMattos of Matthews Studio Group.

Another recent award recipient is Frank D. Robinson, the founder of Robinson Helicopter. Robinson Helicopter is the number one manufacturer of light helicopters in the world and, since its founding in 1973, has expanded a dealer/sales network to 200 locations around the world. "Our company is a good example of what the award is all about," says Robinson from his 260,000-square-foot facility at the Torrance Airport in the South Bay area. "We started in my garage and now we have 600 employees."

The Measurement of Success

The award program was established to honor entrepreneurs whose ingenuity, hard work, and perseverance have created and sustained successful, growing business

The Entrepreneur Of The Year® program, through the Entrepreneur Of The Year Institute, was established by Ernst & Young in 1986 to celebrate the accomplishments of the world's outstanding entrepreneurs and to make the general public more aware of the benefits they provide to society. Each June, outstanding entrepreneurs are chosen at 47 regional conferences throughout the United States and in another 80 locations around the world. In 1998, there were 28 finalists in the Los Angeles area, and nine award recipients were chosen at a gala banquet sponsored locally by J&H Marsh & McLennan; The Citibank Private Bank; Wedbush Morgan Securities; Riordan & McKenzie; Paul, Hastings, Janofsky & Walker LLP; and Capital Resources Consulting (top).

Joe Kaplan, founder of Superior Bankcard Service, was a 1998 award recipient (bottom).

ventures. Nominees for the award must meet the criteria outlined by the institute, and their companies should be at least two years old. Nominees from private businesses must be from the ranks of the owner or manager responsible for the company's successful financial performance. If the company is public, the founder must be active in management. All nominees are interviewed and must disclose some limited, recent financial information.

Candidates are nominated by customers, colleagues, employees, or vendors. The process requires only the completion of the official nomination form, which can be submitted from January through April. The judging process encompasses several key areas. The nominee's background—including special skills, experience, and major accomplishments—is considered along with participation in business, community, or civic involvement.

In addition, the history of the nominee's company is thoroughly evaluated. This assessment includes the source of the idea for the original strategy, the financial risk involved, innovative approaches to management and marketing, the company's current stage of development, and future prospects. Part of the evaluation includes a description of the company's major products and/or services, and how the company has demonstrated excellence in its field or industry.

Recognition of Excellence

Since winning the award in 1998, Robinson says his company has received significant recognition. "This award helps your credibility in the business world, and in the industry as well," he says. Entrepreneur Of The Year finalists and award recipients benefit from local, regional, industry, and national media recognition. In Los Angeles, media outlets, such as radio stations KCRW-FM, KNX-AM, and KFWB-AM, as well as the *Los Angeles Business Journal,* help disseminate news about winners.

The honor also benefits marketing and public relations efforts. Each year, a survey of prior Entrepreneur Of The Year award recipients is conducted by the Ewing Marion Kauffman Foundation, the largest such organization supporting entrepreneurship in the United States.

The Entrepreneur Of The Year award stands for excellence, and participation in the awards program benefits individual entrepreneurs, their companies, and their colleagues. In turn, the community benefits through the dynamic innovation and growth accomplished by fostering new ideas, new risk taking, and new triumphs—the true description of entrepreneurship.

1998 award recipient Jim Ellison of Sierra Concepts Corporation, flanked by Mark Lamensdorf of Citibank Private Bank (left) and Tommy Hawkins, former Lakers All-Star

Ed Gavaldon of Peerless Systems Corporation was an award recipient in 1998, and is shown here with actress Cathy Lee Crosby and Rick Welch of Riordan & McKenzie.

ViewSonic Corporation

I n less than a decade, ViewSonic Corporation has gone from start-up to industry leader in one of the world's most competitive fields. Under the visionary leadership of founder and President/CEO James Chu, ViewSonic has introduced an array of award-winning display technology products, and today competes successfully with some of the world's largest and best-known companies. ▨ The ViewSonic story began in 1987, when Chu launched Keypoint Technology Corporation, a distribution company specializing in computer peripherals such as power supplies

and keyboards. Before long, Chu perceived a need for high-quality, competitively priced computer monitors and responded by introducing the first ViewSonic monitor in 1990. Sales grew rapidly and the company was twice included on *Inc.* magazine's list of the nation's 500 fastest-growing companies.

By 1998, the company—since renamed ViewSonic to acknowledge its exclusive focus on computer monitors and other display technologies—had been recognized by industry analyst Stanford Resources as the nation's leading producer of branded computer monitors. ViewSonic is one of the largest privately owned companies in Los Angeles County and the county's largest minority-owned business. Today, the ViewSonic logo—three brightly colored Australian finches—is a powerful visual icon that symbolizes the rich, vibrant colors produced by the company's wide range of computer monitors and other display technology products.

The company has enjoyed exceptional revenue growth since introducing its first computer monitor in 1990. ViewSonic generated more than $830 million in 1997, nearly tripling its 1994 revenues and earning the firm a spot on Deloitte & Touche's

list of the fastest-growing high-tech companies in the United States. During that same period, the number of ViewSonic employees jumped from 200 to more than 600.

ViewSonic's rapid growth led the company to relocate its worldwide headquarters in 1997 to a 300,000-square-foot, state-of-the-art facility in Walnut, 30 miles east of Los Angeles. Approximately half of the company's employees are based there; the remainder work at various locations throughout the United States and in France, England, China, Taiwan, Germany, and Canada.

A Monitor for Every User

According to company officials, ViewSonic's remarkable success can be attributed to several factors. For example, the company enjoys close, trust-based relationships with a variety of marketing partners, including distributors, resellers, systems integrators, and retailers. Its products have been highly touted for their consistent quality and high performance. ViewSonic also boasts the broadest product line in the industry, selling more than 60 display products in over 70 countries under three brand names: ViewSonic, Optiquest, and CyberVision.

The company sold more than 2 million ViewSonic brand monitors in 1997. Models under this brand—Professional, Graphics, E2, Multimedia, and ViewPanel series—are carefully designed for a variety of specific applications, including graphic design, imaging, and desktop publishing. They are used in an array of computing environments, from major corporations and government agencies to small businesses and homes.

ViewSonic's Optiquest brand is designed to fulfill the need for cost-effective monitors that offer quality and performance superior to those brands that compete primarily on the basis of price. The CyberVision brand is ideally suited for system integrators, who purchase components and assemble custom computer systems for clients ranging from individuals to large corporations.

In 1997, ViewSonic introduced its first computer-based LCD display projector, extending the company into small- and large-audience presentation markets.

ViewSonic's superior product quality is evidenced by the numerous product awards it has received from ratings organizations and industry trade publications such as *PC Magazine, PC World, Computer Reseller News, MacWorld,* and *Computer Shopper.* The company itself has also been honored by various industry publications. For example, it was named Channel Champion by *Computer Reseller News* and received the prestigious Apex Award from *VARBusiness* two years in a row. *PC Magazine* twice included ViewSonic on its list of the 100 most influential companies in the personal computer industry. And Ernst &

President/CEO James Chu founded ViewSonic in 1987; today, the company has introduced an array of award-winning display technology products and competes successfully with some of the world's largest and best-known companies (top).

ViewSonic's worldwide headquarters is located in a 300,000-square-foot facility in Walnut, 30 miles east of Los Angeles (bottom).

Young honored Chu in 1994 when it named him Entrepreneur of the Year.

Technology Provider

Company executives claim that a large part of ViewSonic's success stems from an innovative business model that often enables the company to design, produce, and distribute products more quickly than its competitors. Eschewing traditional approaches to product design, manufacturing, and assembly, ViewSonic is able to exploit technologies from research laboratories and manufacturing facilities around the world in order to fulfill market demands.

Before providing product specifications to manufacturers and assemblers, ViewSonic consults with value-added resellers, system integrators, distributors,

retail chains, and others in order to anticipate which features, technologies, and prices will be sought by consumers. The company's powerful partnerships allow it to route a product from concept to shipping in as few as 12 weeks—significantly below the industry standard.

ViewSonic's success is arguably a direct result of Chu's philosophy toward hiring and motivating employees. The company's distinct corporate culture continually attracts top-quality people who share an entrepreneurial spirit that combines individual aspiration and group cooperation. These employee-partners (Chu's term for his staff) work assiduously toward a common goal: total customer satisfaction. In return, they share company profits and are rewarded with generous bonus

plans. Moreover, they enjoy a work environment designed to promote fun and excitement.

Chu and his employee-partners have ambitious dreams, seeking nothing less than to become the preferred provider of display technology products worldwide. Achieving that dream will require the company to maintain its commitment to customer satisfaction; continuously deliver new technologies and products faster than its competitors; and maintain close relationships with its various business partners. Reaching this goal also will necessitate cultivating the firm's powerful entrepreneurial culture. Chu and his employee-partners are confident of their ability to lead the display technology industry in the new millennium.

Clockwise from top:
The company's distinct corporate culture continually attracts top-quality people who share an entrepreneurial spirit that combines individual aspiration and group cooperation.

ViewSonic's superior product quality is evidenced by the numerous product awards it has received from ratings organizations and industry trade publications.

The ViewSonic logo—three brightly colored Australian finches—is a powerful visual icon that symbolizes the rich, vibrant colors produced by the company's wide range of computer monitors and other display technology products.

Koo Koo Roo, Inc.

Designed with today's active lifestyles in mind, Koo Koo Roo, Inc. caters to the health-conscious diner who demands food that's big on flavor as well as nutrition. From its beginnings as a two-outlet, fast-service eatery to today's multimillion-dollar national restaurant chain, Koo Koo Roo has provided fresh, savory meals that are "good for yoo" for more than a decade. ◆ "The market was ripe for a fresh, new concept," says John Kaufman,

president and COO of the chain. "Today's consumer is much more educated and aware of nutrition, diet, and its correlation with disease. This has helped pave the way for Koo Koo Roo's success."

Koo Koo Roo appeals to a wide range of people who look for good-tasting, freshly made, moderately priced food, and who also appreciate menu items that are wholesome and healthy. For those dining in, Koo Koo Roo also creates an appealing atmosphere, including bright, clean dining rooms, fresh flowers at every table, comfortable chairs, and spotless flatware. The sights and smells of fresh food preparation are displayed in glass-enclosed stations featuring chefs in whites and toques.

Koo Koo Roo's Original Skinless Flame-Broiled Chicken® is a menu mainstay, as are the country herb-garlic rotisserie chicken; fresh, hand-carved turkey; specialty sandwiches on freshly baked rolls; hearty soups; and made-to-order, crisp garden salads. Two dozen signature side dishes are freshly prepared every 20 minutes in small, home-style quantities. The restaurant offers a variety of freshly made, hand-tossed salads, including its award-winning Chinese chicken salad.

A Decade of Good Food

The Koo Koo Roo restaurant concept began in Southern California in 1988. Two brothers, Michael and Raymond Badalian, opened two outlets that offered skinless chicken prepared in a secret marinade and broiled over an open flame. Then, in 1990, restaurateur Kenneth Berg paid the Badalian brothers $2.5 million for a 50 percent interest in the business.

Berg upgraded the Koo Koo Roo concept by adding new dishes, like salads, fresh vegetables, and hand-carved turkey, and by 1992, the chain had grown to seven outlets. The restaurant went public shortly afterward, and the Badalian brothers sold their stock in the chain. Still, the brothers' recipe for skinless chicken has never changed.

Koo Koo Roo has since expanded to nearly 40 locations across the United States. The national restaurant chain added a variety of new stores in 1997, including locations in Florida and California. Nearly 20 more restaurants opened in 1998

throughout Southern California. Today, Koo Koo Roo operates 52 restaurants in California, Las Vegas, Florida, and the Washington, D.C., area, including 14 Hamburger Hamlet restaurants. The company's Canadian partner also operates three Koo Koo Roo California Kitchen restaurants in Toronto.

In 1998, Berg resigned his position as chairman of the board, and Lee A. Iacocca, a current board member and the former chairman of the board of Chrysler Motors, assumed the role of acting chairman. Along with new CEO William Allen, Iacocca and the board will take the Koo Koo Roo vision into the next century.

Koo Koo Roo creates an appealing atmosphere, including bright, clean dining rooms, flowers at every table, and comfortable chairs. The sights and smells of fresh food preparation—such as hand-carving a freshly roasted turkey— are displayed in glass-enclosed stations featuring chefs in whites and toques (top).

Two dozen signature side dishes are freshly prepared every 20 minutes in small, home-style quantities. The restaurant offers a variety of freshly made, hand-tossed salads, including its award-winning Chinese chicken salad (bottom).

On December 16, 1997, the Getty Center art and cultural complex opened its doors in Los Angeles. Among the most expensive art institutions built in American history—a $1 billion undertaking—the Getty Center unites the organizations of the J. Paul Getty Trust on one site. Situated in the foothills of the Santa Monica mountains in the historic Sepulveda Pass, the 110-acre campus is expected to draw more than 1.3 million visitors a year. But this massive undertaking had its beginning in one piece of art. When J. Paul Getty bought his first notable work of art in 1931, few in the world had heard of the oil magnate. But within the next two decades, he would establish a nonprofit trust to oversee a museum founded from his ranch house in Malibu. And by the late 1960s, Getty would have committed $17 million to building a new museum, on the same grounds, that was modeled after a Roman villa.

When Getty died in 1976, he left the museum $700 million in Getty Oil stock. In the 1980s, the trustees dramatically expanded the trust's mission and created four new organizations under the Getty Trust umbrella. After a massive undertaking that took 14 years from its conception, the Getty Center in Los Angeles was born, becoming a unique urban monument that has brought to the region a new, world-class museum and research center.

J. Paul Getty Museum

From the Getty Center's front entrance, visitors ascend the hill in an electric tram for a five-minute ride to the center's central plaza. Eighty-six acres of landscaped gardens and terraces, including the Central Garden designed by artist Robert Irwin, provide sweeping views of the Los Angeles basin, the mountains, and the ocean.

The center houses the Getty Research Institute for the History of Art and the Humanities, which is dedicated to interdisciplinary scholarship in the arts, and features an 800,000-volume research library; the Getty Conservation Institute, a commitment to preserving the world's cultural heritage; the Getty Education Institute for the Arts, which seeks to improve the quality and status of arts education in American schools; the Getty Leadership Institute for Museum Management, which helps professionals acquire the business knowledge needed to operate art institutions; and the Getty Grant Program, which has awarded nearly $69 million, and provides crucial support for projects in the areas of art history, museum practice, and conservation. The campus also includes a full-service restaurant, two cafés, a museum bookstore, and a 450-seat, multipurpose auditorium.

The highlight of the Getty Center is the new J. Paul Getty Museum. The museum's collection includes European paintings, sculpture, drawings, and decorative arts before 1900; illuminated manuscripts; and photographs. The museum also features collections on loan from other institutions around the world. Its collection of Greek and Roman antiquities will provide the core of the exhibition program at the Getty Villa in Malibu, which will reopen in late 2001 as a study center devoted to comparative archaeology and culture.

From a one-piece collection to the definitive symbol of art and culture in Los Angeles, the Getty Center has fulfilled J. Paul Getty's dream of bringing the world of art to the City of Angels. With its ongoing mission of education and leadership and its dedication to preserving culture and the arts, the Getty Center is creating an enduring legacy that will last for generations to come.

The Getty Museum's collection includes European paintings before 1900, such as *Irises*, by Vincent van Gogh (top).

The museum's collection of paintings, sculpture, decorative arts, drawings, illuminated manuscripts, and photographs are exhibited in five gallery pavilions around a central courtyard (bottom left).

Designed by Richard Meier & Partners, the Getty Center opened to the public on December 16, 1997 (bottom right).

JOHN STEPHENS

NELSON SHELTON & ASSOCIATES

While Southern Californians can count on sunny skies just about any given day of the year, the region's real estate climate isn't so dependable. But for more than a decade, the Beverly Hills real estate firm Nelson Shelton & Associates has ensured that sellers and buyers of Los Angeles' prime properties have felt the constant warmth of friendly, reliable service. Formed by real estate veterans Elsa Nelson and Mark Shelton—who have

been in the industry for more than 20 years—Nelson Shelton & Associates covers all the aspects of real estate sales: residential, residential-income, and commercial. Centrally based in Beverly Hills, the firm's agents are a cross section of the community, and cover a service area that ranges from downtown Los Angeles west to Malibu, north to the San Fernando Valley, and south to the Marina del Rey-Venice Beach area.

Nelson and Shelton believe their company's success comes from its ability to be as diverse as the city it serves. "We'll sell a $5 million estate in Bel Air, or a

$60,000 home in South-Central; a $15 million hotel, or a $500,000 home in Westwood," Nelson says. "It's because we have our eyes on the community, and on the pulse of the market."

In an industry dominated by large national corporations with faceless offices that are often not sensitive to the local market, the seasoned professionals at Nelson Shelton & Associates ensure that each client is treated as the only one. "The highest-quality service ensures the best results for all parties," Shelton says. The difference between working with Nelson Shelton & Associates and a national fran-

chised organization can be compared to eating at a fast-food chain versus a gourmet restaurant.

Shelton makes the analogy this way: "There's no question that there are a lot of Ford Tauruses sold. We are the Mercedes-Benz or the BMW of the real estate world. We are not going to have an office at every corner of the city. What we are going to have is a very high quality service. That's a throwback to traditional real estate service."

Seasoned Agents

In 1996, when Nelson and Shelton broke away from the large national organization they helped form, the partners decided they were going to assemble the best team of real estate agents they could possibly get. The 100 handpicked associates were, like the principals, independent and experienced in their field. To attract talented professionals, Nelson and Shelton made sure the firm's associates were paid above the industry standards. Today, the firm has some 320 agents. The average Nelson and Shelton associate has more than 10 years' experience in the field.

Providing associates with high commissions has given them the freedom to be creative in their marketing strategies, Nelson says. Nelson Shelton & Associates advertisements in local trade publications stand out from the rest of the ads. A full-page ad consists of a handful of large photographs showcasing homes, as opposed

◄ HEADSHOTS ETC. TOMORROW PHOTOGRAPHY

"Our philosophy is doing right by people, doing the right thing at the right time," Elsa Nelson says. "That's why we have positive results. Mark [Shelton] and I are in this heart and soul, because our company bears our names."

For more than a decade, the Beverly Hills real estate firm Nelson Shelton & Associates has ensured that sellers and buyers of Los Angeles' prime properties have felt the constant warmth of friendly, reliable service.

Formed by real estate veterans Elsa Nelson and Mark Shelton—who have been in the industry for more than 20 years—Nelson Shelton & Associates covers all the aspects of real estate sales: residential, residential-income, and commercial.

to a dozen or so words describing what a property looks like.

The firm also invests in the latest technology to support its staff. In 1998, it spent a substantial amount of money to upgrade the company's telecommunications system, purchasing not only state-of-the-art telephone, messaging, and paging systems, but also the latest computers tailored to real estate brokerage specifications. To further add support, the firm recently launched a Web site: www.nelsonshelton.com.

While most real estate companies put a lot of time and effort into creating independent offices, Nelson and Shelton have found advantages to being all under one roof. Because Nelson Shelton & Associates has only one office, one standard of quality is enforced. "Rather than 15 different managers with their own interpretations of how to service customers, there is one voice speaking for the company.

That way there is one level of expectation," Shelton says.

Proven Results

In 1998, the *Los Angeles Business Journal* rated the firm among the top 25 real estate brokers in Los Angeles County. The newspaper article, which listed the firm as number 16, stated that Nelson Shelton & Associates had the highest increase in sales that year of any company that did not acquire another firm. In addition, the firm was number one in growth in the Westside area. In the two-year period between 1996 and 1998, the number of units the firm sold doubled. In 1998, the firm had $450 million in sales and more than 1,000 units sold.

"Our philosophy is doing right by people, doing the right thing at the right time," Nelson says. "That's why we have positive results. Mark and I are in this heart and soul, because our company bears our names."

NORTHERN TRUST BANK OF CALIFORNIA

Northern Trust Corporation has been a leader in providing trust and investment management services to individuals, families, corporations, and not-for-profit institutions for more than 100 years. The company takes the very personal approach of forming a partnership with clients, developing innovative approaches to planning for trusts and estates, investing and monitoring funds, and maintaining leading-edge technology to support a complete range of private banking services.

Northern Trust Corporation is committed to continued growth and has expanded to 78 locations nationally. With a growing network of subsidiaries in 12 states, international offices in five countries, and some 7,800 employees worldwide, Northern Trust's style of business has made it a financial leader, with trust assets under administration totaling $1.2 trillion and banking assets of $26 billion.

The California Presence: The Private Bank

In January 1988, Northern Trust Bank of California opened its first office in Santa Barbara. Later that year, offices were opened in Los Angeles and San Francisco. By the end of 1992, the bank had expanded to Westwood, Newport Beach, and San Diego, and then to Montecito and La Jolla in 1997, and Beverly Hills in 1998. Northern Trust Bank has grown to be the sixth-largest trust company in California, with trust assets exceeding $11 billion.

Northern Trust President and CEO Sherry S. Barrat says, "While being the largest bank is not our goal, clearly more than a century of experience and $1.2 trillion in assets testify that many people believe we are very good at what we do."

Northern Trust Bank, "The Private Bank," provides its clients with personal attention and professional service, a return to the idea of private banking, which was

used as a model for the private banks that have served the titled families and the affluent of Europe for centuries. "The bank treats customers as family," Barrat says. "We consider each person's individual financial profile, as well as the

needs of other family members. Northern Trust's services go beyond the usual banking relationship to meet the individual requirements of its clients and their families."

The People behind the Service

In the gallery of the bank's headquarters in Los Angeles, the words "integrity," "tradition," and "trust" are emblazoned in large letters over picturesque California landscapes. Barrat points out that at the center of everything the bank does are its people, who provide the service to every client. "Our people don't have jobs with us, they have careers," says Barrat, who has been with the company since 1990. "About 80 percent of the employees own stock in our company, which is their company." Northern Trust has the highest employee ownership of any major financial institution—nearly 20 percent of the company's stock. The bank's employees are experts at what they do and are con-

Northern Trust Bank of California President and CEO Sherry S. Barrat says, "Northern Trust's services go beyond the usual banking relationship to meet the individual requirements of its clients and their families."

Chief Investment Officer Lynn J. Danielson states, "At Northern Trust, our primary focus is our commitment to our clients, and to providing them with the most updated financial information and personalized service available."

stantly working to remain at the forefront of their areas of specialization.

Community Partnership

Northern Trust Bank is known as a bank that returns resources to the local communities it serves through the support of art, music, dance, theater, health care, education, sports, and cultural events. In addition, the corporation has been recognized for eight consecutive years by *Working Mother* magazine as one of the country's top 100 companies for programs and benefits that support the balance of work and personal responsibilities. All senior officers of Northern Trust hold positions on boards of cultural and other charitable and community organizations.

With more-than-a-century-old tradition of being a well-managed, conservative, but progressive, bank and a premier provider of trust and private banking services, Northern Trust Bank is committed to providing superior products and services in the communities it serves.

In January 1988, Northern Trust Bank of California opened its first office in Santa Barbara. Later that year, offices were opened in Los Angeles and San Francisco. By the end of 1992, the bank had expanded to Westwood (pictured), Newport Beach, and San Diego, and then to Montecito and La Jolla in 1997.

Northern Trust Bank, The Private Bank, opened its 10th statewide office in Beverly Hills during the fall of 1998.

Bragman Nyman Cafarelli, Inc.

Whoopi Goldberg, L.L. Cool J, Cameron Diaz, Miramax, Paramount, Universal, Nickelodeon Movies, Levi Strauss & Co., Salvatore Ferragamo, Dom Perignon, and Guinness Stout. What do they all have in common? They trust Bragman Nyman Cafarelli, Inc. (BNC) with their public relations and marketing concerns. With offices in Beverly Hills and New York City, BNC is one of the only public relations marketing agencies in the country to combine the corporate

and entertainment worlds, providing a mixture of public relations and marketing strategies both for Fortune 500 companies and for celebrities, special events, television shows, movies, and productions. BNC has about 150 clients and projects, and currently bills more than $6 million in fees annually, putting it among the 10 largest public relations firms in Los Angeles and among the top firms in the country for the entertainment industry. The agency employs a staff of 80 in its two offices and maintains a client-to-staff ratio of 3-to-1.

A Public Relations Partnership

After more than a decade in public relations and marketing, Howard Bragman founded his own public relations firm in 1989 in a spare bedroom in his house. The following year, seasoned professionals Michael Nyman and Brad Cafarelli joined him and, in 1991, the three officially established the agency of Bragman Nyman Cafarelli, Inc. In the ensuing decade, BNC evolved into a public relations powerhouse, attracting a team of associates with an impressive array of marketing and public relations credentials under their belts. The firm's areas of specialty are entertainment marketing, personality and special event publicity, television/film, consumer product/event marketing, and corporate entertainment.

"The world of entertainment is more than just film, television, and music," says

agency president Nyman, "and our firm's success has been based greatly on our ability to guide and position our clients in the convergence of the entertainment and corporate worlds. BNC's business philosophy is simple: We strive to be the best, and in doing so, we want to change the way public relations is viewed in the business world."

BNC has created a partnership structured along the lines of accounting and

law firms, a strategy that has benefited not only its clients, but its employees as well. Observing that most creative service businesses suffer from untimely staff departures, BNC has developed a partnership plan that rewards and encourages employee growth and retention. Employees don't simply have jobs—they have true career paths, which encourage quality work and promote loyalty.

Bragman Nyman Cafarelli, Inc. (BNC) is one of the only public relations marketing agencies in the country to combine the corporate and entertainment worlds, providing a mixture of public relations and marketing strategies both for Fortune 500 companies and for celebrities, special events, television shows, movies, and productions. Pictured is actress Salma Hayek at the 1998 Fire & Ice Ball (top).

Participants toast the immortal memory of Robert Burns at the Scotsfest '98 Whiskey Ball (bottom right).

Thousands of kegs are loaded on the Guinness airplane in Dublin and shipped to America for St. Patrick's Day. More than 11 million perfect pints of Guinness will be consume worldwide on this Irish holiday (bottom left).

The New Wave in Entertainment PR

As the demographics of the nation shift in the new millennium, the under-25-year-old age group is becoming the most significant consumer demographic—a fact not lost on BNC. With a staff whose average age is in the early 30s, the firm is poised to develop and execute public relations and marketing programs that speak directly to this audience.

Inside PR magazine characterized BNC as the new wave in entertainment public relations and marketing. Citing the agency's knowledge and understanding of both the entertainment industry and consumer product public relations, the magazine called it "the preeminent marketing public relations firm in Southern California."

"Not only do we understand how to create a strategic public relations plan, but we also understand how corporate America and Hollywood operate," Nyman explains. "Because we can speak both languages, we are able to give the clients strategic thinking and understanding of their business, as well as the solid results they need to drive their business."

The recognition BNC has recently received is a good indication of its success in these efforts. Among the awards BNC has garnered are *Brandweek* magazine's Gold Medal awards in 1996 for sports and event marketing and cause-related marketing, and *Inside PR*'s Creativity in PR award in 1996 for cause-related marketing. BNC also won the Women Executives in PR award in 1997 for cause-related marketing, and the Gay and Lesbian Alliance Against Defamation (GLAAD) Fairness Award in 1998.

Nyman says that he and his two founding partners established BNC on the principle that they could combine their expertise with their passions. That commitment has moved them to serve the community in a variety of ways. Bragman sits on the board of directors of AIDS Project Los Angeles, communications advisory board of the Magic Johnson AIDS Foundation, and board of governors of the Los Angeles Gay and Lesbian Community Services Center. Nyman is a member of the board of directors of the Neil Bogart Memorial Fund for Children's Cancer, Leukemia, and AIDS Research, is a member of the ERAS Center and serves on the Alumni Board for the Harvard-Westlake School. Cafarelli serves on the board of directors of the Starlight Children's Foundation.

Bragman Nyman Cafarelli looks forward to a future of growing along with its client base. Its targets for growth are the areas of consumer products business, entertainment marketing, television, film, and new media.

The founding partners, Howard Bragman, Michael Nyman, and Brad Cafarelli, also contribute their expertise to serve the Los Angeles community. The partners sit on the boards of directors and advisory boards of many organizations, including AIDS Project Los Angeles, the Neil Bogart Memorial Fund for Children's Cancer, Leukemia, and AIDS Research, and the Starlight Children's Foundation. At left, Madonna speaks at the 1998 AIDS Project Los Angeles AIDS Walk.

Participants of the California AIDS Ride Five, presented by Tanqueray, make their triumphant arrival in Los Angeles (bottom).

BAKER & HOSTETLER LLP, COUNSELLORS AT LAW

Since its beginnings in Cleveland, Ohio, the law firm of Baker & Hostetler LLP, Counsellors at Law has grown to become one of the largest law firms in the country. With nearly 500 lawyers, the firm has offices in 10 cities: Los Angeles, Beverly Hills, and Long Beach, California; Cincinnati, Cleveland, and Columbus, Ohio; Denver, Colorado; Houston, Texas; Orlando, Florida; and Washington, D.C. The firm was founded in 1916 by Newton D. Baker,

Joseph C. Hostetler, and Thomas L. Sidlo. Baker served as secretary of war for President Woodrow Wilson. The Los Angeles office opened in 1990 with the acquisition of McCutchen, Black, Verleger & Shea, which also has offices in Long Beach and Houston, further expanding Baker & Hostetler's practice.

Baker & Hostetler defies the stereotypical image of Los Angeles lawyers. "There are several aspects that make this firm unique," explains Jack I. Samet, the Los Angeles office's partner in charge. "We offer our clients all the resources that come with being part of a large national firm, while maintaining the atmosphere of a small firm."

Adds Samet, "The strength of the Los Angeles office lies in the quality, depth, and diversity of its attorneys, combined with client-oriented customer service." The firm's attorneys strive to create successful, long-term relationships with clients, and are dedicated both to the legal profession and to the cities in which they live and work. Many of them have experience in technical and nonlegal fields, including petroleum, engineering, computers, public accounting, economics, finance, psychology, business, international relations, physics, education, and government service.

Practice Areas

Sheldon Gebb is the managing partner of the firm's three California offices. As the largest of the state's offices, the Los Angeles division is headquarters for the Business Group, led by Tom Roberts; the Litigation Group, under the guidance of David Destino; and the Employment Law and Benefits Group, managed by Terri Tracy.

The Business Group handles a broad spectrum of general corporate law, providing legal counsel to businesses of all sizes. The practice includes forming, dissolving, and reorganizing corporations, joint ventures and partnerships, distributorships, and franchises. The Los Angeles office represents a number of California-based for-profit and nonprofit corporations, as well as out-of-state corporations with local operations, and has particular experience in international business and financial transactions, including banking, currency exchange controls, export controls, intercompany pricing, and customs rules.

The Litigation Group represents businesses, industries, and individuals in commercial litigation settings. It has experience in cases including contract disputes, securities litigation, construction litigation, employment law issues, intellectual property, product liability, environmental and hazardous waste litigation, and maritime-related disputes. The group has handled appeals before the U.S. Supreme Court, U.S. Court of Appeals, U.S. Court of Claims, California Supreme Court, and the California Court of Appeals. Intellectual property attorneys in the Litigation Group regularly handle the prosecution and defense of claims for copyright, trademark, patent, and unfair competition litigation. Its international practice in trademark and copyright law emphasizes the protection and enforcement of licensing and merchandising properties.

In the Employment Law and Benefits Group, employment and labor law attorneys counsel and represent employers on employment law issues that range from wrongful discharge lawsuits, individual and class action statutory claims (such as race, sex, and age discrimination), and claims arising from the employment relationship (such as trade secret disputes and unfair competition by former employees). The firm represents employers before administrative agencies, and works closely with clients to address their human resources issues.

The Los Angeles office has a broad range of clients, including many of the major national and international corporations doing business in Southern California. These companies engage in the business of manufacturing, shipping, transportation, distribution, personal services, real estate development, oil and gas (exploration, production, and distribution), insurance, retailing, banking and finance, manufacture and sale of automobiles, and international trade. The office also repre-

(From left) Attorneys Patrick J. Cain, Penny M. Costa, and Cranston J. Williams are shown on the grounds of the Los Angeles Public Library, with downtown Los Angeles in the background.

sents trade associations, governmental agencies, and nonprofit entities.

Commitment to Communities

In addition to Baker & Hostetler's commitment to its clients and to the legal profession, the firm is dedicated to the community, as demonstrated by its active participation and financial support for cultural landmarks such as the Los Angeles Library, the Cabrillo Marine Aquarium, and the recently opened Long Beach Aquarium. Many of the firm's attorneys participate each year in Public Counsel, a pro bono project of the Los Angeles County Bar

Association, as well as other pro bono and community activities. Others participate in political activities and have been members of volunteer and elected bodies such as area city councils, school boards, commissions, and civic committees. As part of the firm's 75th anniversary—and marking a link with its beginnings—the Los Angeles office formed a partnership with Woodrow Wilson High School, located in the inner city, and established a scholarship program for minority students. In addition, every summer, the firm hires a Wilson student as an intern, and introduces him or her to the field of law as a career opportunity.

The vital business environment in Los Angeles has created a growing need for sophisticated, national law practices with the ability to meet the demands of a diverse client base. The Los Angeles office has effectively kept up with this multifaceted, fast-changing environment. With its national resources and wealth of experience, Baker & Hostetler continues each day to meet the many challenges of the Los Angeles business community— for both established and newly arriving businesses in a wide range of industries— and will continue to do so for many years to come.

Consumers spend almost $4 billion a year on bottled water, ranging from the familiar five-gallon bottle perched atop the office watercooler to the sport-top bottles that show up in almost every sports venue across the nation. When Southern Californians get thirsty, chances are they reach for Sparkletts, the flagship brand offered by McKesson Water Products Company (MWPC) of Pasadena. ♨ As the world's largest American-owned bottled water company,

MWPC reported more than $350 million in sales in fiscal year 1999, with annual sales of more than 100 million bottles of water through retail outlets alone. The company employs more than 2,000 workers, who operate 11 bottling and 41 distribution facilities—all dedicated to producing top-quality water products. Each day, MWPC processes an average of 830,000 gallons of pure drinking water under three well-known brand names available through retail outlets, as well as delivered to homes and offices.

Sparkletts Water, founded in 1925, is today MWPC's largest brand and has become a category leader in its market areas, which include Southern California, Washington, Nevada, Texas, New Mexico, Oklahoma, and Mexico. McKesson Water Products Company's other labels are Alhambra Water, established in 1902 and today the leading brand in northern California, and Crystal Water, established in 1948, now the leading brand in Arizona.

The 1998 purchase of the Ephrata Diamond Spring Water Company in Ephrata, Pennsylvania, and Keystone Natural Water Company in Yardley, Pennsylvania, enabled MWPC to expand into the mid-Atlantic region, one of the fastest-growing bottled

water markets in the country. McKesson Water Products Company is a division of San Francisco-based McKesson HBOC, Inc., the world's largest health care services company, which is publicly traded on the New York Stock Exchange under the symbol MCK.

Meeting Consumer Demands

MWPC and its brands have long been pioneers in the bottled water industry. In addition to producing fluoridated drinking water, mountain spring water, purified water, and distilled water, the company supplies Premium Ice, the nation's first branded ice. Sold in California, Sparkletts Premium Ice is available in containers of three three-pound packs. MWPC also pioneered the sport-top bottle as well as the three-gallon bottle, and was the first company to introduce personal-size fluoridated bottled water for children. Recent innovations include the Travel Pak, a bottle style that is specifically designed for in-car cup holders, and an attractive two-liter decanter that fits conveniently in the refrigerator and also looks great on the dinner table.

In keeping with the company's unwavering commitment to quality, MWPC draws

its water from aquifers ranging from 200 to 900 feet beneath the earth's surface. It goes through a multistage purification process to remove salts and minerals, gases, organic compounds, and particulate matter. Selected minerals may be added for taste.

For the past four years, MWPC has received the International Bottled Water Association's Excellence in Manufacturing award. This award indicates that the company's facilities have received top scores on National Sanitation Foundation quality assurance audits. The company's products are also regulated by Food and Drug Administration guidelines, as well as state regulators. Across the entire spectrum of its brands and products, the company is dedicated to freshness and purity, and to ensuring that high-quality water is available to consumers whenever and wherever they need it—at home, at work, and at play.

Commitment to the Environment

MWPC prides itself on innovative ideas that reach beyond the company's water. In 1998, for example, Sparkletts began delivering its products via an environmentally friendly electric truck. The Sparkletts Electric Route Truck is the first midsize vehicle of

Known as the bottled water industry's leading product innovator, McKesson Water Products Company and Sparkletts offer a variety of sizes and water types to consumers in the retail market. Sparkletts also offers delivery of three- and five-gallon sizes to homes and offices.

its kind to hit the road and is the prototype for future models. Traveling about 70 miles on one charge, the truck carries up to 1,000 gallons of water, while producing no smoke, odors, emissions, or noise.

MWPC's environmental concerns extend to wildlife conservation. In 1997, the company donated 2,300 acres of land, valued at $7 million, to the Nature Conservancy, one of the largest gifts the organization has ever received in California. These desert wetlands, which at one time had been earmarked for development into condominiums, a golf course, and a hotel, are now a protected home to more than 200 plant and animal species, including the desert bighorn sheep, mountain lion, black bear, and peregrine falcon, all of which are considered threatened species.

Giving Back to the Community

During emergencies, particularly in such natural disasters as earthquakes, floods, droughts, and fires, MWPC generously supplies water to those in need. The company is concerned with children's literacy as well, and its employees participate in

an Adopt-a-School partnership with Pasadena's Unified School District, where they volunteer time to tutor elementary students. MWPC also supports a variety of family, fitness, and educational programs.

In the past few years alone, bottled water has become the hottest beverage

category in the United States, growing annually at a rate of 9 percent. McKesson Water Products Company, in response to the increasing demand for a variety of quality products, has risen to the challenge, tapping its history of innovation to provide a pure, healthy beverage for an ever expanding market base.

▶ TIM HAWLEY

Clockwise from top left:
Children who visit the Petersen Automotive Museum, a part of the Natural History Museum of Los Angeles, can enjoy a visit to an interactive Sparkletts truck exhibit. For more than 75 years, Sparkletts has supported community events and educational programs in Los Angeles.

Sparkletts Jr. Sport, a 12-ounce sport-top featuring lively, multicolored graphics, is the leading kids' water in Southern California. It fits easily in a lunch pack and comes in a fluoride version for consumers who are concerned about healthy teeth.

Sparkletts customers can count on dedicated, service-oriented employees who make sure that they deliver top-quality water along with customer satisfaction each day.

Think of Nestlé, and most likely chocolate comes to mind: Nestlé Butterfinger, Baby Ruth, and, of course, Nestlé Crunch. But think again. Think of the very best foods that consumers rely on every day: Libby's Juicy Juice 100 percent juice, Hills Bros. coffee, Nestlé Carnation Instant Breakfast, Ortega Mexican meals, Stouffer's Lean Cuisine entrées, Nestea iced tea, and Nescafé coffee. And think of what the family pet craves: Friskies, Fancy Feast, Mighty Dog,

and Alpo pet foods. These are but a few of the members of the Nestlé family of foods, which include dozens of trusted brands that provide tasty, nutritious meals and snacks for every member of the family. Nestlé's strength comes from the quality and diversity of its brands, which have been in almost every household for years.

In 1998, for the second year in a row, Nestlé USA was voted the nation's most admired food company in a poll conducted by *Fortune* magazine. Part of Swiss-based Nestlé S.A., the largest food company in the world, Nestlé USA has 19,500 employ-

ees working in 67 facilities in the United States, and its annual sales in 1998 were $8 billion.

Addressing Specific Needs

Nestlé has an impressive history of focusing on specific nutritional needs; in fact, this is how the company got its start. In Switzerland in 1867, neighbors of the young pharmacist Henri Nestlé consulted him because their child could not be breast-fed. Nestlé developed a formula of natural ingredients to substitute for the mother's milk, saving the child's life. Out

of this came the method for condensing milk and producing the world's first formulas for infants, which have evolved into Nestlé Carnation baby formulas. Throughout the world, Nestlé S.A. still has a special interest in developing nutritional products for babies and children as their specific needs dictate. In addition to an array of baby formulas and foods, Nestlé also produces nutrient-fortified beverages for older children throughout the world whose diets are likely to be inadequate.

Nestlé continues its efforts to meet families' needs, including the need for foods that can be prepared quickly (think Stouffer's frozen entrées), the need for nutritious alternatives for dieters (think Stouffer's Lean Cuisine frozen entrées and Nestlé Sweet Success diet shakes), and the need for well-balanced meals for the family pets (think Alpo and Friskies). In fact, the company's pet food division has more than 2,000 professionals, including veterinarians, nutritionists, and animal behaviorists, who are dedicated to developing pet foods that are both nutritious and tasty.

The company's FoodServices division is among the largest food-service suppliers in the United States, with some 500 products bearing such familiar brand names as Carnation, Ortega, and Stouffer's. These and other Nestlé products provide the very

Clockwise from top left:
Nestlé USA Chairman and Chief Executive Officer Joe Weller

Nestlé USA is headquartered in Glendale, and has some 19,500 employees working in 67 facilities.

Although the name Nestlé brings to mind chocolate, the company offers many products and brands that touch consumers' lives every day.

best in taste and nutrition in restaurants, hotels, schools, stadiums, cafeterias, and offices across the country.

What sets Nestlé apart from the competition is the strength of its brands and its global resources. In Nestlé kitchens throughout the United States and around the world, food experts dedicate themselves to product development to ensure that, indeed, Nestlé makes the very best.

Commitment to Community and Family

Nestlé USA is actively involved in the community and is committed to education. To these ends, it takes an active role in the community through the Nestlé Very Best Volunteers Adopt-A-School program. Backing up its assertion that giving back

to the community means more than simply writing a check, Nestlé sends more than 1,000 employees, including Chairman and Chief Executive Officer Joe Weller, into local classrooms to share their knowledge and passion for food. They assist students at the local level in after-school tutoring and mentoring programs, and participate with them in book fairs, field trips, reading programs, and pen friend programs. The company encourages participation by allowing employees two hours off per month to give to these programs. Nestlé also contributes significantly to Reading Is Fundamental (RIF) and the United Negro College Fund (UNCF).

Nestlé operates on the premise that food should provide for the spirit as well as for the body, and that preparing and

enjoying food enriches the experience of life among family and friends. Nestlé is committed not only to producing foods that are wholesome and delicious, but to monitoring the evolving needs of its consumers so that it can continue to develop high-quality products to meet those needs. The Nestlé logo, featuring a family of birds in a nest, is based on Henri Nestlé's family coat of arms, and is a graphic representation of his name. This symbol was chosen because it evokes security, maternity and affection, nature and nourishment, family, and tradition. The company is still dedicated to this today in its work to develop the very best foods that nourish and sustain consumers through all the stages of their lives.

for many, it's hard to imagine being able to lean back and enjoy a massage while working in an office or while flying on a commercial airline. But today, thanks to the innovations of Relaxor®, the country's leading developer, manufacturer, and marketer of a vast array of massage furniture and electronic personal massage products, it's a reality. ▼ Founded in 1990, Relaxor is today a privately held company with corporate offices in Bellflower, California, and manufacturing in

China. In 1997, the company was selected by the *Los Angeles Business Journal* as number 22 on its list of the top 100 of the fastest-growing private businesses in the Los Angeles area.

To what does Relaxor attribute its ongoing success? Says Chairman of the Board Dorothy Lorentz, "Our finest asset is our personnel. They are dedicated, determined, and loyal. It is a family-oriented culture." Indeed, Relaxor is a family business, established in Los Angeles by President Gayle Benaron Gerth; Consumer Products Director and Executive Vice President Teri Benaron; their father, furniture industry veteran Joe Benaron; and Lorentz. In 1998, Richard F. Clayton joined Relaxor as chief executive officer, bringing a vast array of retail and manufacturing experience to support the company strategically with its growth into the 21st century.

Selling Relaxation in the 1990s

High-tech gadget stores have discovered a key trend among consumers in the 1990s: They lead stressful lives, and therefore crave opportunities to relax and be pampered. Relaxor has contributed to the popularity and availability of products that allow consumers to lie back and enjoy a shiatsu massage in the privacy of their homes—anytime they want one. A number of the company's home-use massage products are marketed through upscale stores such as the Sharper Image, Brookstone, Bloomingdale's, Macy's East, Robinson·May, Sears, JCPenney, and many others. Many well-known furniture manufacturers, including Action Lane, La-Z-Boy, Benchcraft, and Stratolounger also install Relaxor's electromechanical massage seating components in their recliners and sofas.

The early success of these products led the company to explore beyond the individual consumer market. Relaxor has since expanded from its focus on furniture for home use and moved into the sale of office, automotive and truck, airline, and health care massage components. A number of truck seat manufacturers install Relaxor's tactile massage units in their products to help alleviate fatigue for drivers by providing massage to the mid-back, lumbar, and thigh regions.

As the company wraps up its first decade in business, its products have achieved popularity internationally, as well as in the United States. Furniture manufac-

Relaxor's goal is to develop products to help people live fuller, richer lives, bringing to the consumers products to make their fast-paced, stressed lives healthier, more livable, and more enjoyable.

turers from Europe to South America to Asia are installing Relaxor's massage and heating systems in their chairs and sofas. In addition to its seating components for automobiles, airlines, private jets, and recreational vehicles, the company produces a line of personal wellness and relaxation products for an array of uses, including aromatherapy, sound and light therapy, hot and cold therapy, and foot therapy.

Looking to the future, Relaxor's plans include extending its product lines and moving into more clinical and scientific areas of personal care and relaxation. The company was founded on the premise that research and development in these areas would lead to new, innovative products and provide a better environment for its customers. Relaxor's goal is to develop products to help people live fuller, richer lives, bringing to the consumers products to make their fast-paced, stressed lives healthier, more livable, and more enjoyable.

All of Relaxor's products are UL and TUV listed with in-factory inspections. In addition, the company's manufacturing facility is ISO 9002 certified, and Relaxor is in the process of becoming ISO 9001 certified for the engineering and design of its products.

Making a Difference with Youth

Relaxor strives to play an active part in the community, particularly in promoting spe-

cial programs for young people. The company has sponsored college scholarships in the name of Pioneer Educators for deserving students, who were honored at the Dorothy Chandler Grand Hall in downtown Los Angeles. Relaxor has also sponsored a meal, toys, and a special showing of the movie *Babe* for 2,400 homeless, foster care, handicapped, and poverty-level children during the holiday season.

The company has taken a special interest in children with cystic fibrosis, holding a kickoff reception for the Cystic Fibrosis Foundation, handing out Furbys at Christmas to area children stricken by the disease, and cosponsoring an auction that netted $100,000 for cystic fibrosis research. In addition, in 1998, Relaxor gave more than $300,000 to various other charities in the name of its customers, vendors, and employees.

Whether through its relaxation products, personal safety innovations, or community involvement, Relaxor strives to make a positive difference in its customers' lives.

Relaxor is the country's leading developer, manufacturer, and marketer of massage furniture and electronic personal massage products.

AREF & ASSOCIATES

As the global corporate landscape has changed over the course of the 1990s, so has the prevailing corporate culture. This evolution has created a shift in the way "the new workplace" is viewed as well, with space becoming an important tool of productivity, rather than just a place to work. Refining this concept, Aref & Associates has become an industry leader in space planning and interior design. ▼ Aref & Associates' progressive attitude about the nature of work and the

workplace has helped set the trend of compressing the traditional pyramid shape of interior design into the contemporary flattened design that reflects the organizational changes taking place in the corporate world.

"While offices in the 1980s reflected their success and stability by making an opulent statement about their image, the 1990s have seen the opposite occur," says Mohammed Aref, cofounder of the Los Angeles-based design firm. "Many firms—large and small—have changed their look to reflect the business culture of today, priding themselves on efficiency and functionality."

BIELENBERG

The success of Aref & Associates' projects can be seen in their results: a very efficient and functional space with sensitivity to ergonomics and human factors; a flexible and mobile environment that is adaptable to changes in the work process, organizational patterns, and technological advances; and a space that is reflective of the corporate culture in a collaborative and open environment that allows for greater interaction and knowledge sharing. The planning concept is an integral part of the design of the space, carefully blending interior architectural details with articulated forms, textures, and colors that create an open and inviting space. This concept, accentuated with contemporary art, results in a dramatic and soothing environment.

BIELENBERG

The firm has come to be respected in the industry through the work of its designers, who emphasize a stable and professional image for rapidly growing and fast-paced firms. With a high rate of repeat business, Aref & Associates has developed close ties with the business community and its corporate clients, who come from many different industries, including law, entertainment, management consulting, technology, development, financial, public utility, and corporate firms.

In working with Aref & Associates, clients have the opportunity to experience a visual sample of what they can expect before designing their offices. Using the latest state-of-the-art technology, Aref designers can give virtual tours of their new floor plans using animation computer software, such as 3D Studio and 3D MAX. All designs are done in-house, helping to save time in the delivery of the product.

Aref & Associates counts on highly talented and passionate designers that range from young innovators to established professionals. "The young designers we have bring fresh and innovative concepts that are our bridge to technology and the

Aref & Associates was founded in 1991 by Mohammed H. Aref and Frozan Akbar-Aref. The firm has conceptualized the new workplace by creating multifunctional spaces that encourage creativity and the free exchange of ideas.

With a high rate of repeat business, Aref & Associates has developed close ties with its clients, who come from many different industries, including law, entertainment, management consulting, technology, development, financial, public utility, and corporate firms.

new workplace," Aref says. "In contrast, we have well-established professionals whom we count as mentors to the young staff in making sure that special attention is given to details that make for the successful completion of a project."

Workplace of the Future

Aref & Associates was founded in 1991 by Mohammed H. Aref and Frozan Akbar-Aref. Their philosophy was to establish long-term collaborative relationships with clients based on a clear understanding of each company's cultural environment, work process, long-term business plan, and corporate identity. The firm's goal is to ultimately create an intelligent working environment to meet these objectives.

Over the course of its history, the design firm has thrived by developing strategic planning concepts, while adhering to its basic design philosophy that allows form to follow function. The spaces the firm creates have a functional requirement in a multitask environment. Whether it's an office or a workstation, there are spaces for roundtable team interaction in a non-hierarchical environment. The firm believes that design is also driven by the functionality of each work group, and therefore one solution is not the answer for all work groups.

Aref & Associates helps clients come to better understand the planning concept developed for their offices. The firm guides companies wishing to modernize their workplaces to be more flexible, mobile, and adaptable to change in order to better deal with the constant challenges facing its clients. Aref's designers then balance these qualities with aesthetics to create an environment that workers will enjoy. To do this, Aref & Associates have conceptualized the new workplace by creating multifunctional spaces called "the commons," where there is soft seating, modular tables, a cappuccino machine, chess tables, audiovisual equipment, and video-conferencing, among other amenities that may encourage creativity and an exchange of ideas.

"People spend most of their time at work," says Akbar-Aref. "We want to make the workplace as pleasant for workers as possible, which leads to higher productivity, retention of employees, and recruitment of new talent."

As a highly motivated design firm, Aref & Associates has become known for its ability to think differently, and for its hands-on involvement in each step of the design process. This philosophy has led to the many long-term relationships built by the Aref team over the years, and it will continue to guide the firm as it moves into the next millennium.

92.3 THE BEAT

mid one of the most media-saturated cities in the country, The Beat, 92.3 on the FM dial, stands alone for delivering top entertainment while maintaining a high level of community commitment. ✓ The Beat's music reflects the melting pot synergy of Los Angeles by blending a unique mix of current R & B, funky old school, and contemporary hip-hop music to create its own special lifestyle sound and flow. The Beat also features many nationally recognized specialty

shows that showcase everything from underground cutting-edge music, reggae music, slow jams, and dedications, to even a show featuring strictly local West Coast music. "We have a commitment to being real with the music we play," states Michelle Santosuosso, program director for The Beat. "That means that we do not follow national charts or trends . . . we want to make sure that we are representing the music in a way that's true and unique to Los Angeles. I'm more interested in setting up our own musical vibe that fuses with The Beat's commitment to the community and No Colorlines® sentiment!"

Owned by Chancellor Media Corporation, a Dallas-based, publicly traded company, The Beat combines talented radio personalities spinning the latest urban music hits—from Janet Jackson to Ice Cube—with social awareness campaigns that are identified as crucial by listeners. The station's No Colorlines slogan, which has become part of its logo, encourages positivity and unity through music and commitment to action.

"When we hit the air in 1991 and looked at what was being done by the radio stations in this town, we saw that there wasn't a great deal of substance, or soul, taking place," says Craig Wilbraham, senior vice president and general manager. "After the 1992 civil unrest, we saw some glaring needs that we felt we would be able to help meet in some way."

No Colorlines®

The award-winning station is consistently a top performer among listeners from 18 to 54 years old, and its loyal audience reflects the multicultural Los Angeles population. Typically, radio stations with similar formats attract audiences that are 70 percent African-American. By comparison, The Beat's audience base goes beyond the traditional mix. African-American listeners make up a third of the station's audience, while Latino listeners constitute a third, as well.

On-air radio personalities include African-Americans, Asians, Latinos, and Caucasians. The racially diverse team has helped position the radio station as one of the top three in the market. "The station's staff reflects the audience," says Eileen Woodbury, director of marketing and promotions. "It's important for us to walk the way we talk."

The Beat's No Colorlines campaign has helped bridge the gap between the ethnic populations of Los Angeles. The station has won commendations by the County of Los Angeles, city council, California state legislature, and police department for its involvement with the community in such issues and projects as AIDS Dance-A-Thon and AIDS Walk; Gay & Lesbian Pride Festival; Black History Month; food, toy, and clothing drives; Kids Care Fair; Youth Leadership Conference; Summer Jam Benefit Concert; Holiday Cooldown; Mexican Independence Day; *Street Science*-hosted town hall meetings; and voter registration drives with Rock the Vote.

No other radio station in Los Angeles has dedicated an entire department to reach out to the community. The Beat created the Community Action Department, supervised by Dominique DiPrima, who hosts

Clockwise from top:
Craig Wilbraham, senior vice president and general manager of 92.3 The Beat (left), poses with Los Angeles Mayor Richard Riordan during his on-air guest appearance on the station's community action talk show *Street Science*.

92.3 The Beat afternoon DJ Theo (right) visits backstage with world-renown artist and producer Kenneth "Babyface" Edmonds (left) and the president and CEO of Yab Yum and Edmonds Entertainment, Tracey Edmonds.

Michelle Santosuosso, The Beat program director, joins the morning crew of *John London and The House Party*, broadcasting live from the Grammys in New York City, with Motown recording artists Boyz II Men.

ARNOLD TURNER

her own hard-hitting show, *Street Science,* on Sundays from 9 p.m. until midnight. The department consists of four staff members who do outreach to neighborhoods throughout the radio station's coverage area—from San Diego in the south to Santa Barbara in the north—to find what people on the streets are talking about, discover what their needs are, and find ways to meet them.

DiPrima says, "One of the big goals of the Community Action Department is to make sure that what we do isn't isolated to our department. The idea is to have a philosophy that permeates the station in every aspect.

"We want to make an impact block by block, rather than being a drop in some huge bucket," states DiPrima. It's this philosophy that makes the station stand out from the others, and has awarded the station significant recognition from its peers. The Beat recently received the prestigious Crystal Award from the National Association of Broadcasters, an award for community service presented to the top 10 radio stations across the county. "L.A. is so big, but it's made up of many little neighborhoods. We leave a lasting bond on each neighborhood we touch," DiPrima adds.

DJs for each 92.3 time slot dedicate personal time to social awareness. On their own, they have taken up pet programs or a topic to champion. Top-ranked *John London and The House Party,* which airs mornings from 5:30 to 10, consists of a five-member, multiethnic team that interacts with the audience with humor, while focusing on families and children. Each year, they host the John London and the House Party Celebrity Golf Tournament, with the proceeds benefiting local Boys and Girls clubs. DJ Theo, a Japanese-American, ranks number one among Los Angeles radio listeners during afternoon drive time, between 2 and 6, and uses his clout as a role model to emphasize education. Julio G, who airs from 6 p.m. to 10 p.m., concentrates on gang intervention and violence prevention. Kevin Nash, who takes listeners into the night with romantic slow jams, is a bridge to church groups that work with nonprofit organizations. In addition, the station takes The Beat's fleet of vans for live broadcasts from sites where hot topics are being debated: juvenile halls, homeless shelters, schools, parks, and even coffee shops.

"You'll hear a thread of positivity and messages throughout the day on the air:

racial tolerance, AIDS awareness, gay and lesbian rights, gang and violence prevention, single parenting, and education. These are some of the things that other stations are afraid to tackle because they are gritty and sometimes make people uncomfortable," says Wilbraham. "It's a fun, entertaining radio station; but there is a dose of reality that we include every day."

▶ ARNOLD TURNER

Clockwise from top:
Dominique DiPrima (right), The Beat community action director and *Street Science* host, interviews Angela Davis, civil rights activist.

DiPrima and Los Angeles Chief of Police Bernard Parks

(From left) EEG recording artist Missy Elliott, Atlantic recording artist Aaliyah, and Universal recording artist Erykah Badu go live on-air with 92.3 The Beat while broadcasting live backstage at the Soul Train Music Awards.

▶▼ ARNOLD TURNER

From the microwave oven to the world's first electronic depth sounder to the Patriot missile, Raytheon Company has made significant scientific and technological contributions to the quality and safety of our lives throughout its more than 75-year history. Raytheon has successfully built upon its pioneering traditions to become a global technology leader. ▼ Headquartered in Lexington, Massachusetts, Raytheon today is a $20 billion, global technology leader operating in three core business segments: defense and commercial electronics, engineering and construction, and business and special mission aircraft. With more than 100,000 employees worldwide, Raytheon is one of the largest industrial corporations in the United States. Its extensive U.S. and international operations serve customers in more than 80 countries throughout the world.

Early Days

Raytheon was founded in Cambridge, Massachusetts, in 1922 as the American Appliance Company. Building upon the company's early success in the field of radio tubes, company officials adopted the Raytheon name in 1925.

The company went on to play a key role in World War II through its technological innovations. Raytheon was the leading producer of radar tubes and complete radar systems during the war, providing the most important military advantage for Britain and the Allied forces. An important Raytheon development was the microwave SG radar, a shipboard radar that was far superior to those carried in planes because German submarines could not tune in on their frequencies as they could with aircraft radar. In 1942, Raytheon began manufacturing the radar for PT boats, a feat other manufacturers previously had claimed was impossible, and by the end of the war, every U.S. PT boat was equipped with the Raytheon radar. Following the war, Raytheon became a pioneer in the field of missile guidance. In 1948, Raytheon became the first company to develop a missile guidance system that could hit a flying target.

In 1964, the company embarked on a major diversification program to broaden its business base by adding commercial operations. By the end of the decade, the company had increased its commercial business to 45 percent of overall sales.

Defense Technology in the Kitchen

Raytheon was the first to apply microwave energy to cooking with the invention of the microwave oven. It was Raytheon's 1965 acquisition of Amana Refrigeration, Inc.—an Iowa-based manufacturer of refrigerators and air conditioners—that ultimately made the microwave oven a fixture in U.S. households. In 1967, Raytheon introduced the Radarange®, the first countertop, domestic 100-volt microwave oven, which retailed for just under $500.

The company continued to grow and evolve in the ensuing decades, but in 1991, Raytheon captured the world's attention. The Persian Gulf War put Raytheon's Patriot

Clockwise from top:
From refineries—such as this one designed and built by Raytheon—to power plants and light-rail lines, Raytheon Company provides full-service, turnkey engineering and construction capabilities to diverse markets around the world.

Raytheon is a world leader in designing and building air traffic control (ATC) systems.

Raytheon's Patriot is the world's most advanced air defense system, capable of defending against the entire spectrum of air defense threats. Here, Patriot antennas undergo tests during adverse weather conditions.

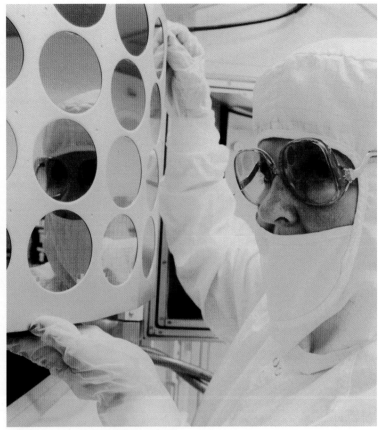

technology to the test in a real military conflict when upgraded Patriot Advanced Capability Phase 2 (PAC-2) missiles successfully intercepted and destroyed Iraqi Scud missiles fired at Israel and Saudi Arabia. Credited with saving lives and changing the course of the war, the Patriot earned worldwide recognition as the first missile in history to successfully engage a hostile ballistic missile in combat.

At the end of the Cold War in 1991, the U.S. Department of Defense, Raytheon's largest customer, reduced defense procurement by 60 percent. Since that time, Raytheon has focused on converting its sophisticated defense technology for commercial markets where appropriate. Raytheon today is successfully expanding its defense technologies into nondefense electronics markets such as air traffic control, data, image and information management, transportation, and communications.

In 1997, Raytheon completed a $9.5 billion merger with the defense operations of Hughes Electronics, a leading supplier of advanced defense electronics systems and services. From that merger—the largest transaction in Raytheon's history—came the creation of Raytheon Systems Company (RSC), now the third-largest U.S. military contractor. One of Raytheon Systems Company's five segments, Sensors and Electronic Systems (SES), is headquartered in El Segundo.

Education, Community, and the Environment

Raytheon's commitment to quality, ethical standards, and teamwork extends to the company's community involvement. Recognizing the complexity of today's social, educational, and environmental problems, Raytheon believes it is important to be involved in various facets of the community to find long-term solutions. In 1998, the company was honored with the National Trustee Award from Citizens' Scholarship Foundation of America; supported the Hispanic Engineers Conference sponsored by the Society of Hispanic Professional Engineers; was a major corporate sponsor of the Academic Decathlon; and won recognition for employee participation in California Recycle.

Working in communities where its facilities are located, Raytheon's corporate contributions program focuses on the strategic priorities of science and math education, with an emphasis on K-12 teacher professional development, student academic achievement, and postsecondary engineering education.

As Raytheon continues to establish itself as a valued corporate citizen in Southern California, the company, as always, is looking toward the future. Raytheon plans to become an even more global company, to remain a leader in defense and government electronics, to continue growing its commercial business in both sales and profitability, and to continue expanding defense technology into new commercial markets.

Clockwise from top left:
Raytheon's aircraft are distinguished by superior workmanship, advanced technology, and larger, more commodious cabins, such as those found in Raytheon's Beechjet 400A light jet.

Originally developed for defense applications, Raytheon's gallium arsenide monolithic microwave integrated circuit wafer technology is helping to advance the art of wireless communications.

Raytheon volunteers visit classrooms to help students better understand industry's impact on the environment.

As recently as 1996, the name Washington Mutual was virtually unknown in California. Today, the name is highly visible on nearly 600 bank branches throughout the state; its total deposits exceed those of any other California bank, save one; and the bank is a California leader in home mortgages. ⚜ This remarkable transformation came about through a series of mergers that paired Washington Mutual with some of the oldest and most familiar

names in California community banking—American Savings, Great Western Bank, and Home Savings of America. These acquisitions, completed between late 1996 and the end of 1998, added a major California presence to Washington Mutual's network in the Pacific Northwest. They also produced the eighth-largest banking company in the United Sates, with more than $90 billion in total deposits and $150 billion in total assets.

A Clear Focus

To hear Washington Mutual's management tell it, however, size is not the most important element in the story. The bank's overriding goal is to create a community-oriented financial institution with the size and scope of the largest commercial banks, but with a clear focus on individual consumers and small businesses.

This focus is evident in Washington Mutual's list of product offerings. The flagship product is Free Checking—so named because there is no minimum balance obligation, no direct-deposit requirement, and no fees for teller service. The no-fee approach to in-person banking reflects a belief that technology, while important, hardly renders obsolete the delivery of high-quality customer service through neighborhood branch offices. In fact, although Washington Mutual has one of the largest automated teller machine networks in the western United States and offers both telephone and on-line banking ser-

vices, traditional branch banking remains central to the company's business strategy.

Other Washington Mutual deposit and investment products include interest-bearing checking, money market accounts, certificates of deposit, and individual retirement accounts. A separate affiliated company offers investments in securities and mutual funds.

On the credit side, Washington Mutual's preeminent business is shelter-related lending. Perennially ranked among the nation's top home mortgage providers in terms of loans made and serviced, the bank offers home buyers a wide array of

adjustable- and fixed-rate mortgage loans, as well as construction and lot loans, manufactured housing loans, and other specialty real estate loans. In addition, Washington Mutual is California's largest apartment lender.

Consumer and small-business lending are growing business segments at Washington Mutual. Consumer credit products include home equity credit lines, credit cards, personal lines of credit, student loans, savings-secured loans, and auto, boat, and recreational vehicle loans. For small-business owners, the bank offers lines of credit up to $100,000.

Clockwise from top:
Washington Mutual's goal is to create a community-oriented financial institution with the size and scope of the largest commercial banks, but with a clear focus on individual consumers and small businesses.

Washington Mutual loan consultants help home buyers choose mortgage loans that meet their needs.

Shelter-based lending is the bank's core business.

MAURY L. PHILLIPS

MAURY L. PHILLIPS

Committed, Active Neighbors

A simple listing of Washington Mutual's business lines and product offerings paints an incomplete picture of the company. Washington Mutual was founded in Seattle in 1889 as part of that city's efforts to rebuild following a devastating fire. A commitment to community involvement has been a hallmark of the bank's approach ever since.

Washington Mutual supports local neighborhoods by actively establishing partnerships with community agencies, encouraging volunteerism among its employees, and contributing funds to nonprofit organizations.

The Washington Mutual CAN! Program (Committed Active Neighbors) operates with a dual emphasis: to improve public education and to increase the amount of affordable housing in communities served by the bank. Grants are made to nonprofit organizations working primarily in these areas. In addition, hundreds of Washington Mutual CAN! volunteers lend a hand to a wide variety of community projects.

A Historic Commitment

The bank's California acquisitions have been accompanied by a major expansion of Washington Mutual's community reinvestment programs, with California cities and communities as major beneficiaries. Early in 1998, the bank announced a historic $120 billion, 10-year commitment to lend and invest in low- to moderate-income communities in its service areas.

This commitment is larger, as a percentage of total assets, than any other similar commitment previously made by any U.S. banking company. It has been praised by community activists and housing advocates for its specificity and for Washington Mutual's willingness to consult the community in the process of developing a plan.

The specific 10-year targets for Washington Mutual's community reinvestment programs include $81.6 billion in affordable housing loans to minority borrowers and borrowers in low- to moderate-income neighborhoods; $25 billion in loans to small businesses and consumers with low to moderate incomes; $12.1 billion for apartment and manufactured home park developments in low-income communities; and $1.3 billion in investments and loans to community-development and low-income housing initiatives, tax-exempt housing revenue bonds, and minority financial institutions.

As part of the 10-year commitment, Washington Mutual has pledged to continue its long-standing goal of returning 2 percent of its pretax earnings to the communities it serves, with an emphasis on underserved areas. These resources are distributed through grants, sponsorships, discounted loans, in-kind donations, and paid employee volunteer time.

The bank's entry into the California market has given it a significant stake in the economic future of the state and its many communities. By accompanying that entry with a pledge to function as a community bank in the best sense of the word, Washington Mutual has provided clear acknowledgment that it sees California and its many communities as critical to its own success as an enterprise.

▶ MAURY L. PHILLIPS

Washington Mutual deposit and investment products include interest-bearing checking, money market accounts, certificates of deposit, and individual retirement accounts.

▶ MAURY L. PHILLIPS

Support for education is a major focus of Washington Mutual's corporate grant and employee volunteer programs.

THE BOEING COMPANY

The Boeing Company, respected around the globe as a pioneer and leader in the aircraft building business for nearly a century, became the largest aerospace company in the world after its 1996 acquisition of the defense and aerospace units of Rockwell International and its merger in 1997 with McDonnell Douglas. ⚜ With the merger and acquisition, Boeing established a corporate presence in the Southland through the McDonnell Douglas units in Long Beach and Huntington

Beach—and formed the Space & Communications Group in Seal Beach, which had been the site of Rockwell's world headquarters.

Today, the Boeing presence in the Southland has become vital to the region's economy: With more than 40,000 employees in locations throughout Los Angeles and Orange counties, Boeing is the largest private employer not only in Southern California, but in all of California. Also, Southern California is the second-largest center of operations for Boeing nationally, after the Puget Sound area.

Boeing Operations in Southern California

Boeing's Commercial Airplanes group is located in Long Beach, and is the home of the newest member of the Boeing commercial jet family. Introduced to the world in October 1995 as the McDonnell Douglas MD-95, the relaunched 717-200 twinjet is the product of a global program meeting the needs of the growing worldwide demand for full-size jetliner comfort on short-range flights.

The 717-200 has been designed specifically for efficient short-hop service,

short-field operations, fast turnaround at airport gates, and the ability to sustain eight to 12 one-hour flights on a daily basis–day after day.

Also in Long Beach is the Airlift & Tanker Programs division, where Boeing is under contract to build and deliver 120 C-17 Globemaster IIIs through 2004. The C-17 is an advanced, high-wing, four-engine, T-tailed aircraft with a rear loading ramp–174 feet in length–and a wingspan of 169 feet. With a payload of 160,000 pounds, a C-17

can take off from a 7,600-foot airfield, fly 2,400 nautical miles (much more with in-flight refueling), and land on a small, austere airfield in 3,000 feet or less.

The C-17 can carry army wheeled vehicles in two side-by-side rows. Three Bradley fighting vehicles comprise one deployment load. Similarly, the army's newest main battle tank, the M1A2, can be carried in conjunction with other vehicles.

The Space & Communications division is in Seal Beach, where Boeing has

Clockwise from top:

The Boeing Company established a corporate presence in the Southland in 1997, and is now a vital part of the region's economy. Here, Boeing holds the rollout of its first 717-200 passenger jet at its Commercial Airplanes operations in Long Beach.

Reusable Space Systems, based in Huntington Beach, designs, develops, builds, and manages programs for both manned and unmanned space vehicles, and has developed supporting hardware on programs ranging from the Apollo command and service modules to the reusable space shuttle fleet.

Canoga Park-based Rocketdyne Propulsion & Power is the world leader in liquid fuel rocket engines, which include the next-generation RS-68, destined for the Boeing Delta IV.

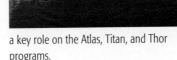

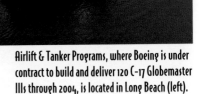

gathered the aerospace businesses of Boeing, McDonnell Douglas, and Rockwell into a single unit. Under this headquarters, there are 15 businesses–11 of which are located in Southern California or have significant operations there.

Boeing is a leader in human space flight as the builder of the space shuttle orbiters and their main engines and, through its family of Delta rockets and the unique Sea Launch program, a major player in government and commercial launch services.

Expendable Launch Systems is based in Huntington Beach and is responsible for the Delta family of expendable rockets. These vehicles have earned a worldwide reputation for reliability, affordability, and flexibility in placing a wide range of government and commercial payloads into orbit.

Reusable Space Systems—formerly based in Downey and now also based in Huntington Beach—designs, develops, builds, and manages programs for both manned and unmanned space vehicles, and has developed supporting hardware on programs ranging from the Apollo command and service modules to the reusable space shuttle fleet. Today, in addition to developing orbiter upgrades that will enable the shuttle fleet to fly well into the 21st century, the unit is also pursuing advanced launch vehicle technologies and concepts.

The Sea Launch Home Port is in Long Beach, where commercial satellite payloads will soon be processed and integrated for launch from a sea-based launch platform located at a site on the equator deep in the Pacific. Boeing is a 40 percent partner in this multinational consortium.

Boeing is NASA's prime contractor for the International Space Station, a project that draws upon the resources and the

scientific and technological expertise of 16 cooperating nations, including the United States, Canada, Japan, Brazil, Russia, and 11 member nations of the European Space Agency. Although Boeing's International Space Station operation is headquartered in Houston, Canoga Park-based Rocketdyne Propulsion & Power is responsible for the end-to-end electric power system for the space station. In Huntington Beach, the Boeing Space Station team developed and built the station's pre-integrated truss structure, pressurized mating adapters, node modules, and the mobile transporter—as well as performed cupola outfitting.

This team is also involved in various support systems for the station, such as communications and tracking; guidance, navigation, and thermal control; and command and data handling.

In the San Fernando Valley for more than 40 years, Rocketdyne has an unparalleled track record of designing and building advanced rocket propulsion systems, including the main engines for the space shuttle—the only reusable liquid fuel rocket engines ever built. Rocketdyne engines powered Apollo astronauts to the moon. In addition, Rocketdyne engines played

a key role on the Atlas, Titan, and Thor programs.

Today, Rocketdyne engines also power the Boeing Delta II and Delta III, and the unit's new RS-68 engine will propel the next-generation Boeing Delta IV rocket. The unique Rocketdyne linear aerospike engine will power NASA's X-33 reusable launch vehicle.

Boeing has several business units in Southern California managing high-technology products and services that focus on commercial and military information and communications needs. These include such programs as the global positioning system navigation satellites; Ellipso, a satellite-based global communications system; unmanned aerial vehicles; and a series of missile defense programs.

Satellites & Ground Control Systems, based in Seal Beach, designs, develops, produces, tests, and integrates satellites from small, individual units to large, complex constellations. The unit is the home of the U.S. Air Force's highly successful Navstar Global Positioning System, and has recently built and integrated a sophisticated research and development satellite for the air force—the Advanced Research

Airlift & Tanker Programs, where Boeing is under contract to build and deliver 120 C-17 Globemaster IIIs through 2004, is located in Long Beach (left).

The Sea Launch Home Port is in Long Beach, where commercial satellite payloads will soon be processed and integrated for launch from a sea-based launch platform located at a site on the equator deep in the Pacific (right).

The Boeing Electronic Systems & Missile Defense business in Anaheim is a respected, long-time force in the markets of strategic missiles, missile defense systems, and marine system products, as well as electronic products and sensor systems for global defense and commercial markets.

Clockwise from top:
Satellites & Ground Control Systems, based in Seal Beach, designs, develops, produces, tests, and integrates satellites from small, individual units to large, complex constellations. The unit is also the home of the U.S. Air Force's highly successful Navstar Global Positioning System.

Together with the U.S. Department of Defense, Boeing is spearheading a team of companies to develop a comprehensive national missile defense system to protect the United States and its allies from any limited ballistic missile attack in the 21st century.

Expendable Launch Systems is based in Huntington Beach and is responsible for the Delta IV family of expendable rockets.

and Global Observation Satellite (ARGOS).

Boeing is a major developer of high-power laser and electro-optical systems, and the Laser & Electro Optical Systems business in Canoga Park is adapting chemical oxygen iodine lasers to tactical weapon applications for army, navy, and air force applications. The unit has developed high-resolution real-time compensated imaging capabilities, as well as electro-optical remote sensing capabilities as a result of several ongoing and proposed programs for the U.S. Department of Defense.

The Boeing Electronic Systems & Missile Defense business in Anaheim is a respected, longtime force in the markets of strategic missiles, missile defense systems, marine system products, as well as electronic products and sensor systems for global defense and commercial markets. Electronic Systems & Missile Defense is now leading a team of contractors to re-

place the aging guidance system electronics in the Minuteman III ICBM, designated to be the backbone of the land-based strategic missile U.S. fleet.

Communications & Battle Management Systems, headquartered in Anaheim, produces many of the company's highly specialized military products and space- and ground-based information systems and services. One of the key programs being worked on in Anaheim is the Combat Survivor Evader Locator system, a complete over-the-horizon search and rescue system. Outside of Southern California, this unit is responsible for the high-profile Airborne Warning & Control System (AWACS) surveillance aircraft.

Boeing serves as the lead system integrator of the national missile defense program. Together with the U.S. Department of Defense, Boeing is spearheading a team of companies to develop a comprehensive national missile defense system to protect the United States and its allies from any limited ballistic missile attack in the 21st century. The company is building on its experience in systems engineering, integration, testing, guidance, sensors missiles, and spacecraft to satisfy the national missile defense requirements.

Building the Community

Because it recognizes the responsibilities that come with being a good corporate citizen, Boeing is committed to bettering the communities in which it does business. In addition to providing an environmentally safe workplace and offering its em-

ployees top-notch health care benefits, Boeing helps support projects that enhance the community as a whole via company and employee contributions, including financial donations, volunteer work, and in-kind gifts.

In 1997, company and employee contributions totaled $90.5 million nationwide, of which more than $4.5 million was donated to communities in California. In addition, employees have logged volunteer time at the Great Los Angeles River Clean-Up, Christmas in April neighborhood project, Habitat for Humanity, Southern California region Special Olympics, KCET-TV spring pledge drive, and March of Dimes Walk-A-Thon, among many other local and regional events.

The Boeing volunteer program is active throughout the Southern California region, and includes a host of educational outreach projects, teacher enhancement programs, and charity functions. Boeing can only estimate the enormous number of volunteer hours employees and retirees and their families put in throughout the year to enhance and enrich their communities. Boeing also produces communications materials and videos for nonprofit agencies, and donates computers, office supplies and furnishings, transportation for community activities, and material for volunteer projects.

Boeing and the Arts

Since the early 1960s, Boeing has been providing general operating and project support to the arts in its operating communities throughout the United States. It's a reflection of the company's commitment to enhance the quality of life where its employees live and work. In 1997, Boeing received the prestigious Business in the Arts Award for its long-standing commitment to the arts. From 1986 to 1996, Boeing grants and in-kind services to the arts totaled nearly $35 million. In 1998, Boeing became a supporter of the construction of Disney Hall.

Employees serve on the boards of cultural organizations throughout the United States, and many provide extensive volunteer services. Employees and retirees are also encouraged to support the arts through the company's gift-matching program. Much of the Boeing staff is actively involved in the cultural landscape of Southern California.

Through its dedication of unparalleled resources and time, both in local involvement and national policy, the Boeing Company is as much a powerful force in the shaping of its host communities as it is in the global aerospace industry.

ediaOne, the nation's leading broadband services company, provides entertainment,

information, and communication services to more than 5 million people. The company traces its roots to the 1963 founding of Continental Cablevision in Ohio, and entered the Los Angeles market in 1988. Today, MediaOne is the third-largest cable television operator in the country, serving customers in 60 of the top 100 cable markets in the United States.

In recent years, MediaOne has also become a world leader in the development, design, and deployment of hybrid fiber coaxial (HFC) networks, which offer the best technical and economic choice for cable and telephone operators. HFC provides a combination of speed, interactivity, signal quality, and bandwidth to integrate voice, video, and data services over a single network. Through its focus on HFC, MediaOne has pursued its aim to simplify the process by providing voice, video, and high-speed data—all through a single fiber-optic wire that runs right into the home of every customer. The company also plans to launch digital television in the near future.

MediaOne Express, the company's high-speed Internet access service, amassed more than 10,000 customers within the first year of its introduction. MediaOne Express offers customers access to the Internet at speeds up to 50 times faster than what is available through a standard 28.8-kilobit-per-second dial-up modem, enabling users to download graphics-rich files almost instantaneously.

Following the 1998 merger of MediaOne's and Time Warner's high-speed on-line services into a joint venture, MediaOne Express evolved even further. Bringing together the best content and features of MediaOne Express and Road Runner, the new service was launched in the first quarter of 1999.

"Broadband is a strategy we envisioned years ago, and now other companies only confirm the value of our approach," says Gisselle Acevedo-Franco, company spokesperson, MediaOne, Western Region.

"We're upgrading our broadband networks to offer multiple services, including video, high-speed Internet access, and telephony. We want to be positioned as a company of the future here today."

More Industry Changes

MediaOne has changed things in another arena, also. Its president and CEO, Janice Peters, is currently the only woman to head a major cable company. A seasoned telecommunications professional, Peters entered the cable industry after the buyout of Continental Cablevision by the Denver-based employer, U S WEST Communications. When Continental's CEO declined to move from Boston to the new Denver headquarters, Peters found herself poised to assume the top position with the cable enterprise, renamed MediaOne and later split off from U S WEST as a separate public company. Her strong business and management background and fresh perspective are helping energize this rapidly growing company.

Traded on the New York Stock Exchange under the symbol UMG, MediaOne is now the largest broadband services provider in Los Angeles and the second largest in the state. The company employs 1,500 dedicated individuals in the metropolitan area, where it serves some 900,000 subscribers.

MediaOne's focus is fixed firmly on the future as it watches for new and better opportunities to provide comprehensive services via a single fiber-optic wire. But despite this forward-looking approach, customer service is still the company's priority. "While it's easy to talk about bigger, better, and faster, our commitment is to our customers by consistently providing superior customer service," says Acevedo-Franco. "Our broadband service is how we can bring simplicity into people's lives."

Clockwise from top leftt:
Mark Kaplan and his son Tszvi, one of MediaOne's many broadband families, enjoy the simplicity of broadband living.

Customer Paul Ash enjoys the high-speed Internet access that MediaOne Express provides.

MediaOne, a broadband company, launches a free Internet education program, Community Outreach and Online Learning (COOL), in Los Angeles.

A MediaOne technician prepares to install service for a new customer at the first broadband community, Park LaBrea in Los Angeles.

▲ SUSAN GOLDMAN PHOTOGRAPHY

▲ SUSAN GOLDMAN PHOTOGRAPHY

TOWERY PUBLISHING, INC.

From its beginnings as a small publisher of local newspapers in the 1930s, Towery Publishing, Inc. produces a wide range of community-oriented materials, including books (Urban Tapestry Series), business directories, magazines, and Internet sites. Building on its long heritage of excellence, the company is today global in scope, with cities from San Diego to Sydney represented by Towery products. In all its endeavors, this Memphis-based company strives to be synonymous with service, utility, and quality.

A Diversity of Community-Based Products

Over the years, Towery has become the largest producer of published materials for North American chambers of commerce. From membership directories that enhance business-to-business communication to visitor and relocation guides tailored to reflect the unique qualities of the communities they cover, the company's chamber-oriented materials offer comprehensive information on dozens of topics, including housing, education, leisure activities, health care, and local government.

In 1998, the company acquired Cincinnati-based Target Marketing, an established provider of detailed city street maps to more than 300 chambers of commerce throughout the United States and Canada. Now a division of Towery, Target offers full-color maps that include local landmarks and points of interest, such as parks, shopping centers, golf courses, schools, industrial parks, city and county limits, subdivision names, public buildings, and even block numbers on most streets.

In 1990, Towery launched the Urban Tapestry Series, an award-winning collection of oversized, hardbound photojournals detailing the people, history, culture, environment, and commerce of various metropolitan areas. These coffee-table books highlight a community through three basic elements: an introductory essay by a noted local individual; an exquisite collection of four-color photographs; and profiles of the companies and organizations that animate the area's business life.

To date, more than 80 Urban Tapestry Series editions have been published in cities around the world, from New York to Vancouver to Sydney. Authors of the books' introductory essays include former President Gerald Ford (Grand Rapids), former Alberta Premier Peter Lougheed (Calgary), CBS anchor Dan Rather (Austin), ABC anchor Hugh Downs (Phoenix), best-selling mystery author Robert B. Parker (Boston), American Movie Classics host Nick Clooney (Cincinnati), Senator Richard Lugar (Indianapolis), and Challenger Center founder June Scobee Rodgers (Chattanooga).

To maintain hands-on quality in all of its periodicals and books, Towery has long used the latest production methods available. The company was the first in the country to combine a desktop workstation environment with advanced graphic systems to provide color separations, image scanning, and finished film delivery under one roof. Today, Towery relies on state-of-the-art digital prepress services to produce more than 8,000 pages each year, containing well over 30,000 high-quality color images.

An Internet Pioneer

By combining its long-standing expertise in community-oriented published materials with advanced production capabilities, a global sales force, and extensive data management expertise, Towery has emerged as a significant Internet provider. In keeping with its overall focus on community-based resources, the company's Internet sites represent a natural step in the evolution of the business. There are two main product lines within the Internet division: introCity® and the American Community Network (ACN).

Towery's introCity sites introduce newcomers, visitors, and longtime residents to every facet of a particular community, while also placing the local chamber of commerce at the forefront of the city's Internet activity. The sites include newcomer information, calendars, photos, citywide business listings with everything from nightlife to shopping to family fun, and on-line maps pinpointing the exact

Towery Publishing President and CEO J. Robert Towery has expanded the business his parents started in the 1930s to include a growing array of traditional and electronic published materials, as well as Internet and multimedia services, that are marketed locally, nationally, and internationally.

location of businesses, schools, attractions, and much more.

ACN, Towery's other Internet product, is the only searchable on-line database of statistical information for all of the country's 3,141 counties and 315 metropolitan statistical areas. Each community's statistical profile includes vital information on such topics as population, workforce, transportation, education, taxes, and incentives. ACN serves as a national gateway to chambers of commerce, private companies, and other organizations and communities on the Web, making it an ideal resource for finding and comparing data on communities suitable for a plant or office location.

Decades of Publishing Expertise

In 1972, current President and CEO J. Robert Towery succeeded his parents in managing the printing and publishing business they had founded nearly four decades earlier. Soon thereafter, he expanded the scope of the company's published materials to include *Memphis* magazine and other successful regional and national publications. In 1985, after selling its locally focused assets, Towery began the trajectory on which it continues today, creating community-oriented materials that are often produced in conjunction with chambers of commerce and other business organizations.

Despite the decades of change, Towery himself follows a long-standing family philosophy of unmatched service and unflinching quality. That approach extends throughout the entire organization to include more than 130 employees at the Memphis headquarters, another 60 located in Northern Kentucky outside Cincinnati, and more than 50 sales, marketing, and editorial staff traveling to and working in a growing list of client cities. All of its products, and more information about the company, are featured on the Internet at www.towery.com.

In summing up his company's steady growth, Towery restates the essential formula that has driven the business since its first pages were published: "The creative energies of our staff drive us toward innovation and invention. Our people make the highest possible demands on themselves, so I know that our future is secure if the ingredients for success remain a focus on service and quality."

Towery Publishing was the first in the country to combine a digital desktop environment with advanced graphic systems to provide color separations, image scanning, and finished film delivery under one roof. Today, the company's state-of-the-art network of Macintosh and Windows workstations allows it to produce more than 8,000 pages each year, containing well over 30,000 high-quality color images.

The Towery family's publishing roots can be traced to 1935, when R.W. Towery began producing a series of community histories in Tennessee, Mississippi, and Texas. Throughout the company's history, the founding family has consistently exhibited a commitment to clarity, precision, innovation, and vision.

STEVE BAKER is an international photographer who has contributed to more than 100 publications. With a degree in journalism from Indiana University, he is the proprietor of Highlight Photography, specializing in assignments for clients such as Eastman Kodak, Nike, Budweiser, the U.S. Olympic Committee, and Mobil Oil, which has commissioned seven exhibitions of his work since 1994. Baker is author and photographer of *Racing Is Everything*, and he has contributed to Towery Publishing's *Jackson: The Good Life*; *Baltimore: Charm City*; *Indianapolis: Crossroads of the American Dream*; *Nashville: City of Note*; *Chicago: Heart and Soul of America*; and *Dayton: The Cradle of Creativity*. Currently, Baker resides in Indianapolis.

NOELLA BALLENGER is a professional nature and wildlife photographer. A member of the American Society of Media Photographers (ASMP), she has traveled throughout the world in search of unspoiled areas to photograph—from the spectacular coast of Oregon to the desolate Namib Desert of Africa. Ballenger has led master classes and given lectures on photography for various museums and organizations. Her images have been displayed in Children's Hospital Los Angeles, the Ninth Federal Circuit Court of Appeals in San Francisco, and private collections across the United States and around the world.

JAMES BLANK began his career at age 15, taking pictures of professional wrestling matches in Cedar Rapids, Iowa. After selling 40 pictures to wrestling magazines, he began a career in landscape photography. A resident of Chula Vista, he is employed by Scenics of America, and his clients include Kodak, Hallmark, World Book, *Reader's Digest*, and *Beautiful America*. Blank has also contributed to Towery Publishing's *San Diego: World-Class City*.

JAMIE BRISICK, a one-time professional surfer, specializes in portraiture and fast-action photography. He fills a variety of roles at *Surfing* magazine, including photographer, writer, and executive editor. Brisick's images have appeared in *Women's Sports & Fitness*, *Tracks*, and *Snowboarder Germany*.

JIM CORWIN earned a bachelor's degree from the University of Washington and a degree in photography from Everett Community College. He spent 12 years working for photo labs in the Seattle area before opening his own business in 1990. A native of Portland, Oregon, Corwin specializes in travel, nature, people, and sports photography, and he has worked for such clients as the Boeing Company, Safeway, US West Communications, GTE, and Microsoft. His work has been published in *National Geographic Traveler*, *Audubon*, *Mother Earth News*, and *Business Week*, in addition to Towery Publishing's *Seattle: Pacific Gem* and *San Diego: World-Class City*.

LINDA DELAY-JOSEPH began her career as a photographer after receiving grand prize honors in a nationwide Nikon contest in 1987. Her work is included in the permanent collection of the California Museum of Photography in Riverside, as well as in numerous private and corporate collections. Her articles and images have appeared in Sierra Club publications, *Wyoming Wildlife*, the *Territory Ahead*, *Zoom*, *Photo District News*, and *Explorer*.

MICHAEL FARR, owner of Michael Farr Photography, specializes in music industry and live performance photography. Farr's clients include Warner Bros. Records, Interscope Records, and House of Blues, and his images have appeared in *Juxtapoz*, *Grindstone Magazine*, and *International Tattoo Art*.

JEAN FERRO began her career in the visual arts in the 1970s as a press photographer and portraitist for the recording industry. Her work has been commissioned by Paramount Studios and the Southern California Regional Rail Authority. Ferro is the recipient of a City of Los Angeles Cultural Affairs Artist in the Community Award for her documentary portrait, "Through Our Own Eyes," in which 30 homeless people were commissioned to photograph themselves and their world with disposable cameras.

IRENE FERTIK is a staff photographer for the University of Southern California News Service. Her images have appeared in the *Los Angeles Times*, *Time*, the *New York Times*, *Encore*, and *Black Sports*, as well as the books *Women and Work* and *In Spite of Everything, Yes*. A three-time recipient of the Los Angeles

Cultural Affairs Endowment Grant, Fertik is currently working on a book documenting the integration of Ethiopian Jews into the Israeli Jewish culture.

Lee Foster is a veteran travel writer and photographer who lives in Berkeley. His work has been published in a number of major travel magazines and newspapers, and he maintains a stock photo library that features more than 250 worldwide destinations. Foster's travel publishing efforts can be viewed on his Web site at www.fostertravel.com. His work can also be seen in Towery Publishing's *Salt Lake City: Welcoming the World*.

Ewing Galloway, Inc., based in Rockville, New York, opened in 1920 as one of the country's original stock agencies. During its almost 80 years of operation, the company has provided imagery for advertising agencies, design studios, corporations, publishers, and record companies.

Mike Greenlar graduated from the Rochester Institute of Technology (RIT) with a bachelor of arts degree in journalism. Currently self-employed and boasting seven years of newspaper experience, Greenlar has had images published in *Time, Newsweek, Life, Forbes, Fortune*, and *Business Week*, as well as Towery Publishing's *Greater Syracuse: Center of an Empire*. He specializes in editorial photography of people and technology, as well as contemporary images of Native Americans. In addition to giving frequent

lectures at RIT, Greenlar has taught photojournalism at the S.I. Newhouse School of Public Communications.

James W. Jeffrey Jr., owner of Los Angeles-based James W. Jeffrey Photo Illustration & Motion Pictures, specializes in film/video production stills, and commercial and advertising photography. His client list includes Holloway House Publishing, NBC 4, FOX 11, Los Angeles County Public Library, and Proline Hair Products. Jeffrey received the 1977 CIBA Award, the 1981 Charles White Award, and the 1998 DEA Certificate of Appreciation.

Kenneth Johansson moved to the Santa Monica area from Sweden in 1976. His specialties include magazine features, editorial portraiture, and travel, interior, and architectural photography. Johansson's images have appeared in publications throughout Scandinavia and Europe.

Gil Kofman received a bachelor of arts degree from Cornell University, a master of fine arts degree from Yale University, and a master of arts degree from New York Graduate Film School. His work has appeared in *New York Times Magazine*.

Robert Landau graduated from the California Institute of the Arts with a bachelor of fine arts degree in photography/design. His work has been included in four books, as well as publications such as *Forbes, In Style, Los Angeles Magazine, Merian* (Germany), *Mode International* (France), and *Rolling Stone*. Landau

has received numerous honors, among them inclusion in the 1997 National Trust for Historic Preservation calendar and first place in the 1987 *Sierra* photography contest.

Bud Lee studied at the Columbia University School of Fine Arts in New York and the National Academy of Fine Arts before moving to the Orlando area more than 20 years ago. A self-employed photojournalist, he founded both the Florida Photographers Workshop and the Iowa Photographers Workshop. Lee's work can be seen in *Esquire, Life, Travel & Leisure, Rolling Stone*, the *Washington Post*, and the *New York Times*, as well as in Towery Publishing's *Treasures on Tampa Bay: Tampa, St. Petersburg, Clearwater; Orlando: The City Beautiful; Jacksonville: Reflections of Excellence*; and *Greater Syracuse: Center of an Empire*.

James Lemass studied art in his native Ireland before moving to Cambridge, Massachusetts, in 1987. His areas of specialty include people and travel photography, and his work can be seen in publications by Aer Lingus, British Airways, and USAir, as well as the Nynex Yellow Pages. Lemass has also worked for the Massachusetts Office of Travel and Tourism, and his photographs have appeared in several other Towery publications, including *New York: Metropolis of the American Dream; Treasures on Tampa Bay: Tampa, St. Petersburg, Clearwater; Washington: City on a Hill; Orlando: The City Beautiful*; and *San Diego: World-Class City*.

Gary Leonard received a Ralph M. Parsons Foundation Grant to document the neighborhood of Echo Park for the Los Angeles Public Library Archives. His images have also appeared in the book *Make the Music Go Bang*, a photographic essay on the early L.A. punk scene.

Jeff Novak, a native of Manhattan Beach, received a 1997 Best Album Package Grammy nomination for his Tool album cover. A former professional surfer, he specializes in art, music, and fashion photography.

Bill Parr, owner of Bill Parr Photography, specializes in surfing and ocean images. His photographs have appeared in *Surfer*, *Surfing*, *Surfer's Journal*, *Longboard Magazine*, and the *Los Angeles Times*. Parr enjoys photographing exotic surf locales.

Joshua Paul graduated from the University of Washington with a degree in English and attended Parsons School of Design. He has won two Absolut Vodka Student Showcases and has provided images for Nike Design, Nordstrom, the DEP Corporation, and Hotel Bel-Air.

David Peevers, owner of Peevers Creative Services, specializes in writing and photography for the travel industry. He is currently producing guidebooks on Los Angeles and California for Lonely Planet Publications. The staff photographer for *German Life*, Peevers has amassed one of the largest stock photograph collections on Germany to be found in the United States.

Photophile, established in San Diego in 1967, is owned and operated by Nancy Likins-Mastern. An internationally known stock photography agency, the company houses more than 1 million color images, culled from more than 90 contributing local and international photographers. Photophile's 200-plus subject areas range from extensive coverage of the West Coast to business and industry, people and lifestyles, health, medicine, travel, scenic images, wildlife, and adventure sports.

Chuck Place received a camera as a graduation present after earning his degree in biology. Plans for graduate school quickly faded as his interest in photography grew. Assignments have taken Place from the Mayan ruins in Mexico and outrigger canoe races in Hawaii to orchid cultivation in California and Native American ceremonies in the Southwest. His clients include *Time*, the Smithsonian Institution, and the National Geographic Society. Place's images have appeared in *Pueblo and Mission, Cultural Roots of the Southwest* and *The Smithsonian Guide to Historic America*.

Laura Rohrer, an L.A. native since 1991, works as a location coordinator for Walt Disney Studios in Burbank. An amateur photographer, she has done freelance production work on commercials and music videos. Rohrer enjoys the artistic aspects and photographic challenges of black-and-white photography and plans to continue documenting people and places in the L.A. area.

Lisa Romerein received a bachelor of arts degree in psychology and communications from Stanford University. A native of Seattle, she specializes in travel, portrait, and lifestyle photography. Romerein's clients include *W*, *Los Angeles Magazine*, and *In Style*.

Jim Russi travels internationally three-fourths of the year for 52 magazines. He specializes in photographing water sports, and enjoys capturing the largest waves around the world. Russi frequently uses remote control to photograph sports such as luge, skateboarding, snowboarding, and surfing.

Robert D. Stout enjoys photographing subjects ranging from buildings to people. His images have appeared in various brochures and books—including Towery Publishing's *Celebrating Greater Kansas City*—and as the subject of several postcards. A freelance photographer, Stout is from Osawatomie, Kansas.

Jason Lawrence Todd specializes in atmospheric night photography. A Las Vegas native, he has been published in *CMYK*, *Los Angeles Times Magazine*, and *American Photography Annual* #8.

D.J. Waldie is the author of *Holy Land: A Suburban Memoir*. A lifelong resident of Lakewood, he is the recipient of honors from the National Endowment for the Arts, the California Arts Council, the California Book Awards, and the Whiting Writer's Awards.

NIK WHEELER, a native of Hitchin, England, began his photographic career in Bangkok, where he copublished a travel supplement and guidebook to Thailand. In 1967, he worked in Vietnam as a combat photographer. Since that time, Wheeler has covered the 1968 Tet Offensive, the Jordan Civil War, the fall of Saigon, the Montreal Olympics, and the coronation of the king of Nepal. His clients include *Time*, *National Geographic*, *Newsweek*, *Geo*, *Travel & Leisure*, and *International Wildlife*. Wheeler has published four books; has copublished and photographed for the *Insider's Guide* series, including Japan, Hawaii, California, and Spain; and has appeared on *The Merv Griffin Show* and Regis Philbin's *The Morning Show* (New York).

DAUNA WHITEHEAD, a native of Las Vegas, received a degree in chemistry from the University of California, Los Angeles. Her images have appeared in *Architecture California*, *Artweek*, *Downtown News*, *L.A. Architect*, and *Los Angeles Times Magazine*, and are included in numerous corporate, public, and private collections. Whitehead has received awards from the American Institute of Architects, Hollywood Arts Council, and Los Angeles County Fair.

ZUMA PRESS is an international assignment and stock photo agency formed in 1993 by a group of photographers and award-winning journalists. Its unique photography files encompass a range of subjects, from the military to politicians, business leaders, movie stars, medical and scientific trends, and circus performers. Zuma is also committed to developing human interest features and in-depth documentary photo-essays for immediate syndication.

Other photographers and organizations that contributed to *Los Angeles: City of Dreams* include Jonathan Alcorn, Allsport, Carlos Ballantyne, D. Boone, James Caccaid, Corbis-Westlight, Otto Creule, Richard Cummins, Greg DeGuire, Danny Feld, Robert Ginn, Elsa Hasch, Richard Hewett, Harry How, N. Irvine, Jed Jacobsohn, Nancy Kaszerman, Robert Laberce, Andy Lyons, Sal Maimone, Scott McKiernan, Zoran Milich, H. Miller, Lisa O'Connor, John Post, Bill Ross, Marissa Roth, R. Sinbran, J.R. Stangler, Chase Swift, David Taylor, Peter Taylor, Tecmap, Underwood Photo Archives, Todd Warshaw, William Warren, and Aubrey Washington. Special thanks to Jim Heinman and Eddie Morris for their assitance to the photo editor.

© LISA POMFREN

LIBRARY OF CONGRESS CATATLOGING-IN-PUBLICATION INFORMATION

Boyarsky, Bill.
    Los Angeles : city of dreams / by Bill Boyarsky ; art direction by
Brian Groppe.
      p.   cm. – (Urban tapestry series)
    Includes index.
    ISBN 1-881096-63-7 (alk. paper)
    1. Los Angeles (Calif.)–Civilization. 2. Los Angeles (Calif.)–
Pictorial works. 3. Los Angeles (Calif.)–Economic conditions.
    4. Business enterprises–California–Los Angeles. I. Title.
    II. Series.
F869.L85B69   1999
979.4'94–dc21   98-56459

TOWERY PUBLISHING, INC.,
THE TOWERY BUILDING,
1835 UNION AVENUE,
MEMPHIS, TN 38104

PUBLISHER: J. Robert Towery
EXECUTIVE PUBLISHER: Jenny McDowell
ASSOCIATE PUBLISHER: Michael C. James
NATIONAL SALES MANAGER: Stephen Hung
MARKETING DIRECTOR: Carol Culpepper
PROJECT DIRECTORS: Andrea Glazier, Jim Tomlinson, Robert Delmar, William Thomason

EXECUTIVE EDITOR: David B. Dawson
MANAGING EDITOR: Lynn Conlee
SENIOR EDITOR: Carlisle Hacker
EDITOR/PROFILE MANAGER: Jana Files
EDITORS: Mary Jane Adams, John Floyd, Brian Johnston, Heather Ramsey
ASSISTANT EDITOR: Rebecca Green
EDITORIAL ASSISTANT: Sunni Thompson
PROFILE WRITER: Enrique Levin
CAPTION WRITERS: David Peevers and Andrea Schulte-Peevers
EDITORIAL CONTRIBUTORS: Hope Hamashige, Lesley Wright, Carol Penn-Romine

PHOTOGRAPHY EDITOR: Jonathan Postal
PHOTOGRAPHY COORDINATOR: Robin McGehee
PROFILE DESIGNERS: Laurie Beck, Kelley Pratt, Ann Ward
PRODUCTION ASSISTANTS: Loretta Drew, Melissa Ellis
PRODUCTION RESOURCES MANAGER: Dave Dunlap Jr.
PRODUCTION COORDINATOR: Brenda Pattat
DIGITAL COLOR SUPERVISOR: Darin Ipema
DIGITAL COLOR TECHNICIANS: Eric Friedl, Brent Salazar
PRINT COORDINATOR: Tonda Thomas

URBAN
TAPESTRY
SERIES
TOWERY
PUBLISHING, INC.